THEATER
IN THE
AMERICAS

A Series from
Southern
Illinois
University
Press
SCOTT
MAGELSSEN
Series Editor

SYSTEMIC DRAMATURGY

A HANDBOOK FOR THE DIGITAL AGE

Michael Mark Chemers
and Mike Sell

Southern Illinois University Press ○ *Carbondale*

Southern Illinois University Press
www.siupress.com

Copyright © 2022 by the Board of Trustees,
Southern Illinois University
All rights reserved
Printed in the United States of America

25 24 23 22   4 3 2 1

Cover illustration: In The Builder's Association's *Elements of Oz* (2016), Glinda (Moe Angelos) appears in an augmented reality (AR) bubble. Photograph by Larry Shea. *Courtesy of The Builder's Association.*

Library of Congress Cataloging-in-Publication Data
Names: Chemers, Michael M., author. | Sell, Mike, 1967– author. | Weems, Marianne, writer of foreword.
Title: Systemic dramaturgy : a handbook for the digital age / Michael Mark Chemers and Mike Sell ; foreword by Marianne Weems.
Identifiers: LCCN 2021034964 (print) | LCCN 2021034965 (ebook) | ISBN 9780809338313 (paperback) | ISBN 9780809338320 (ebook)
Subjects: LCSH: Dramaturges—Interviews. | Dramaturges—Effect of technological innovations on. | Drama—Technique. | Theater—Production and direction. | Technology and the arts.
Classification: LCC PN1661 .C48 2022 (print) | LCC PN1661 (ebook) | DDC 808.2—dc23/eng/20211118
LC record available at https://lccn.loc.gov/2021034964
LC ebook record available at https://lccn.loc.gov/2021034965

Printed on recycled paper ♻

Southern Illinois University System

CONTENTS

List of Illustrations   vii
Foreword by Marianne Weems   ix
Acknowledgments   xi

Introduction: Thinking and Making Systemically   1

    Interview 1. *Dramatizing Systems*:
    Noah Wardrip-Fruin on Storytelling in the Digital Age   21

1. Sokyokuchi   35

    Interview 2. *Layers of Mediation*:
    Marianne Weems on the Dramaturgy of the Digital   63

2. Playing with Play   75

    Interview 3. *Play Matters*:
    Elizabeth Swensen on the Theatricality of Games   103

3. The Empathy Machine   117

    Interview 4. *Empathy for Whom?*
    micha cárdenas on Activism and Digital Performance   145

4. Toward a Dramaturgy of Videogames   155

    Interview 5. *Generations*:
    Jennifer Haley on the Theater Game   185

5. The Uncanny Mountain and *Neighborhood 3: Requisition of Doom*   195
6. Systemic Dramaturgy Roundtable   217
Afterword: Systemic Dramaturgy Then, Now, and Tomorrow   243

Notes   251
Bibliography   257
Index   265

ILLUSTRATIONS

I.1. Phone augmenting the experience of the Builders Association's *Elements of Oz*   17
1.1 A Bunraku performance by the Hitomi-Za Puppet Troupe   39
i2.1 Screens surrounding a performer in *Super Vision*   66
i2.2. Multiple forms of mediated representation and those who are creating them in *Elements of Oz*   69
2.1. Two automatons designed and constructed in the late 1800s   92
3.1. Screenshot from *Depression Quest*   128
i4.1. A view of the augmented reality game *Sin Sol/No Sun*   153
4.1a and 4.1b. Digital avatars mimicking the user's gestures and lip-syncing with the user's voice in VoicingElder   165
4.2a and 4.2b. Interplay of computational and digital technologies with live actors in *Bad News*   170
i5.1. Two images from the Royal Court's 2012 production of *The Nether*   188
5.1. A diagram from Masahiro Mori's "Uncanny Valley"   200
5.2. From the 2015 Flea Theater production of *Neighborhood 3: Requisition of Doom*   209
6.1. The actor's face projected onto large screens in *Strange Window*   220
6.2a and 6.2b. Screen captures from *Redshift and Portalmetal*   234

vii

FOREWORD

When we began the Builders Association in 1995, a lot of people were interested in what we did, but we were often asked, "But is it theater?" My typical response was, perhaps too obviously, "It takes place in a theater." That mostly holds true to this day, though some of our work is migrating to technology such as personal electronic devices and headsets. In any case, some people thought the distribution of media onstage somehow compromised the theatrical experience and fretted that the large screens and multiple cameras onstage would result in the obliteration of the live presence of the actors. Despite the frequently-predicted death of this *liveness*, it persists, and our work turned out to be only the first wave of the incorporation of digital elements into performance, which are now de rigueur in commercial theater. But these were ultimately dramaturgical debates: we were doing things that didn't fit into conventional dramaturgy as we knew it, and there has been a lingering need for a dramaturgy expansive enough to encompass the future directions of performance.

In this light, *Systemic Dramaturgy* is a singularly valuable book. Even though there are several good studies on the arguments around blending presence and liveness with new technological systems (which have kindly included discussions of my stage productions), this book expands the discussion. For Michael Chemers and Mike Sell make clear that the challenges and opportunities offered to performance by digital media extend in two directions, both into the past and into the foreseeable future. By starting with Zeami's observations of puppetry in fourteenth-century Japan, the authors connect digital performance to the *longue durée* blending of the natural and artificial systems in theater. *Systemic Dramaturgy* articulates a radical connection between these operational systems in theater and the contemporary systems that inform digital games, social media, interactive media, and artificial intelligence. The book gives us useful, real-world tools to explore how this systemic dramaturgical approach informs how we experience, make,

Foreword

and use those technologies on and off the stage. It engages us in exploring the responsibilities and powers that we bring to bear in combining performance with media systems. It's timely and topical, and it reaches out directly to the kinds of things that not only my collaborators and I are working with, but also visionaries in the digital realm, including Noah Wardrip-Fruin, micha cárdenas, Sandy Stone, and many others in these pages.

We are surrounded by systems and we learn from systems, but in performance we haven't been given a critical language to talk about them. Chemers and Sell make the point that systemic dramaturgs embrace, as they put it, a historically informed, multifaceted, capacious understanding of play and performance. This puts them in a unique position to help others engage critically and consciously with what it might mean to learn something from a system, be it a play or a videogame, and what it might mean to challenge something through a system by pointing to its hidden biases, assumptions, or methodological flaws.

When Michael Chemers and I met in 2005, we were colleagues at Carnegie Mellon University's School of Drama. I was struck by his facility for thinking outside the box and his ability to recognize and articulate several systems at play in my work. In talking to him and Mike Sell for this book, we touched on our early experiments with technology and performance. They brought to those discussions an expansive dramaturgy that is both forward-facing and historically grounded and enriched my thinking about my own history. This book speaks to dramaturgs, devisers of new performance, game designers, media artists, and everyone in between. It is passionate, is full of much-needed wit, and brings new insight into what "theater" was, is, and will be.

Marianne Weems, artistic director
of the Builders Association
February 2021

ACKNOWLEDGMENTS

Dramaturgy is a collaborative endeavor and so is this book. We thank micha cardenás, Jen Haley, Nick Junius, Sandy Stone, Elizabeth Swensen, Noah Wardrip-Fruin, and especially Marianne Weems for their contributions. For travel support, we are grateful to the Department of Theater Arts at the University of California–Santa Cruz and the College of Humanities and Social Sciences at Indiana University of Pennsylvania. We had the opportunity to try out our ideas at a systemic dramaturgy event at the Humanities Center at the University of Pittsburgh, and we benefited from the intellectual company provided by codirector David Marshall; our hosts, Shatasha Reeves and Dan Kubis; our respondents, Patrick McKelvey and Megan Monaghan Rivas; and Michelle Granshaw and her students. We also wish to acknowledge the following: For publishing our early research on systemic dramaturgy, Jeanmarie Higgins, editor of *Teaching Critical Performance Theory: In Today's Theatre Classroom, Studio, and Communities*, and Lisa Jackson-Schebetta, editor of *Theatre History Studies*. For infinite help in shepherding this volume to completion, Kristine Priddy and Scott Magelssen at Southern Illinois University Press. We value the time we've spent exploring the ideas in this book with undergraduates at Indiana University of Pennsylvania and students in the Graduate Program of Literature & Criticism, and students of DANM, theater arts, and AGPM at the University of California–Santa Cruz. Our thoughts on videogames and theater benefited from the series of working sessions held at the annual conference of the American Society for Theatre Research (ASTR).

And of course, we thank Farhana, Zain, Kate, Brando, River, and Dylan.

SYSTEMIC DRAMATURGY

INTRODUCTION: THINKING AND MAKING SYSTEMICALLY

Imagine the following scenarios:

You're graduating next semester with your dramaturgy specialization. You've taken courses in the history of theater, script analysis, set design and construction, and acting. The school's production of *The Master Builder*, which you dramaturged, received a rave review from the reviewer at the *Post-Gazette*—and she usually doesn't attend university productions! But you're facing a dilemma. Your other passion is videogames. You've played them since you can remember. And you've been taking videogame design courses, organized a couple of game jams, even attended the annual Game Developers Conference. So, what's it going to be? Is there even a career path for someone like you?

During a board meeting to discuss next year's season, your managing director announces that she's been approached by a well-known tech manufacturer who wants to donate a significant amount of money to your production company. Great news! But there's a catch: you'll have to use the manufacturer's infrared sensors and proprietary software in at least two productions. The artistic director leans over and whispers sorrowfully, "I guess that means *The Inspector General* is off the table."

While preparing the syllabus for a contemporary theater course, you learn that the Builders Association will be performing its latest production at a local theater. You'd love to bring your students to see this legendary company, but your expertise is in traditional script-based, realistic theater. The kind of experimental, process-based, multimedia work that the Builders Association does is unfamiliar, even a bit frightening to you. But you can't possibly pass up this opportunity, can you?

Introduction

So you sit down with your laptop and start Googling "technology and performance." You quickly grow confused and overwhelmed.

Each of these scenarios presents different professional, creative, imaginative, and personal challenges. Each presents different *dramaturgical* challenges. The first concerns how we integrate cutting-edge technology into what we make without harming our commitment to the time-tested texts we love and the soulful, beautiful art that matters to us and our creative communities. The second concerns how we can build on what we know as theater historians, performance theorists, and script analysts to educate ourselves and others about the amazing things that artists are doing today with digital technology and social media. And the third concerns the ways we can become knowledgeable, critically minded people in a world of pervasive social media and digital entertainment by using our understanding of how actors create roles, how audiences see and hear, and how scripts and stage communicate values. But regardless of the challenge, a smart, flexible, *systems-conscious* dramaturg should be able to win the day.

THE TECHNOLOGICAL DRAMATURG

We've written this book to empower the technology-curious dramaturg to understand the special requirements of the digital era. We've also written this book to encourage the technology-savvy codemaster to make the leap into the predigital theatrical past. We argue that the challenges and opportunities posed by digital lighting consoles or intermedia platforms aren't fundamentally different from those that tallow candles posed to the Renaissance stage designer, or at the very least, we feel it's worth considering what these challenges have in common. Regardless of the particular technical capacities of a particular theatrical technology, the questions raised by their use are ultimately questions of perception, understanding, and feeling. What matters is that the impact of those technologies on perception, understanding, and feeling is thoroughly understood before they're implemented. Do we deny that the emergent technologies of our moment are creating unprecedented challenges and opportunities for directors, designers, actors, and audiences? Of course not. But those challenges can best be approached by positioning them within a broader cultural, historical, and practical framework. Ultimately, we've written this book to empower dramaturgs, no matter what their attitude toward technology might be, to apply their dramaturgical knowledge in innovative ways. We've written this book so that dramaturgs may use their skills as script analysts, creative collaborators, askers of questions, and solvers of problems to think and use technology in ways that are critically minded and creatively focused no matter where they find themselves, in the theater or out.

In some ways, we see this book as a sequel to Chemers's *Ghost Light: An Introductory Handbook for Dramaturgy* and we are just as committed in these pages to effective dramaturgical practice, but we emphasize here the philosophical and analytic. After all, the first step toward successful making is successful thinking. You won't find in these pages a five-step guide to installing hanging mics or synchronizing actor movements to procedurally generated images. But you will find chapters that explore the historical, conceptual, and ethical dimensions of play and empathy; investigate different ways of thinking about the relationship of live performance, audience experience, and theater technology; and provide useful critical perspectives for those who want to try the tools of dramaturgy with other performance-based media, such as videogames. We'll show you how to apply the concepts of systemic dramaturgy to dramatic works, both old and time-tested and new and paradigm-shattering. And we'll allow you to sit in on our conversations with some of the most forward-thinking, innovative, and creative people working in live media today.

In sum, this is a handbook for *thinking theatrically about technology*. We believe that this kind of thinking can empower dramaturgs to do better the work they have always done and to do new kinds of work beyond the conventional dramaturgical haunts of the library, rehearsal room, and stage.

Because of the remarkable ways that dramaturgs think about performance (what Geoff Proehl calls "the dramaturgical sensibility"[1]), we are in an exceptional

The Elements of Effective Dramaturgical Practice

o Meticulous analysis of both the dramatic script (if one is being used) and the performance text, as it comes into being.
o Effective collaboration with all members of the production team, answering and asking questions that enable the best possible production process and audience experience.
o Thoughtful outreach to the audience, both potential and actual, to ensure the best possible understanding of the performance.

position when it comes to understanding how these factors intertwine. Depending on the needs of a given production, a dramaturg might be a historian, an aesthetic theorist, a critic, a useful gadfly, a practical problem solver, a teacher, a carnival barker, or even a visionary. Dramaturgs are, regardless of the situation, both thinkers and makers—and, without a doubt, thinkers and makers whose curiosity leads us to places and problems that might not be on the radar of directors, designers, actors, and department chairs. That's just what we do!

Not everyone is comfortable with that combination of conceptualization and fabrication. In his biography of Ludwig Tieck, Edwin Zeydel characterizes the dramaturg as a "man of letters who rashly interferes in the business of theater."[2] We don't consider ourselves rash (nor, of course, are we all men). The dramaturg's perspective, as illustrated in *Ghost Light*, is that thinking about what theater is, was, and might be and actively working with a creative community to make *this* production in *this* space at *this* time for *this* audience are two sides of the same coin—inhaling and exhaling, if you will. Because we play so many roles and are concerned with so many aspects of theater generally and productions specifically, dramaturgs do what we do in a unique way, always conscious of vast networks of interlocking processes. Dramaturgs are *systemic thinkers and makers*.

Thus our concern about how dramaturgs ought to respond to advances in new technology drives an approach we call *systemic dramaturgy*, which we consider as part of a wave of scholarship and creative practice that has dramatically expanded the very notion of dramaturgy: the premise that theater must be

> The process of trying to unravel the mysteries and indeterminacies of a play's meaning creates in those who undertake this work—the work of dramaturgy—an awareness of the limits and potential of knowledge. . . . Attaching sensibility to dramaturgy may only confound the confusion that still clings to dramaturgy, but the field needs a way to talk about a kind of awareness that is as much felt as thought. . . . One of our challenges is the need to dislodge dramaturgy, the dramaturg, and ways of knowing from schemes that reduce them to cognitive, analytical, usually Apollonian functions. A heart that thinks, or what archetypal psychologist James Hillman more elegantly calls the "thought of the heart," comes closer, particularly if we understand that with this phrase Hillman suggests not only mental and emotional qualities but also physical sensations, both pleasurable and painful.
>
> —Geoff Proehl, *Toward a Dramaturgical Sensibility*, 17

understood as a concatenation of people, places, things (scripts, props, structures, tools, and so on), and processes (writing, casting, rehearsal, direction, design, publicity, and so on) that work together (hopefully!) in an organized fashion (hopefully!) to accomplish the goal (particularly hopefully!) of entertaining and edifying an audience. Theater itself is an interlocking set of conceptual systems: interpretive systems, production systems, teaching systems, and research systems. The systemic dramaturg understands not only how these systems work but how they work together *and* how they work in concert with larger, ongoing systems, including aesthetic, political, and economic ones.

BACKWARD COMPATIBILITY

We tend to think of technology as exclusively forward-looking, as providing innovative solutions to never-before-encountered problems and better ways of dealing with existing problems. But the book you are reading is a book about *dramaturgy*, which means that its authors have a predisposition to look for aesthetic solutions in the historical record—sometimes far back in that record. What is to be gained from this is the realization that our modern problems, especially ones relating to aesthetics and ethics, aren't really new at all, and theater artists have been solving them for millennia.

Technology is not a new thing and it is not monolithic. Technologies develop at different rates and in different forms in different places. Engineers understand this and often design systems and products so that they can be used alongside older tech without any kind of special modification. We've all encountered this: the new videogame mercifully plays on your old system or the brand-new malware security blessedly doesn't crash your new hard drive. Engineers call this "backward compatibility," and it is highly valuable to the ongoing

The Systems of Dramaturgy

Commercial: donors, funding agencies, markets, sponsors

Interpersonal: cast, crew, administration, commercial interests, community

Institutional: theaters, universities, religious or community organizations that produce theater

Professional: for-profit theaters and other exhibition spaces

Processual: writing, design, directing, acting, movement

Social: organizational dynamics, audience development

Technological: electrics, computers, robotics

Textual: scripts, choreographies, outlines

Introduction

evolution of popular usable technology.[3] Similarly, the term "forward compatibility" is used to describe the design of systems or products to anticipate new evolutions in technology.

Theater is a good example of a backward-and-forward-compatible technology. *Theatron* (θέατρον, from the root verb meaning "to view" in Greek) originally meant "seeing place," an actual but also conceptual space in which ideas important to a culture could be embodied and played out for the purpose of being witnessed. Indeed, the ability of theater to both keep old technologies alive and absorb new technologies is an important source of its power to preserve and protect the past and peer into the future. Marvin Carlson calls the theater "among the most haunted of human cultural structures" and a "repository of cultural memory," but he explains that "like the memory of each individual, it is also subject to continual adjustment and modification as the memory is recalled in new circumstances and contexts." The theater is a place that favors the "retelling of stories already told, the reenactment of events already enacted, the reexperience of emotions already experienced," but also "the bodies and other physical materials it utilizes to tell them, and the places in which they are told." Carlson writes, "Any theatrical production weaves a ghostly tapestry for its audience, playing in various degrees and combinations with that audience's collective and individual memories of previous experience with this play, this director, these actors, this story, this theatrical space, even, on occasion, with this scenery, these costumes, these properties."[4]

Since every encounter with, say, *Hamlet* is both utterly familiar and utterly new, we do not merely experience a single cultural artifact when we see a performance. Instead, we witness and are part of the creation of an *assemblage* composed of not only our immediate impressions and reactions to this particular performance but also our memories of all the other *Hamlet*s we have seen and all other live performances of any kind we have already seen. Witnessing a performance is engaging with a system composed of recursive instances of signification, representation, innovation, and history. This experience enables us to connect with the action of the particular performance in a way not limited to our presence in conventional space and time. This transcendent experience is the everyday bread and butter of the dramaturg.

Theater has a unique facility to absorb new technologies to tell old stories. But this facility can also lead to confusion and constricted creativity. In his *Environmental Theater*, Richard Schechner decries the way "new theaters designed by people who want to keep up to date try to keep 'the best' from previous ages." Invited to develop a production of the Performance Group in one such theater, he was horrified by the monstrous amalgam he encountered: traces of the Greek amphitheater, the vomitoria of the Roman stadium, the wagons of the medieval pageants, the fly systems of the Italian renaissance, the orchestra pits of nineteenth-century opera, and the turntable of the early twentieth. "These theaters are like old trees weighted down by so many branches that they break," he says. Schechner and his company chose to use the theater's scene shop instead, "an honest, large, irregular space that could be made into anything."[5]

Though it feels more "natural" because it involves arms and legs and eyes and heart, performance is also a technology. Indeed, performance is among the oldest and most enduring technologies of communication. In fact, it has been in use for so long and has proven so durable that in some places it is a medium for preserving some of the oldest historical records. As Diana Taylor has demonstrated, in places where colonial powers have imposed their disastrous regimes, performance preserves the indigenous cultural record and provides a set of useful tools for resistance against colonial culture. This record, these tools she calls the "repertoire," distinguished from the printed records preserved in the "archive." She describes the repertoire in a way that illuminates its backward and forward compatibility: "The repertoire . . . enacts embodied memory: performances, gestures, orality, movement, dance, singing—in short, all those acts usually thought of as ephemeral, nonreproducible knowledge. . . . As opposed to the supposedly stable objects in the archive, the actions that are the repertoire do not remain the same. The repertoire both keeps and transforms choreographies of meaning."[6] Ultimately, we think about performance as a tool that has many uses and technology as a tool that enables many different kinds of performance.

If Aeschylus's play *Prometheus Bound* is any indication, the Greeks felt that technology was not only sacred but also intimately connected

Introduction

with the development of humans into, well, humans. Some scholars say it was not "fire" that Prometheus stole, but techne: a term that refers not just to tools but to a way of being in the world, of perceiving the world, of imagining what the world—and we ourselves—might be. Techne shapes the way we live with each other—for example, the communities, institutions, and organizations that are built around the acquisition and dissemination of knowledge and the practices and skills to apply that knowledge. These skills include efficiency, objectivity, and calculation, as well as collaboration and compassion. Indeed, according to philosophers, humanity is itself both the cause and the result of techne.

As theater historians, we are certain of two things: first, that humanity would not exist without drama, theater, and performance; and second, that drama, theater, and performance as we know it could not exist without scientists and engineers. Without a counterweight crane system, could Euripides have written the climax of *Medea*, when the antiheroine escapes from Jason on a chariot pulled by dragons? Which more frightened medieval Christians into taking seriously the whims and wanderings of sin and desire: the concept of hell shouted at them by their local religious authority or the horrific hellmouths, brightly painted and with articulated jaws that bellowed smoke and fire, on their stages? From Vitrivius to Zeami to Richard Wagner to Adolphe Appia to David Belasco to Oscar Méténier to Ariane Mnouchkine to Julie Taymor to Hatsune Miku, the story of theater is the story of audiences taking instruction and delight from stage magic. In turn, it is the story of experimentation and innovation by producers, playwrights, actors, and designers to use and conceive and devise ever more cunning and useful devices to thrill and move us. For millennia, the stage has been a welcome home for technological innovation. Ultimately, despite the fears of theater lovers through the ages, technology has neither obviated nor erased

---

The Greek word *theatron* . . . was both a physical and perceptual space ordered by technology: an architectural zone where the spectator sat to watch the drama unfold, and a perceptual one that mediated the visual and acoustic relationship between the worlds of stage and audience. In other words, technology in the performance arts reveals itself not only in the machines that descend from heavens by their own will, but also in how—through craft, skill, construction, or making (what the Greeks called *techne*)—it orders the world."

—Chris Salter, Entangled, xxii

the ancient relationship between audience and actors, between mind and heart, between art and life. When used judiciously, thoughtfully, cleverly, with an awareness of the manifold systems that surround that moment of encounter between artists and audience, technology has instead significantly enhanced that relationship.

But the collaboration between theater and tech is not—and never has been—limited to stage spectacle. Advances in anatomy, nutrition, and medicine have been incorporated by actors since before Quintilian wrote about the importance of breath and before Bharatamuni described the physical exercise and diet required of an actor in the *Natyasastra*. Playwrights have been interested in what motivates human behavior at least since ancient Greece, and the writings of Aristotle, Aeschylus, and Sophocles predicted and influenced the psychological writings of Schopenhauer and Freud and the political writings of Burke and Paine, who were hardly alone in relying on the language of the stage to illustrate their ideas. In 1881, the same year the Savoy Theatre in London became the first building to be lit entirely by Edison's incandescent electric lamps, the French novelist Émile Zola wrote that he was waiting "until the playwrights return to the source of science and modern arts, to the study of nature, to the anatomy of man, to the painting of life in an exact reproduction more original and more powerful than anyone has so far dared to risk on the boards."[7] He did not have to wait long. The twentieth century witnessed an explosion of theater technology and experimentation, leading to the astonishing variety of live performance events occurring all over the world today.

SYSTEMIC VERSUS NEW MEDIA DRAMATURGY

Live performance is increasingly imbricated with digital technology. However, despite a century of warnings from well-meaning (if overweening) theatrical traditionalists, live performance has not perished but instead evolved into new, exciting, and culturally and politically pertinent forms. This raises a number of questions: Exactly what should dramaturgs be asking about the digital, the cybernetic, the robotic, and the virtual in relation to live performance? What questions can help us define the theoretical foundations for a renewed dramaturgical practice that takes political, social, technological, historical, and psychological discourses into account? How can dramaturgs better serve directors,

Introduction

designers, and audiences so that they can think about technologies both old and new, technologies that can not only create memorable experiences in the theater but also facilitate creation and collaboration by those who want to make those kinds of experiences? Although many excellent scholarly works on new media and performance have emerged in the last few decades, we argue that the ability of theater artists to rise to the challenges and opportunities of computers, digital media, social media, and other so-called new media is hampered by both conventional understandings of dramaturgy and inadequately historicized understandings of technology.[8]

We follow in the footsteps of the dramaturgs who, in the words of Peter Eckersall, Helena Grehan, and Edward Scheer, envision dramaturgy "as an artistic activity that operates conceptually and procedurally between dramatic literature and performance, and at the same time links theatre aesthetics and practices with questions about ideology and culture."[9] We share the desire to implement "a new, collaborative dramaturgical model that . . . would be inquiring and provisional rather than already decided. It would need to accentuate the materiality of performance and include stage materials, bodies, light, duration, and dramatic context in a 'ceaseless dialogue.'"[10]

We are excited and edified by this growing body of work because we also believe that digital media, information networks, intermediality, cybernetics, robotics, social media and other aspects of technoculture are changing how we understand, make, and experience theater and performance. We are particularly fascinated by the "new media dramaturgy" practiced by artists like Kris Verdonck and dumb type, who stage digital, robotic, and computer technologies not simply as an adjunct to or vehicle of performance, but as "objects in performance for their own sake."[11] And like them, we don't buy the idea that these technologies pose an existential threat to live performance and audience experience. With Philip Auslander, we believe that liveness is always mediated in some fashion or other; therefore, we see emerging around us not the mortification of liveness, but rather its diversification. We affirm the idea that new media can be more than "simply scenographic elements" but can and should be considered as potentially "core components of the dramaturgy" of a production, as it is in the work of Marianne Weems and the Builders Association.[12]

But unlike these dramaturgical scholars of new media, we do not see the challenges posed to live performance by advanced technology as particularly new. On the contrary, *we understand the relationship of performance and technology as the original problem of theater.* The first human who stood in front of their friends to tell a story was the first human who asked the question, "What if the light were different? What if I stood *here* instead of there? What if I spoke like *this* instead of like that?" Theater history is shaped by the technologies of light, sound, architecture, and costume. It is shaped by those who thought deeply about the relationship of theatrical representation and technology. Theater, historically and across cultures, is an art form that has attracted innovators, tinkerers, inventors, interdisciplinary explorers, hucksters, and visionaries. August Strindberg, for example, felt there was no way to stage a story that reflected cutting-edge psychological and biological science with the lighting, scenography, makeup, and acting techniques of his time. In the preface to *Miss Julie*, he advocates a radical reformation of theater technology: the abolition of footlights in favor of a design that would highlight the subtleties of the actor's face and eliminate the need for actors to stand downstage and speak directly to the audience, the creation of more naturalistic makeup, and the construction of theaters that were smaller and darker, providing the audience surer insight into the interior lives of the characters. But if Strindberg's ideas about the human being were new, though the technologies he had available to him were new, the questions he was asking were essentially no different from those asked by Kaˉlidaˉsa, Aeschylus, Zeami, Hrosvitha, or Richard Wagner.

> Is there a dramaturgy for movement, sound, light, and so on, as well? Is dramaturgy the thing that connects all the various elements of a play together? Or is it, rather, the ceaseless dialogue between people who are working on a play together—or is it about the soul, the internal structure, of a production. Or does dramaturgy determine the way space and time are handled in a performance, and so the context and the audience, too. And so on. . . . We can probably answer all these questions with, "Yes, but."
> —Marianne van Kerkhoven, "Looking without Pencil in the Hand," 5

THE SYSTEMIC DRAMATURG

The problem with historicizing technological innovation as *either-or* in relation to performance is that it fails to recognize the broader forces

Introduction

that affect the development of an art form—any art form. When a biologist is considering the evolution of a species, she does not restrict herself to collecting data only about a few individuals and how they compete with other species for resources. On the contrary, the biologist must collect data on the relationships between predators and prey in the environment, changes (sudden or gradual) in climate or geography, genetic variations, and any number of other forces that can alter the way an organism adapts, including time itself. Biologists refer to those relationships as an *ecosystem*. And because ecosystems are vast and dynamic, the biologist's model must be supple enough to allow for new information or for a reexamination of well-known relationships at any time. Could dramaturgy follow suit by examining dramaturgical *systems* of theatrical signification? If so, why haven't we already done it? Or have we?

The answer, as with many dramaturgical questions, is "Well, yes and no." Chris Salter likens the set of detailed instructions on music, gesture, architecture, rhythm, actor training, and performance aesthetics in the *Natyasastra*, Bharatamuni's classical text on Indian performance, to a "software manual." He points out the self-consciousness of the *Natyasastra* on the interactions of a variety of systems at work in performance and visual art, comparing these interactions to those of the classical Greek *theatron* described by Aristotle. In both cases, the theater-makers understood performance as an art form that exists at a complex intersection of aesthetics and technology, imagination and manufacture, and the creation and interpretation of shared truths.[13]

We assert that modern dramaturgs, even as they have been quick to adapt to new technologies, aren't broad enough in their curiosity and intervention. How may we understand all these discourses—aesthetic, historical, political, social, and scientific—as part of a *system* or, better yet, of *multiple systems* of play, communication, and representation? Traditional dramaturgy does this to some extent. Following Marianne van Kerkhoven, we might call attention to the difference between the "micro-dramaturgy" of a single production and the "macro-dramaturgy" that understands individual productions as part of massive social processes. In her State of the Union speech at the 1994 *Theatrefestival* in Brussels, van Kerkhoven stated, "We could define the minor dramaturgy as that zone, that structural circle, which lies in and around a production. But a production comes alive through its interaction, through its audience, and through what is going on outside its own orbit. And around the production lies the theatre and around the theatre lies the city and around the city, as far as we can see, lies the whole world and even the sky and all its stars. The walls that link all these circles together are made of skin, they have pores, they breathe."[14]

When dramaturgs get involved in season planning, sitting on arts councils to affect public policy, or sitting on awards and grants committees to support certain types of work over others, the impact is more obvious. When plays change hearts and minds, laws and policies can follow, and injustices may be abated. That is one of the things that make our moment unprecedented. Mass media and mass interactive technology like the internet means that any single act of cultural production may now affect and be affected by hundreds, thousands, even millions of people—indeed, may be designed to do just that, as was the case with the Lysistrata Project, the 2003 global protest organized by Kathryn Blume against the U.S. invasion of Iraq.

If we are to recognize a *systemic dramaturgy* that takes a broader and more dynamic view, we must recognize that performance and technology, like the actor and the audience, are not two separate entities but, to borrow a term from Salter, "entangled." He writes, "Technologies are not simply inert or neutral artifacts that are, as Heidegger termed it, *ready to hand*: waiting for human presence to activate them and thus extend human action into the world, revealing it and framing it in a particular manner. Instead, technologies are . . . constructing and ordering socio-cultural-political relations. Technology does something in and to the world by modifying existing relations and constructing new ones between humans, tools, processes, and the environment in which all are deeply entangled."[15]

In an entangled theatrical system, a dramaturg holds multiple positions at once. She can fluidly occupy or at least surrogate the traditional positions of playwright, director, designer, or audience member. But she can also be network analyst, social media designer, new media philosopher, communications expert, engineer, field operative, entrepreneur, innovator, and diplomat. And she can do this in the theater or out, as a professional or an amateur. The relationship we are describing is one that Gilles Deleuze and Felix Guattari call an "assemblage," a big, messy, dynamic, living machine composed as much of desires, behaviors, beliefs, mores, and norms as it is of moving parts and bodies.[16]

The need to understand how systems work has never been more important than right now. The explosive proliferation of digital technology and information networks has fundamentally altered how we communicate, learn, play, think, and live. This intertwining of new technologies and everyday life is called technoculture. Living in a technoculture poses distinctive challenges and opportunities to those who hope to promote creativity, critical thinking, and political agency. The tools that enable us to communicate and create—social media, cloud storage, mobile phones, computer-aided design software—come with serious downsides, ranging from unexpected obsolescence and technical failures to unwanted surveillance that can lead to persecution and violence. Jon McKenzie reminds us that the diffusion and saturation of digital technologies has created a situation in which we "perform or else."[17] The structures and forces of organizational efficiency shape how we work, how we play, how we communicate, how we eat and drink and move. However, although these structures and forces are designed to squeeze out every drop of efficiency and although they tend to promote political and social homogeneity, they also provide opportunities for transgressive creation and new forms of social, political, and artistic interaction.

> Technoculture: the relationship between technology and culture and the expression of that relationship in patterns of social life, economic structures, politics, art, literature, and popular culture. . . . [The study of technoculture addresses] the kinds of questions that arise when we consider the role of technology in determining culture and the role of culture in structuring how we use, produce, define, and relate to the technologies with which we effect change in the world and which, in turn, effect changes in our understanding of ourselves.
> —Debra Benita Shaw, *Technoculture*), 4, 6

This is an opinion shared by game designer Eric Zimmerman, who argues that the information systems of the twentieth century have been rendered "flexible and organic" by way of digital networks that obligate us to play. He writes, "The ways that we work and communicate, research and learn, socialize and romance, conduct our finances and communicate with our governments, are all intimately intertwined with complex systems of information—in a way that could not have existed a few decades ago." Like Erickson, Zimmerman sees opportunities for creative response: "It is not enough to merely be a systems-literate person; to understand systems in an analytic sense. We also must learn to be playful in them. A playful system is a human system, a social system rife with contradictions and with possibility. Being playful is the engine of innovation and creativity: as we play, we think about thinking and we learn to act in new ways."[18] Dramaturgs are specialists in performance and play, so it behooves us to understand how the alterations and opportunities of technoculture affect how theater works and what it means.

Because the dramaturg is capable of addressing theater as a system of systems, we are uniquely poised to address some of the daunting cultural problems of the digital age. This is the reason that other kinds of media, including film, television, and more recently, videogames, have been seeking out and hiring specialists with dramaturgical skills. In different industries, these specialists go by names other than dramaturg. They're called researchers, fact-checkers, analysts, strategists, consultants, and editors. The producer of the smash hit *Assassin's Creed* videogames, Ubi-Soft Montreal, known for its spectacular re-creations of historical periods, employs a small army of academic advisors, professional historians, educators, and in-house specialists it calls "franchise historians." Because all these positions are focused on the employment of text analysis, historical research, and critical theoretical engagement toward the creation of moving dramatic art, they may all be categorized as dramaturgical. And we might also point to the network of "amateur" dramaturgs who shape the experiences of their friends and families as they play videogames or tabletop roleplaying games. The dramaturg's systemic approach to drama, theater, and performance enables us to make an important contribution to how we understand and make works that engage, practically or thematically, with technology, whether that work is intended for the stage, the videogame console, the weekly session of *Dungeons & Dragons*, or some as-yet-unimagined new media platform.

Because dramaturgs understand the multiple systems that constitute theater as a creative process and artistic experience, we guide our artistic and technical teams toward exciting new forms of performance made possible by emergent technologies. Does the systemic dramaturg always advocate for the use of digital technologies? Absolutely not. The systemic dramaturg affirms the doughty pragmatism of the theatrical

Introduction

arts. If necessity is the mother of theatrical invention, the dramaturg is the doula. Our job is to help find the best solution, whether that happens to be something new and shiny, all well and fine. But if the problem would be better served by the time-tested and "low tech," then just as well. The show must go on regardless of the technology in question. What matters is that we ask the right questions about technology for *this* show in *this* place at *this* time.

As dramaturgs, we are committed—mind, heart, body, and wallet— to creating theatrical experiences that are moving, memorable, shocking, and transformative. But we are just as committed to the idea that dramaturgy isn't only about aesthetics. Exploring the practical and conceptual challenges of new media empowers us to engage it both "as an enabling part of everyday life and culture, and as something that threatens it."[19] To that end, we explore in these pages the remarkable creations of contemporary theater makers like Blast Theory, the Builders Association, and Jennifer Haley, creations that explore the ways computers, social media, and robotics challenge how we understand and experience our relationships to other people, to our own bodies, to the spaces in which we live and work. We apply our dramaturgical tools to the diverse modes and communities of videogame performance, as well as to the misogyny, homophobia, and trollish terrorism of Gamergate.

Again, the central imperative of dramaturgy is to create the most interesting and significant performance possible, using all available means and avoiding anything that distracts or undermines the important themes of the drama. For example, we might be consulting with a director and sound designer to create the voice and sound for the Walk-through sections of Jennifer Haley's *Neighborhood 3: Requisition of Doom*, a play about augmented reality games and the emotional isolation of the U.S. suburb. We might push back against their desire to make the voice cold and robotic and introduce them to the brash personalities of online gaming culture. Designing a voice more in tune with gamer culture would help them amplify the play's themes of intergenerational miscommunication and moral malaise. Or we might advise a production team about how to take advantage of an audience's easy access to mobile phones, normally considered an utter nuisance. This was the case with the Builders Association's 2017 production of *Elements of Oz*. Audience members could download an app for their

16

Introduction

phones. At certain points in the show, they received a signal to look around the theater using their phone's camera, allowing them to see, for example, a tornado raging across the stage, technicolor flowers blossoming, or flying monkeys on the wing (fig. I.1).

As Marianne Weems explained in our interview, incorporating phones into the production was the equivalent of Dorothy walking through the door in the 1939 film, a sudden, delight-inducing movement into a space of fantasy and color, a "Technicolor door." But it was also a "doubled-edged sword and a provocation." So as dramaturgs encountering new technology, what are we really after? Do we seek that which is truly *original* or merely that which is *new*? It can be difficult sometimes to tell the difference.

You are reading this book because you want to understand that difference. You're interested in the newest, most cutting-edge forms of theatrical art available—those made available by digital technology. You're interested in digital projection, robots, augmented reality, multimedia performance, social media, and videogames. You're interested in these because they offer new ways to create performance but also because dramaturgy provides unique insights into how these technologies are shaping who we are, how we relate to each other, and

Fig. I.1. Smartphone augmenting the experience for audience members at the theatrical performance of the Builders Association's *Elements of Oz*. Photo by Larry Shea, courtesy of Marianne Weems.

17

Introduction

So, they were encouraged to turn away from the stage and look up and behind them and all around, and it produced so much anxiety in different members of the audience and people on stage. I mean, a huge amount of pleasure, especially for younger people, but for older people, or a more traditional theater-going audience, it feels impolite to hold this up between you and the actor. The technique was meant to be a kind of double-edged sword and a provocation: something happening on stage, and you can augment it with this fucking Technicolor door that you're carrying around all the time, and not really consciously thinking, "This is how I escape into Oz." But it was very hard for the actors because all of a sudden, everyone in the audience would have their phone in front of their face.

—Marianne Weems,
interview by the authors

how we live in the world. But you're reading this book, too, because you are committed to performance as an ancient and widespread art form, a way of creating and communicating that is far older than that open-source digital lighting-board software being touted by your lighting designer. And because you are a dramaturg, you have a unique set of skills that the digital world sorely needs—and primary among them is your ability to think *systemically*.

HOW TO USE THIS BOOK

In this introduction, we have described the idea of systemic dramaturgy. In what follows, we pair chapters that examine particular aspects of our approach with interviews with leading thinkers and makers to investigate what might be next on the horizon for dramaturgy in the digital age.

In chapter 1, we present the writings of Zeami Motokiyo as one intriguing historical foundation of a dramaturgy that understands performance as a dynamic system that encompasses and is encompassed by many other systems. Zeami's work is particularly interesting for its attention to a dynamic interrelationship (*sokyokuchi*, or "mutuality in balance") between the human performer and the inhuman object (in this case, a puppet). Zeami describes this differently than most Westerners have. However, as we show, Zeami has influenced a line of highly influential Western theater artists—among them Meyerhold, Grotowski, and Schechner—often associated with an antitechnological attitude. From the perspective of sokyokuchi, however, these artists are not antitechnology, but rather they take a different approach to and express a different attitude about technology.

Having established this theoretical foundation, we delve more deeply into our assertion that dramaturgs have unique capacities of particular utility in the digital age. One is covered in this introduction—the ability to think systemically. The second of these capacities is playfulness. In chapter 2, we demonstrate that the understanding of *play* remains, as it has always been, a vital component of the study and practice of performance, and that a reminder of the centrality of play to our enterprise, seen from the perspective of sokyokuchi, can fuel boundary-breaking innovations.

The third important capacity of dramaturgs is our understanding of *empathy and the ways it can be inspired and shaped.* In chapter 3, we assert that the rigor of dramaturgy has always been and must always remain responsible to a critical notion of improving humanity by exercising the human facility for cooperation, encouraging generosity and fellow feeling, and expunging fear and hatred. We demonstrate the urgent need for dramaturgs to engage, playfully and with an eye toward sokyokuchi, with digital culture to ensure that performance always strives toward the purpose for which it was, across times and cultures of this planet, always designed to do—help societies function better by making individual humans more compassionate.

In this introduction, we have also maintained that the advent of digital games and other forms of human-computer interaction have opened new horizons for the aesthetic explorations of dramaturgs. In chapter 4, we explore those new opportunities and discuss how dramaturgical attention to systems, play, and empathy is particularly necessary if these platforms are to realize their artistic potential.

In chapter 5, we provide a case study, a dramaturgical analysis of Jennifer Haley's *Neighborhood 3: Requisition of Doom,* as an example of how the systemic dramaturg might approach a multiplatform drama that weaves digital gaming into its plot—and conversely, how thinking systemically about staging a videogame can lead to surprising insights about theater itself.

Interspersed among chapters 1–5 are interviews we conducted with some of the most interesting cutting-edge thinkers and makers of digital performances, games, and scholarship, chosen because of their diverse backgrounds and approaches to these challenges. Chapter 6 brings these experts together for a roundtable on dramaturgy, multiplatform performance theory and practice, digital culture, gaming, and social media. We discuss the challenges the systemic dramaturg faces and identify paths for future exploration.

We conclude by reviewing the three conceptual frameworks we've constructed:

1. An expanded understanding of the history of theater and performance and, with that, a more flexible approach to the application of technologies to aesthetic problems in theater and out.
2. An understanding of play that engages its historical, conceptual, aesthetic, and practical dimensions and thus opens opportunities for the application of dramaturgy to a wider range of media.
3. A revised understanding of empathy that defines it as a "structure of affect" and treats it as a tool that can be turned to diverse tasks, including those that would seek to demonize and oppress.

At all times in this book, we have struggled against our biases and predilections toward Western thought and artistic traditions. We observe that the wider our field of inquiry, the more international, multicultural, and broadly historical it can be, the better our access to useful theories and solutions. We have struggled against our own gender and sexual biases and that of our society to include the voices of women, LGBTQ+, and transgendered individuals, not merely because we believe these individuals deserve a place at the table but because their concerns have become immediate and vital to the ongoing discourses in which we work—especially discourses about technology, which historically have been articulated against those who aren't straight, male, or cis-gendered. We regret wherever we have failed in these attempts, continue to work to improve our ability to think and act inclusively, and invite our readers to make our systemic approach to dramaturgy even more systemic.

INTERVIEW 1

DRAMATIZING SYSTEMS

NOAH WARDRIP-FRUIN ON STORYTELLING IN THE DIGITAL AGE

Noah Wardrip-Fruin is a professor of computational media at the University of California–Santa Cruz. With Michael Mateas, he codirects the Expressive Intelligence Studio, a technical and cultural research group. Wardrip-Fruin's research areas include new models of storytelling in games, how games express ideas through play, the literary possibilities of computational media, and how cultural software can be preserved, discovered, and cited. He has authored or coedited five books on games and digital media for the MIT Press, including *The New Media Reader* (2003), which has been influential in the development of interdisciplinary digital media curricula. His most recent book, *Expressive Processing: Digital Fictions, Computer Games, and Software Studies*, was published by MIT in 2009. Wardrip-Fruin's collaborative playable media projects, including *Screen* and *Talking Cure*, have been presented by the Guggenheim Museum, Whitney Museum of American Art, New Museum of Contemporary Art, Krannert Art Museum, Hammer Museum, and a wide variety of festivals and conferences. He holds both a PhD (2006) and an MFA (2003) from Brown University, an MA (2000) from the Gallatin School at New York University, and a BA (1994) from the Johnston Center at the University of Redlands.

Interview 1: *Dramatizing Systems*

MIKE SELL: Why does play matter?

NOAH WARDRIP-FRUIN: I tell students in my introductory game design class that the class is about two things. One is "How do you make games?" and the second is "How can a game be *about* something?" I tell them that even though the class has games in the title, and we're talking about making games, I'm really not interested in the question of what a game *is*. I'm interested in things that invite play, and interestingly there's almost no pushback against that anymore. When I originally offered this class in 2006, I usually got the question, "But is that *really* a game?" I almost can't think of a less productive question, unless what you're doing is giving a game award, in which case you might have to answer that. But for me, mostly *play* matters because it's a more open-ended and productive alternative to *game*, even though what *game* is itself is something that's been hugely expanding. It's not as if games are a huge cultural and economic force because more and more people are playing *Centipede*. It's because games are becoming more and more things to more and more people in more and more venues. I guess I'd say play matters for all the other reasons you'd find if you were reading

---

In *The Ambiguity of Play*, Brian Sutton-Smith attempts to define play, a notoriously ambiguous term we attempt a similar task in Chapter 2). Attempting to provide some order to the denotative chaos, he describes seven "rhetorics" or "narratives" that are commonly used to describe, define, and assign particular ideological value to playful activity:

1. Progress: Play is a form of learning, enabling the player (especially the child) to develop and adapt.
2. Fate: Life is comparable to a game of chance in which humans are mere plaything (i.e., a roll of the dice).
3. Power: A "rhetoric of ancient hue," play is conflict and heroic achievement is comparable to the agon of sporting and athletic contests.
4. Identity: Play, especially in the form of festivals or other traditional celebrations, affirms and strengthens community.
5. Imagination: Playful creativity, particularly in its most phantasmagorical forms, enables discovery and provides perspective (i.e., games of make-believe).
6. Self: Play enables the individual to relax, escape, experience heightened physical or emotional states (i.e., bungee jumping) or meditate.
7. Frivolity: Play is an idle activity that threatens order and authority and is associated with both threats to puritanical order and with trickster figures and fools.

Sutton-Smith's *The Ambiguity of Play* and the rhetorics he discusses. Play is a hugely fundamental human activity.

MICHAEL CHEMERS: micha cárdenas mentioned to us that she thinks that the tactics that people use to define what a game is often result in the exclusion of people on the basis of race, gender, or sexuality. Is that something you've observed as well?

WARDRIP-FRUIN: People use definitions to exclude or include things consciously and unconsciously all the time. Far more often, people say, "I really only mean digital games." Then we bring up all the problems of exclusion and so on, and we find out that what they *really* mean are digital games in particular genres they recognize. Then people who are trying to do something that might be innovative and uncomfortable will be excluded. But that kind of exclusion is far from unique to games.

CHEMERS: There are direct connections between right-wing activists and Gamergate, where techniques of harassment were intentionally weaponized or made part of a coordinated political action against those who wanted videogames to be different.

WARDRIP-FRUIN: Gamergate, from my point of view, comes out of the same cultural impetus that gives us the alt-right. It is a recruiting ground for it and is fanned into flames by the same funding sources. I'm writing a book about the game *Gone Home*, which was attacked by the folks from 4chan and so on long before the name Gamergate was ever in use.

SELL: Storytelling is a big part of what you teach and do. You've argued that we need to change the way we think about storytelling.

WARDRIP-FRUIN: I'm interested in new forms of storytelling broadly. For example, there are people who for decades have found ways to take advantage of computer networking to tell new kinds of stories. But what interest me most are kinds of storytelling that are in some ways computational. People are doing interesting things with generative storytelling and with responsive, interactive storytelling, some of which is in the form of games. But it could be in the form of other kinds of digital experiences, hybridizing with other media and so on.

One of the projects that came out of our lab in the last few years is this piece *Bad News*, led by James Ryan, Ben Samuel, and Adam Summerville. In this game, a new North American small town is generated for each participant. But the game is played by a player who, in real life, walks up to a stand with a curtain on it and sits down in the chair in front of it. An actor opens the curtain and tells you that even though this is your first day on the job as their assistant, they've been called away to a nearby town, so you're going to have to inform a family that their relative is dead. But we're not sure who the next of kin is, so you need to go around town trying to find the next of kin without revealing that

Interview 1: *Dramatizing Systems*

you are looking for the relatives of a dead person. And so we need to come up with a cover story.

You are brought into two levels of roleplaying immediately. You start talking about how you're going to move around the town, and each time you decide to interact with someone, the curtain closes and reopens, and that same actor is now playing a new character. But there's a third person, unseen by the player, who is sitting at a computer, who is feeding information about the computer-generated town into an interface with the actor, so the actor can see whom they are playing and to whom they are related in the town. This is just one example of ways I think we're also seeing traditional forms of storytelling being hybridized with forms that are more specific to digital computation.

SELL: This is not the first time that you've made works that require the physical presence and copresence of player and a human mediator working in tandem with a computational process.

WARDRIP-FRUIN: I guess there are a lot of things that might motivate this kind of experience. For example, when we designed *Bad News*, we started with the idea that there are a lot of assumptions that are built into human dialogue systems and also in game genres about what people might say, how they say it, and what kinds of reactions make sense. Why don't we just do it with real people? Then we'll get all these ideas we would never have had if we just sat down and went with the assumptions that were built into the tools. Very quickly, it became clear that this wasn't just another data-gathering exercise. This was an experience.

SELL: What do you worry about when it comes to the body and computational storytelling?

WARDRIP-FRUIN: It depends on the medium.

For CAVE-style virtual reality, I was shocked at how much the thing that really made it different from other forms of virtual reality was that our bodies are there, but were not being made part of the experiences. People would make the walls disappear and then say, "Don't move around, because you might bump into the walls and damage them." What we wanted with *Screen* was to make us free to use our bodies, and so we could have the body's movement be a major

---

CAVE: Invented by Carolina Cruz-Neira, Daniel J. Sandin, and Thomas A. DeFanti at the University of Illinois, Chicago Electronic Visualization Laboratory in 1992, a Cave Automatic Virtual Environment is an immersive theatrical space in which walls, floor, and ceiling all serve as projection surfaces, creating a virtual reality.

Interview 1: *Dramatizing Systems*

part of the interaction. Whereas in the case of something like *Talking Cure* or *The Impermanence Agent*, we were asking, "What is it about this medium and its relationship to the body that seems worth exploring?"

CHEMERS: We're interested in the difference between two kinds of liveness: traditional theater on one end and media that encourage improvisatory or "emergent" experiences on the other. Your work seems to be positioned somewhere in the middle.

WARDRIP-FRUIN: You're right about that. We began having this interest in creating rich simulated worlds from which many possible narratives could emerge, whereas a lot of systems only create as much of the world as needed to tell a particular story. I don't think one or another of these is a good or bad choice: they're different aesthetics. In terms of creating the world on the fly or in response to what the player does, that's been one of my big obsessions. If you look at a traditional play, there are lots of things that might happen in a particular performance. There's that possibility space, but then there's this huge, much larger possibility space of all the ways you might choose to stage that play, right? If you look at something like *Dungeons & Dragons*, then there's whatever the Dungeon Master has got planned, and there's this possibility space of things the players might do and ways that the DM might respond. Most videogames are essentially DMs that railroad the players—perhaps there are moments of player freedom, but the main track is already determined.

CHEMERS: There is an illusion of choice, but it's really just, "Did you shoot the target or not," right?

WARDRIP-FRUIN: But there are also lots of sandbox or simulation games, where there's possibilities to go in lots of different directions; it's just that those possibilities tend to be based either on simulations of physical space, which we have such good ones of because of big military investments for things like training fighter pilots, or on resource simulations, which we also have because of big investments from the military and organizations like the RAND Corporation. There are so many other areas of human life where we don't have those kinds of rich simulations.

So what tends to happen in the research group that Michael Mateas and I run is that often students will come in and tell us they want to make richer simulations for talking with characters, for social interactions, for the many ways that one might complete a quest as opposed to the *World of Warcraft* model of quest as grocery list. Those are ambitious projects that require looking at how things are being done in today's games and other forms of media out in the world, imagining how some of those gaps could be crossed by trying to build

Interview 1: *Dramatizing Systems*

new computational models, trying to build tools that support those models, and trying to build games that use those tools. Unfortunately, these steps don't all always get completed within the course of someone's PhD, especially if we get a negative result somewhere along the way, but from my point of view, it's the role of the university to take those big gambles. It's basic research in games. It's not better pathfinding algorithms; it's trying to create things that would enable whole new genres of experience.

SELL: You and your students do not feel particularly wedded to the notion of creating this rich simulation only in one medium.

WARDRIP-FRUIN: It's a part of being willing to do basic research. If you think about the common model for computing research, often you might say that our lab is really good at reinforcement learning. So we are going to find a bunch of ways of doing reinforcement learning. This is our hammer, we're going to look around for nails, and some of those nails might be involved in games, some of them might be involved in database de-duplication, who knows? You can make progress that way. But I'm much more interested in saying, "Let's think about an ambitious aesthetic goal that matters to us as people, and then let's view everything that's been done in the last seventy years." So computing research becomes a toolbox from which we can go and grab things, but then let's go beyond computing research. Hopefully, we're a whole culture of people who actually are aware of forms of media besides computer games made in the last five years, and we can actually go and borrow from those other boxes as well. It does mean that we do work more slowly than we would if all we did were little nail-hammering projects, but to me, it's a lot more interesting.

CHEMERS: But what do you do when you've got a student who says they want to figure out a way to model better human interaction, better social interaction with characters? Where does that student go to learn how to do that?

WARDRIP-FRUIN: Hopefully, they pilfer a whole lot of places. We tend to recruit students who've got interdisciplinary backgrounds already, and we had one, Josh McCoy, who had done his undergrad both in the social sciences and computer science. His initial thought was, "Okay, well, I know some stuff from the social sciences literature that I might borrow from, someone like Erving Goffman." And we said, "Well, yes, but he's actually making an analogy to theater and performance, and what you want to do in the end is actually produce a piece of media that is legible to people the way things from the arts are."

This student's model ended up having some inspiration from Goffman but also from popular self-help books. Things like that are often widely culturally

Interview 1: *Dramatizing Systems*

In *The Presentation of Self in Everyday Life,* Erving Goffman describes identity in dramaturgical terms, interpreting mundane face-to-face interactions in as theatrical encounters in which the individual engages in diverse strategies of self-presentation in an attempt to guide and control the impression of others.

legible. Then we told him to choose some media that has the kinds of interpersonal conflicts and rapprochements and other experiences that you'd want to see in your digital experience. Go and closely observe them.

So the students who were working on the game—including McCoy, Samuel, Mike Treanor, and Aaron Reed—would have notebook parties where they would watch *Sex and the City* and they'd make notes on what they thought were the units of social interaction going on that might attend a potential model in a game. Are there rules? What are the rules? What do the rules parameterize? What are the patterns of interaction? And then they would compare their notes and begin to get sense of how to build it into a computer model. Eventually, this project led to the game *Prom Week* and the Ensemble "social physics" system, which we just released open source.

SELL: Is that remediation or is it something else?

WARDRIP-FRUIN: I think maybe I'd call it applied media studies. It's basically like you are doing media studies or performance studies or some other humanist research. You're being a humanist to the extent that you're able. Some of our students are trained as humanists. Some of them are coming to it for the first time in the service of trying to make something well. Engineers are like artists in that what we do is we make stuff—sometimes we call it computer science, but that's only because of physics envy, because computer science came out of this weird combination of mathematics and electrical engineering, where it seemed to make sense to call it science but it was really about making things. I think in the arts, people do much the same. You put on that humanist hat for a while, but it's applied humanism—you're trying to learn things from what you're looking at, applied to make something else. Right?

CHEMERS: Which goes against the old idea that the humanities are grounded in analysis rather than making. I think what you're saying is that the emphasis in both engineering and art is creation of a new artifice.

WARDRIP-FRUIN: While public humanities run the other way, as in "Let's take our humanities insights and hybridize with arts techniques in order to share them with the broader public."

Interview 1: *Dramatizing Systems*

CHEMERS: If I were a traditionally trained dramaturg—that is, someone who studies the history and aesthetic principles of the theater for the purposes of enriching performance experiences and who has a very strong understanding of how aesthetic systems, social systems, epistemological systems, heuristic systems, hermeneutic systems, and other systems operate in live performance—and I wanted to become a PhD student in your program, what would I need to know?

WARDRIP-FRUIN: We have in some ways had to address this question, because we started a PhD program in computational media. Our goal was that by the time our students began working on their dissertations, they would have mastered an ability to interpret and critically engage with media made by themselves and other people. We also wanted them to be able to make media and do the level of software development that's necessary for the kind of research they want to do. For different students, different parts of these are going to have different levels of importance. We had a PhD student, Chaim Gingold, whose dissertation is focused on doing a software studies interpretation of the original *Sim City* in its original historical and social context. So he certainly knows how to make media and how to program a computer, but his dissertation focused primarily on the interpretive work. Someone from that traditional dramaturgy background, if they came into our PhD program, the assumption would be, "Okay, if you don't know how to program a computer, then that is going to be one of your first orders of business; if you haven't made media, then doing some actual making is going to be another one of the first things you do."

But there's always a distinction between what you want students to know, which is your own declaration of the discipline, and then what is actually useful for someone to know. I taught a collaborative class at NYU for a few years with Adrianne Wortzel, and neither of us knew how to write or direct a movie, or light one, or pick up actors' voices on the microphone, or anything like that. But NYU said, "You bring a useful perspective, and our Oscar-winning directing teacher also doesn't know how to direct a movie." So the dramaturg could come to me as a student who's getting their PhD in the arts or humanities and could participate in projects and never learn to program a computer, or they could come in and sort of be disciplined into computational media. The expectation would be that they become broader maybe even than we expect our own faculty to be.

CHEMERS: Once at Carnegie Mellon, we had a famous alumnus come back and talk to the students. He had studied lighting design at Carnegie Mellon but was now a famous and successful television producer. One of the students in my not-very-popular theater history class said to him, "Look, am I really paying forty

Interview 1: *Dramatizing Systems*

thousand dollars a year here at Carnegie Mellon to learn AutoCAD? Because my little brother just got AutoCAD on the computer and taught it to himself." And the gentleman said, "No, I don't need students who can do AutoCAD. That you could learn. We can pay somebody to teach you how to do that. That's nothing. But every day I go into a room and there's a bunch of images, and I have to turn those images into stories that are compelling. That's what I need you to learn how to do." The students naturally wanted to know where you learned how to do that, and bless him, he said, "I learned it in theater history, dramatic analysis, and playwriting classes." My class got more popular.

WARDRIP-FRUIN: When I was a grad student at Brown, a recruiter came from Pixar and asked me about the undergrad students that I was teaching. I didn't know the rumors going around at the time that Andy from *Toy Story* was based on Andy van Dam, a professor of computer science at Brown who helped design early hypertext systems and pioneered the field of computer graphics. So I said, "Well, what are you looking for?" and he said, "I'm looking for somebody who can tell a damn story. I don't care if they know any particular software, but somebody who can actually make things come to life." Not only do we have a wrongheaded idea that education is vocational training, but we have an extremely wrongheaded idea of what vocational training even is.

CHEMERS: This brings me to something you and Pat Harrigan wrote about in 2009 in your book *Third Person*, "vast narratives," which has been influential in the study of television serials, comic book universes, and crossover culture that exists in multiple operational systems that interact. I'm thinking of Marvel, for instance, which now comprises an enormous mythology in which comic books, television shows, movies, and online material interact vibrantly with each other and with fan fiction, reviews, and who knows what. Critics used to say the "author" is dead, but what we are seeing is the contrary—the "author" is now a position occupied by multiple individuals and even groups. What kinds of new dramaturgical skills of analysis are required by these?

WARDRIP-FRUIN: I think there are tools out there for a lot of these things. There's definitely humanities literature about adaptation, which can be applied to look at how stories exist across difference platforms. Clearly, performance traditions are some of the richest we see for people who want to participate in these media, but I think the missing bit is teaching people to think critically about systems. As far as I can tell, critical thinking about systems is still a really unusual topic, and it gets a lot of pushback. For example, a few years ago on the Games Network mailing list, there was a discussion of a workshop that was going to be held, something

Interview 1: *Dramatizing Systems*

like Against Procedurality. The premise was, "Let's stop paying attention to things like game rules, because game rules really aren't that important. What we really care about is like player behavior player, emotion, et cetera." I wrote back to the list and I said, "This is like saying our understanding of traffic is really being limited by too much focus on how cars operate and the rules of the road, when really all we care about is how drivers feel and what drivers are trying to express as they press down on the accelerator. But let's not talk about that accelerator."

I observe a high level of discomfort, whether people are trained in the humanities or in the social sciences, in dealing with the fact that digital games are made of software. Experts can't understand how the average players play, and we certainly can't understand these exceptional players that were deeply interested in play without engaging this thing as a software object. There's a sense that the software artifact is territory that is owned by engineering, and if we as humanist critics intrude on it, then (A) we're interlopers, and we don't like being interlopers, we want to be seen as experts; and (B) we may just get sucked in, we may end up being taken over by the instrumental values of engineering, as opposed to maintaining our critical stance. There are a couple of things that are able to make me angry in our field, and one of them is basically saying it's inconvenient or difficult to admit that these are technologies. Until we as faculty and students can learn to do that, I think we're going to have real trouble.

SELL: *System* is a fungible term; it can be applied to different things. For those of us who work in performance studies, or for those of us in English departments, we're used to terms that allow us to organize and analyze all kinds of objects. That fungibility is intellectually adventurous and it often allows us to reflect on conventions in performance in ways that enable us to understand more and go beyond that. But we also get into the danger of, if you will, metaphorical or figurative overreach. I wonder if you could talk a little bit about what concerns you have about the benefits or potential risks of the idea that we might be using an analytic model that is wedded to a particular kind of medium or technology or discipline and using it to look at a lot of other things.

WARDRIP-FRUIN: One question is, How do traditional humanities methods travel across fields, if they do? For example, there is a field called critical code studies, which to my mind is essentially asking, "How do we take something like close reading and apply it to software?" Mostly, you can absolutely do this. But most software is not productive to close read as code because questions of, for instance, how variables are named or what comments made by the programmers say are not the most telling elements.

Interview 1: Dramatizing Systems

What's actually interesting about a software system is how it functions. If we want to closely read "collision detection" in *Grand Theft Auto*, do we care what name they gave to the bounding boxes that are used for collision detection on police cars? Or do we want to know that the police will allow you to break any traffic law, but if you sideswipe them, even a little, they'll run you down? That's the part about collision detection that is expressing an idea about the world. The question is, Where's the productive analogy? I'd say critical code studies is more like history of the book. There are great insights that come from that history, but you don't want to apply it all the time, everywhere. Whereas close reading, that is looking closely at how the system operates, is pretty much useful all the time, everywhere. There are no pieces of software where you don't need to know what it's doing to analyze it. That's the thing that requires your close attention.

SELL: I want to make sure I heard you correctly—that close reading for you is a solvent technique. It's one that you feel works across disciplines, across fields.

WARDRIP-FRUIN: There have always been things like "close playing" used in video-game development, in board game creation, and so on. Designers said, "Here we have to pay really close attention and note exactly what happened under these circumstances, then try to trace back why that happened, and so on." But that said, I think there's a question about defining games, and it makes sense that what we call games run a pretty wide gamut. For example, *Myst* is a deck of 3D images with links between certain ones and a tiny little bit of "if" statements. But it's essential to the power of *Myst* that it uses a little bit of system to make it a little bit a game. I don't mean to disparage games like that, but they're using a small bit of gameness to amplify something that's primarily other forms of media.

And then there are things like *Sim City*, which is really just a system with a little bit of other media. In analyzing *Myst*, maybe we might want to close-play it, but we also really, really want to bring visual studies to bear on it. Whereas, maybe visual studies isn't going to tell us much about *Sim City*. Certainly, it could tell us almost nothing about *Hammurabi*. But there are other things, like the way *Sim City* is engaging with ideas of the city, or the way *Hammurabi* is engaging with ideas of history. Those questions are going to tell us more than questions that visual studies would ask. If we draw the right analogy to what close reading is, for games and other systems, it's going to be useful everywhere. And other techniques, like history of media or visual studies, are going to be useful in particular circumstances.

SELL: It's a poetic endeavor in some respects.

Interview 1: *Dramatizing Systems*

WARDRIP-FRUIN: Which is saying we spent hundreds of years developing this box of critical techniques and, again, let's not be the people who have the hammer and just look at everything as a nail.

CHEMERS: When I was a new professor, my mentor was Brian Johnston, one of the greatest theater scholars of the twentieth century. I sat in on his graduate seminar one time when he was doing a close reading of the *Oresteia*. He was talking about the phalanx military formation as a reflection of the notion of democracy and how that's reflected in one particular tiny passage in the play. One of the students raised his hand and said, "Excuse me, Professor Johnston, but don't you think you're reading too much into this?" Without missing a beat, Brian said, "Well, since Aeschylus was a genius and I'm not, I rather think I'm not reading enough into it."

So many factors go into performance that are not controllable or predictable, and the actors know that. It's part of their training to respond to those things and bring them in, whether it's the audience behaving a certain way or not behaving a certain way, or it's raining or it's foggy or there's traffic. But we still see an open hostility to criticality, whether it's theater people questioning the use of computers or computer people questioning the use of theater methods.

I wonder if that same kind of hostility to criticality is what we're seeing when these engineers who want to be game developers suddenly find themselves butting up against the kind of critical apparatus that we traditionally use in the arts. They want to be good storytellers. They want to make stuff that's moving and compelling, but they don't appear to want to engage with that kind of criticality, particularly if they feel that it will restrict their creativity.

WARDRIP-FRUIN: I studied creative writing in undergrad and grad school, and one of the differences was that in undergrad, creative writers didn't think they had anything to learn from literature class, because they were just going to find a story and tell it, and maybe it would just mess up their creative brains if they looked at how other people have constructed stories and were asked to critically examine their own stories and so on. By the time someone is good enough to get into grad school, they've matured beyond that. But it gives me some compassion for those undergrad game development students. I had a group of students who wanted to make their entertaining game about going out and partying and so on. They had essentially made a game where female characters were obstacles, and so I just tried to keep my cool, and I asked them, "Okay, how would you feel if I gave you this game to play, but these characters weren't women, they were African Americans, and you had to get around these Black obstacles in order

Interview 1: *Dramatizing Systems*

to accomplish the things you wanted to in the game?" I just went through this conversation with them where they can pretty immediately see they had said something they didn't mean to say, but somebody had to be there to point it out to them. I think most of them get there by the time they finish.

SELL: Could you speak to where you see your work going, particularly in terms of humanities-oriented computational studies?

WARDRIP-FRUIN: I'm trying to finish a book right now called *How Pac Man Eats*. It's basically about the question of how games can be *about* things on that sort of fundamental level. The argument of the book is that there is a fundamental level that we basically skipped over in game studies. It's as though we were making our arguments all about film genre, and we've never actually had a conversation of cuts and pans. And then the book keeps going right up to that higher level of what we can model and why those are the things that we're able to model and so on. The book is almost entirely focused on that systemic and explicitly humanistic inquiry. As for what we'll do next in the lab, one of our PhD students is interested in building systems that are in part inspired by things like *Dungeons & Dragons*, which has usually been talked about as players telling a story together, and she thinks there's been an underemphasis on the extent to which they are also about creating a world together. She's engaged in that process of humanist evaluation. To my mind, for most students who are really going to make an exciting contribution in this area, humanities is the first step that will lead them into actually having an interesting computational question that will then allow them to make a compelling piece of media.

SOKYOKUCHI

NOVICE: Why did they applaud?
KNOWLEDGEABLE COMPANION: It's hard to explain, but
  basically,
he did that exactly as if he were a puppet.

Some very old approaches to theater articulate a new and useful way of thinking about and working with technology on and off the stage. Here, we delve into the historiographic and theoretical foundations of this idea, keeping in mind the questions we raised in our introduction regarding how we might renew the practice of dramaturgy to respond to emergent technologies while remaining faithful to the enduring principles and practices of the craft. Those questions inform an exchange overheard by Michael at a 1996 performance of Santō Kyōden's *Playboy, Grilled Edo Style* (*Edo umare uwaki no kabayaki*) at Indiana University's Lilly Library. It occurred at the moment when the hero of the play first entered the stage, crossed to the center, and in one smooth movement shifted his stance, bringing his parasol from his left shoulder to his right, earning thunderous applause from members of the audience who understood and appreciated what they had just seen. The challenge faced by the novice spectator of Kabuki is twofold: to fully understand, first, why a human actor would intentionally wish to mimic the movements of a puppet, and second, why an audience would find such mimicry so profoundly moving. As it happens, this doubled challenge provides an excellent starting point for our first case study of systemic dramaturgy.

Sokyokuchi

The conventions of Kabuki are challenging to the novice because they reflect a different way of thinking about and making with technology. To engage that difference, we need to understand the development of Kabuki and Bunraku theater, particularly their interrelations, and the works of the fourteenth-century actor, playwright, and dramaturg Zeami Motokiyo, whose worldwide impact is as far-reaching as G. E. Lessing's. We don't wish to imply that Zeami's is the only way to think about technology and theater. The Black Arts Movement's theory of *muntu*, *nepantlerismo* as employed by the Chicano theater, and Richard Schechner's *rasaesthetics* are equally systemic, grounded in non-European traditions, and deeply concerned with the relationship of theater and technology. However, Zeami's influence on artists like Vsevelod Meyerhold, Erwin Piscator, Jerzy Grotowski, Schechner, and others stands as a good example of how an improved understanding of the history of theater and technology can better prepare dramaturgs to identify diverse understandings and applications of older theater technologies and incorporate emerging forms.

To that end, we explore here a set of questions that will enable dramaturgs to expand their understanding of the relationship of theater and technology to encompass a much broader historical and global perspective:

o To what extent are traditional dramaturgical theories and practices rendered obsolete in the age of digital, robotic, and social technologies?
o How do new technologies alter the way we experience live performance? How do assumptions about liveness inform the understanding and experience of technology?
o How do new technologies alter our understanding of the human—especially the capacity to perceive, think, feel, and communicate? What dramaturgical practices can best engage these alterations to help create theater that is moving, meaningful, and memorable?

We observe that the efforts of Meyerhold to integrate new (to him) technical knowledge were similar in many significant ways to those undertaken by Ka̅lida̅sa, Aeschylus, Hrosvitha, and any other dramaturgical thinkers faced with the emerging technologies and technes of their times. And in fact, Meyerhold's own efforts, which were fundamental to the shape of modern theatrical practice, were profoundly influenced by Zeami. The questions asked by these ancients were no different from the ones dramaturgs ask now: How can we tell *this* story and move *this* audience with *these* tools? If we had different tools, could we tell a different story? Could we inspire different emotions and ideas in our audience?

To illustrate our contention that the challenges facing the dramaturg in the era of social media, cyborg performers, and iPhones are far from exclusively modern, we focus especially on Zeami to demonstrate that the cultivation of a particular kind of aesthetic sensibility, one with roots in the classical Japanese theater, can tremendously aid in our navigation of these advances. Zeami called this sensibility sokyokuchi. And though we find Zeami's dramaturgy particularly interesting—and especially relevant—we acknowledge that there are many ways of thinking about theater and technology, many ways to make theater. What follows is only one of many ways we might essay a historically enriched, culturally diverse practice of systemic dramaturgy.

MUTUALITY IN BALANCE

Zeami Motokiyo (ca. 1363–ca. 1443) was born into a theatrical family. His father, Kan'ami Kiyotsugu, was one of the most celebrated theatrical performers and aesthetic innovators of his day. Kan'ami's specialization was Noh, also called *Sarugaku*, the aristocratic, operatic performance genre that evolved from ministerial performances by Buddhist priests. When Zeami was about ten or eleven years old, the family's performances were attended by Shogun Ashikaga Yoshimitsu, the supreme military and political power in Japan at the time. So impressed was the shogun that he became the family's financial patron, and Zeami spent the rest of his life as a valued courtier near the center of Japan's political power elite. From this position, Zeami advanced the Noh theater not only by acting in and writing dozens of plays but also by writing more than twenty dramaturgical texts that addressed the most pressing questions regarding the dramatic text, the theater, and performance. Like Aristotle's *Poetics* and Bharatamuni's *Natyasastra*, Zeami's texts describe the technical matters of dramatic composition and performance technique and also delve into the relationship of theater to moral and ethical philosophy. Like many other dramaturgs, Zeami argued that performance was one of the best possible ways to encourage audiences to become better human beings—more compassionate, more focused on decency and righteousness, and more concerned for the greater social good. In other words, he had a systemic understanding of performance's relationship with society.

This is nowhere more evident than in his writings about puppets. In his 1424 treatise *Kakyo* (The mirror held up to the flower), Zeami uses the imagery of a puppeteer to describe the project of the actor: "This constructed puppet, on a cart, shows various aspects of himself but cannot come to life of itself. It represents a deed performed by moving strings. At the moment when the strings are cut, the figure falls and crumbles. *Sarugaku* too is an art that makes use of just such artifice. What supports these illusions and gives them life is the intensity of mind of the actor."[1]

Puppetry had been a popular performance tradition in Japan long before Zeami. But stringed marionettes and hand puppet shows were generally considered lowbrow entertainment, not fit for aristocrats who exclusively enjoyed the elegant and serious Noh. Over time, however, puppeteers collaborated with chanters and shamisen players to create a new, sophisticated form that fused these multiple media. It was a smash hit, particularly when it told the romantic story of Princess Joruri ("Pure Crystal"). This new medium in fact became known as Joruri and was popular with the merchant and artisan classes, who wanted to emulate aristocratic culture but were not permitted to attend or participate in Noh. Fed by a steady stream of cash from prosperous merchants, Joruri artists evolved their work into the extraordinary, beautiful genre that is known today as Bunraku.

Bunraku puppets, which have been in use since the eighteenth century, are elegant marvels of technology (fig. 1.1). They require three operators: the lead puppeteer to control the head and right hand, the second to control the left hand and foot, and the third to control the right foot. Puppeteers employ a sophisticated system of pulleys, strings, and rotating sockets to emulate smooth human movement. Though the puppets are made of wood, cloth, and rope, so complex and delicate is this technology—and so rigorous are the standards of artists and audiences—that puppeteers must undergo decades of rigorous training

Fig. 1.1. A Bunraku performance by the Hitomi-Za Puppet Troupe at the III Festival Internacional de Titelles de Barcelona in 1975. *Photograph by Pilar Aymerich. Wikicommons.*

before they are allowed to perform onstage. The masters of Bunraku are deemed "tangible cultural properties" and treated as national treasures by government and citizens alike.

We find it impossible not to make useful comparisons between superbly trained Bunraku masters and the designers and performers of digital spectaculars. It is fascinating to contemplate what, at both a theoretical and philosophical level, the difference is between the three-person performance of a puppet at Osaka's Takemoto theater in 1684 and the thrilling blend of light, sound, and digital projections with old-fashioned practical magic in *Harry Potter and the Cursed Child*, which premiered at London's Palace Theatre in 2016. Whether theater technology is made of rope and cloth or code and Wi-Fi transmitters, dramaturgs consider it first and foremost a tool to bring the artificial to life, enhance the work of live performers, and maximize the experience of audiences. But simply claiming that a puppet and a projection are essentially the same doesn't dispel the deep-seated antipathy that some prominent theater and performance critics feel toward new media performance, cyborg performers, and multiplatform theater (or, for that matter, puppets). And it doesn't make a particularly convincing argument. Any inquiry into the overlap of dramaturgical and technological systems must deal head-on with this antipathy—and do so in a fashion that honors their concerns while addressing their conceptual and historical errors.

The puppet provides an intriguing solution. Zeami's tendency to view the relationship between puppet and puppeteer as a metaphor for human experience is hardly unique. Philosophers of many stripes (aesthetic, spiritual, and political) have used the puppet as a metaphor to underscore the putative divide between the natural and the artificial or the human and the inhuman—two of the most persistent and pernicious dualities in the European philosophical tradition. Most of the time, the image of a puppeteer (clearly alive and natural) being the animating force behind the puppet (clearly unliving and manufactured) is a stereotype that reinforces the notion that these two states might interact in a fashion that is beautiful and moving but are nevertheless, in some essential way, separate and different. In this way of thinking, the live and the artificial reside in separate realms, opposed to one another in fundamental ways.

It is perhaps this notion that inspired Aristotle to put what he called "spectacle" (all the visual tricks and trappings of theater) at the bottom of his hierarchy of Tragedy's constituent elements. At the top, of course, Aristotle put plot, because he believed fervently that the spectator's engagement with a Tragedy's central action ensured the proper emotional and intellectual response. The other elements (character, diction, theme, music, and spectacle) are placed in a subservient latticework in descending order of importance as they move toward the embodied, material aspects of stage business. Aristotle thus privileges the playwright as the genius whose vision all other artists involved in the production must serve—the technical artist being the lowliest.

This hierarchy has been both challenged and ignored at various points in theater history, but since at least the eighteenth century, directors, theater companies, historians, and dramaturgs have been particularly critical when they wanted to bring in technical spectacle. This question was as political as it was aesthetic. In *Environmental*

Theatre, Richard Schechner writes, "One thing is for sure—the play is not the thing. . . . Certainly, Hamlet didn't serve the playwright's intentions, but his own pressing motives." Echoing Lessing, Schechner advocates a dramaturgy that understands the script as part of a multifaceted matrix of transactions that are determined by, among other things, the interpersonal dynamics of company members and the unique characteristics of the space in which the work is developed, as well as the larger social context. In this more holistic understanding of production, Schechner alerts us to the fact that "all production elements speak their own language."[2]

Schechner's ideas have proliferated among scholars and dramaturgs over the last half century. A survey of recent theater reveals a broad spectrum of page-stage relationships, including the deconstructive stagings of classic dramatic works by the Wooster Group, the devised theater of Ariane Mnouchkine's Théâtre du Soleil, and the "new media dramaturgy" associated with dumb type and Kris Verdonck. In light of these, we find ourselves attracted to Geoffrey Proehl's broad-minded conception of "dramaturgical sensibility," which opens the process of critical inquiry and collaboration to "the slow, ambiguous emergence of meaning, particularly those meanings (discursive and aesthetic) we seek with and from our collaborators."[3] This process presumes a radically expanded concept of the dramatic "text." Rather than seeing what Aristotle calls "spectacle" as a necessary evil that distracts from the contemplation of the plot and theme, we believe contemporary dramaturgy broadly holds visual and material aspects of performance as integral parts of the multifaceted matrix of meaning that communicates ideas and emotions.

Zeami's dramaturgy of puppet and puppeteer is quite different from Aristotle's. The passage we quoted earlier

> Plays are produced for all kinds of reasons, rarely because a play exists that "must be done." A producer has or finds money—or needs to take a tax loss; a group of actors want a vehicle; a slot in a season needs to be filled; a theater is available whose size and equipment are suited to certain productions; cultural, national, or social occasions demand performances. One thing is sure—the play is not the thing. Shakespeare's famous sentence ought to be quoted in full: "The play's the thing / Wherein I'll catch the conscience of the king." Certainly, Hamlet didn't serve the playwright's intentions, but his own pressing motives.
>
> —Richard Schechner, *Environmental Theatre*, xli

appears in a section of the *Kakyo* titled "Connecting All the Arts through One Intensity of Mind." This *intensity*, Zeami argues, is a conscious state of dynamic balance between two different kinds of acting methods: *imitation* and *becoming*. By "imitation," Zeami means the skillful analysis and reproduction of human actions (gestures, facial expressions, bodily posture, and so on) by actors in a way that is wholly recognizable to the audience as human. Ironically, Zeami considered this the artificial part of the performance, as it relies on the actor's intellectual comprehension of the library of human gestures and sounds commonly used to communicate inner feelings. In this mode of performance, the actor treats the body itself as a sophisticated avatar, like what denizens of today's virtual spaces might call a "meat puppet."

"Becoming," on the other hand, requires the actor's immersion into the emotional condition of the character. Those trained in the American version of Stanislavski's Method might consider this the more "authentic" part of acting, as it suggests the total embrace by the actor of a self-created emotional state that correlates to that of the character. The Method actor might argue that the audience can sense the underlying sincerity of the performance, and that sincerity whisks away any artifice to express an emotion that is profound, recognizable, and divorced from artifice. But while that would not be an inaccurate reading of the Method, it is certainly a misreading of Stanislavski, who consistently foregrounded the importance of design and technique to the actor's craft and who, in his later years, emphasized the physical training and expression of the actor. The notion that authenticity is somehow the enemy of recognizable artifice would seem very alien to Zeami too. The best actor, Zeami argues, is not the one who manipulates the body in the most precise mimicry of emotional gestures, nor are they the one who forgoes the display of artifice to achieve a more genuine or authentic emotional state. Zeami's best actor is rather the one who can maintain these two contradictory states, intensity and becoming, in constant productive tension with one another. Zeami describes this state as sokyokuchi, or "mutuality in balance," and compares it to the seemingly effortless movement of a bird holding its wings with tension and floating on the air.

The actor's awareness, Zeami argues, should be distributed equally between these states, conscious of both the flow of deep emotion and the adherence to specific actions onstage, of the communication of authentic experience and the effective deployment of technical effects. Further, the performer's eye is turned inward and outward at the same time, keenly aware of their own interior state and the audience's dynamic expectations. Sokyokuchi, then, for Zeami is that frame of mind that is perfectly balanced between seemingly contradictory principles (inward/outward, subjective/objective, natural/artificial, authentic/manufactured) so that the performance, though scripted, staged, and rehearsed, nevertheless flows with every appearance of authenticity and conveys a profound emotional truth. In sum, the actor is both the puppet *and* the operator, and the perfect balance of the craft manifests in the puppet's strings, where the natural and the artificial are inextricably fused. It is, he warns, extremely difficult, but when this fusion occurs, the audience experiences something not merely beautiful and moving, but *virtuosic*, worthy for audience members to interrupt a performance to show their gratitude and respect, say with thunderous applause at the adjustment of a parasol.

Shortly after the emergence of Joruri came Kabuki, a raucous and, at the time, disreputable live-action performance style popular among nonaristocratic audiences who sought entertainment but pooh-poohed the posh Noh and the snobbish elites who patronized it. Kabuki was initially a vibrant and colorful dramatic stylization known as much for mocking the samurai class as for its grand theatricality and exciting action. But from its humble beginning in the red-light district of Edo, the artists and audiences of Kabuki were increasingly drawn to Joruri, first pirating plays that had been written for the more respectable puppet theater by such luminaries as Chikamatsu Monzaemon, then borrowing rhetorical, gestural, choreographic, and musical techniques from the puppets—a tradition that continues to this day, as modern kabuki actors work hard to replicate the motion of puppets.

Would that the poor novice quoted at the start of our chapter had had this information when the actor who performed both puppeteer and puppet did so in a moment of thrilling perfection. Would that this poor novice had had the good fortune to sit next to a voluble dramaturg, preferably one with a systemic understanding of drama, theater, and performance. But that poor spectator isn't the only one who could benefit from a better understanding of Zeami and the history of puppetry in Japan.

Although he was born six centuries before the invention of electronic computers, wireless transmission, and social media, Zeami's way of thinking about technology is profoundly useful to the dramaturg considering whether, and how, to "go digital." Why? First of all, because he reminds us that the "problem" of technology is an old one. Second, because he offers a time-tested way to productively think about and engage that "problem." Whereas many of today's thinkers and makers are frustrated by their inability to reconcile what they perceive to be the contradictory, creatively damaging forces surrounding contemporary drama, theater, and performance, Zeami asks us to ascertain those forces with sensitivity and seek to find a dynamic balance among them. In his dramaturgy, Zeami places innovation on equal footing with that ineffable quality we might call "soulfulness," that sense of authenticity or truthful-feeling emotion that is easy to experience but difficult to explain. To sustain this ever-shifting balance, Zeami describes a third, transcendent way of being, thinking, and making art that affirms both the soulfulness of the machine and the machinery of soulfulness. The strings of the puppeteer are not merely a system of control but a manifestation of mind. This fourteenth-century dramaturg has gifted his twenty-first-century descendants with an intriguing, and we think eminently practical, path out of a thorny theoretical problem that has dominated discussion of theater and technology for decades.

SOKYOKUCHI AND THEATRICAL MODERNISM

As enchanting as Zeami's puppet and puppeteer may be, how do they bring us closer to answering the most fundamental questions that dramaturgs must address as we adapt our minds and hands to the digital age? Most historical overviews of the integration of technology and performance begin in the nineteenth century—Chris Salter, for example, begins his excellent 2010 history *Entangled: Technology and the Transformation of Performance* with the 1876 world premiere of Richard Wagner's *Der Ring des Nibelungen* at the four-day theater festival that attracted thousands of Europe's royalty and artistic leaders to Bayreuth, a tiny town in Bavaria.[4] Wagner's *Ring* was notable for its *illusion*. Almost all its jaw-dropping technical innovations—including an audience arrayed so as to serve as an acoustic resonator, a hidden orchestra pit, and a double proscenium to add the illusion of great depth—were invisible to the audience. Without a doubt, Wagner's *Ring* was a vitally important landmark in the integration of cutting-edge technology with live performance on a truly epic scale. But if we begin our history of theater and technology with Wagner, we fail to comprehend a much longer history and mortgage our thinking to a specifically European way of engaging with technology. Zeami suggests another history and another way of doing that thinking and making.

Theater and performance have been entangled with technology since a performer first used fire to cast moving shadows on stone walls and manipulated the homely objects around them to suggest people, animals, gods, cosmic and natural forces, and ideas. But after Wagner's *Ring*, critics (including Friedrich Nietzsche) and artists became increasingly vocal about the technological accomplishments of the festival opera, arguing that the tricks eclipsed the message and cheapened the experience.[5] Adolphe Appia, for one, challenged the decadent Bayreuth aesthetic by designing sets that provided a more austere look, a lower-tech approach, and implicitly, a more authentic, immediate experience of beauty. In short, after Wagner demonstrated what we *could* do with technology in live performance, critics and artists started to wonder whether we *should* do those things. Technology became a *problem* for performance rather than a solution—at least among elites (popular entertainment gleefully deployed whatever technological tricks could fill the most seats). And the more powerful technology became, the greater the problem appeared and the more poisonous the antitechnology invectives grew.

This is nowhere more evident than in the early years of cinema. The first moving pictures were created in 1895 and were shown around the world over the next two decades, undergoing innovations at an exponential rate and attracting bigger and bigger audiences. Initially, these short silent films were shown in the same theaters as other sorts of communal entertainments, typically accompanied by live orchestras and narrators, and usually as just one part of an evening's theatrical offerings. Movies were considered supplemental entertainment, providing a bit of variety to revues, comedy and vaudeville acts, sometimes full plays or operettas. Even as the film industry exploded in the 1920s and theater impresario Alexander Pantages began converting his network of vaudeville houses into nickelodeons, movies continued to depend on the theater, borrowing (and in many cases never giving back) its writers, actors, directors, designers, and stylists. But here's the rub: although movies were far more expensive to *produce* than theater, they were much, much cheaper and easier to *replicate*. The combination of cheap reproduction and ready access to the distribution network provided by entrepreneurs like Pantages enabled cinema to quickly outstrip its ancient artistic parent in terms of popularity and profit.

No question, this new technology was a threat to the theater, but the threat was economic rather than philosophical. But as is often the case with economic threats, the intelligentsia defending theater's ancient prerogatives perceived the challenge in their own terms. Prominent theater artists and thinkers reacted to the explosive popularity of film by arguing that the cinema was threatening not just the economic viability of an industry but also the moral essence of the form. And that essence was live performance. The performer and the audience were being separated, the essential human link between them sundered by the technology of projector and screen. And this separation by camera, film, projector, and screen robbed all involved, especially the actor and the audience, of the soulful authenticity of aesthetic experience. Yes, the cinema boasts a repertoire of astonishing technical capacities to delight the eye and heart, but, these critics argued, it lacks that special something that theater has always had but no one ever bothered noticing: *presence*.

In a demonstrable sense, cinema replaced space, time, and actors with nothing but light and shadow. Its communication was a one-way street, its imagery fragmented. It forced the viewer into a form of spectatorship that was passive, weirdly unemotional, even *unnatural*. Like any normal human interaction, these critics argued, theater requires the humane and even transcendent coexistence of audience and actor in time and space. Anything else would lose the particular magic of presence and strip theater of its power to elicit strong emotional responses and build empathy.

It's not at all unusual for new artistic media to cast older media in a new light. And it's not at all unusual for cultural gatekeepers—critics, journalists, scholars, and teachers—to recoil from that light. That was the case with theatre and its self-appointed guardians at the dawn of the cinematic era. Though it had rarely figured in discussions previously, *presence* suddenly became an endangered, and therefore valuable, aesthetic commodity and ethical principle. With that rise in philosophical fortune came a host of value judgments about what presence is and what it is not, and how *good* theatre should or should not be using it. Shouldn't theatre, the pundits queried, purify the relationship between spectator and actor rather than cluttering the space with "cinematic" effects? As late as 1968, Grotowski proposed an aesthetic of technical paucity—"poverty"—by asserting that "no matter how much the theater expands and exploits its mechanical resources, it will remain technologically inferior to film and television."[6] Shouldn't directors, designers, actors, and playwrights rally to protect and promote the natural and virtuous community enabled by theater? Or perhaps, is it better for us to read people like Grotowski differently? Although theater may be technologically inferior (actually, we don't believe that, but for the sake of argument . . .), it is still technological. For Grotowski and others at that time, enhancing the "artificiality" of theater with fancy tricks wasn't just a losing battle but also a threat to the essential character of theater.

Grotowski is only the most prominent example of how theater artists moralized technology, deeming the choice

The term *presence* is a hotly contested term in a range of fields, especially after the French philosopher Jacques Derrida "deconstructed" it in a series of essays and books published in the 1960s. In "Jacques Derrida: The Problems of Presence," Derek Attridge sums up the argument as follows:

> When I reflect on my own consciousness, what I experience is self-presence: there seems to be no intervening medium between my sense of myself and that self. Similarly, the world I see and hear is present to me without mediation. The meanings I constantly encounter seem immediately present; it's hard to see how the apparently simple (spatial) here and (temporal) now of being in the world could be divided or complicated. . . . If presence is fundamental and inalienable, anything that threatens to complicate or sully it must be regarded as secondary, derivative and regrettable. For presence is a value; it is what is proper, proper to meaning, to consciousness, to existence, but also good and correct.

to use a film projector or phonograph not as a practical solution to a particular theatrical problem, but rather as a philosophical and ethical judgment, a statement about where one stood in respect to the true, eternal, and authentic essence of theater. Theater historians played no small role in this change. At Cambridge University several decades earlier, a group

Everybody repeats the same rhetorical question: is the theatre necessary? But we only ask it in order to be able to reply: yes, it is, because it is an art which is always young and always necessary. The sale of performances is organized on a grand scale. Yet no one organizes film and television audiences in the same way. If all theatres were closed down one day, a large percentage of the people would know nothing about it until weeks later, but if one were to eliminate cinemas and television, the very next day the whole population would be in an uproar. Many theatre people are conscious of this problem, but hit upon the wrong solution: since the cinema dominates theatre from a technical point of view, why not make the theatre more technical? They invent new stages, they put on performances with lightning-quick changes of scenery, complicated lighting and decor, etc., but can never attain the technical skill of film and television. The theatre must recognize its own limitations. If it cannot be richer than the cinema, then let it be poor. If it cannot be as lavish as television, let it be ascetic. If it cannot be a technical attraction, let it renounce all outward technique.

—Jerzy Grotowski, *Towards a Poor Theatre*, 41

of anthropologists known as the Cambridge Ritualists argued that the origins of classical Greek theater were properly traced to ancient Dionysian rituals, the agricultural ur-religion of sacrifice and revivification. Though based on entirely spurious archaeological evidence and tendentious readings of Sophocles and Aeschylus, the Cambridge Ritualists' romanticized vision of theater as an expression of primal humanity proved durably attractive to artists, who, frankly, should have known better.

The desire to return theater to its pre-technological "ritual origins"—or, thus inspired, abandon orthodox theater in favor of ritualized process and performance—is evident in the work of Adolphe Appia, Edward Gordon Craig, Max Reinhardt, Antonin Artaud, Peter Brook, Jerzy Grotowski, Ariane Mnouchkine, and Richard Schechner, among many others. Surveying this romanticized view of theater and the many critics and artists who bought into it, Eli Rozik concludes that it is motivated by a desire for a pure, unmediated relationship of artist and audience, a relationship that "lend[s] theatre a numinous quality" despite the fact that in the space "between this aura and theatre-historical reality there is nothing."[7] This is not to say that "serious" theater artists didn't use new technologies, but their work was deemed aesthetically and morally valid precisely to the extent that it served the historical progress of mankind, as with the multimedia but rigorously left-wing and didactic theater of Erwin Piscator. The mere fact that commercially viable theater persisted despite its fatal corruption by flashy special effects was proof, for these pundits and putative progressives, that audiences in fact craved something more than the ephemeral titillations of electric light and sound.

But what does this have to do with Zeami and sokyokuchi? As it so happens, in 1908, smack in the middle of this frumious debate about theatrical authenticity, Zeami's writings were "discovered" by European theater makers and their allies among the intelligentsia. The attraction of these texts wasn't just that they had something useful to say about making theater, but that they suggested a different *way* of making theater. Granted, Zeami's writings were never intended for the general public. He believed that the spiritual authority of the actor would be diminished if the most profound wisdom of the theater were available to any Kanada, Tetsuo, or Akira who had an inkling that they might be an actor. So he and his descendants kept the treatises secret.

This wasn't entirely a matter of preserving wisdom. In Zeami's time, Japanese masters of all kinds, from Zen spiritualists to flower arrangers, inscribed secret instructions as a means of protecting the "mystery" of their art from all but the most serious (and elite) practitioners. Not a bad idea if one wanted to keep the supply of great art low enough to keep demand consistent. For centuries, Zeami's writings were shared only among Japanese elites, but in 1908, copies somehow found their way to a secondhand bookstore in Tokyo. Newly edited and mass-published translations of Zeami became de rigueur for the most serious (and elite) practitioners of theater all over the world. The impact of Zeami's writings unfolded in ways that might surprise those who presume that he was interested in the ethereal experiences of the spirit rather than the material stuff of theater. But the ethos of sokyokuchi is evident in a generation of technophilic modernists, including the influential Russian director Vsevolod Meyerhold.

Though Meyerhold is most associated with the Symbolist and Constructivist movements—and he, too, found the separation between performers and audiences a matter of both aesthetic and moral concern—his work was deeply indebted to Asian theater, a fact that is both evident in the theater-historical documents and attested to by his students, audiences, and biographers.[8] In his dramaturgical writings, Meyerhold describes himself as an enthusiastic student of Japanese and Chinese theater, which he began studying through books in 1914. He later witnessed performances in Paris and in 1935 had an important meeting with the celebrated Chinese artist Mei Lanfang in Moscow, after which he declared that socialist realism would be founded on Asian techniques.[9] He freely (arguably, too freely) appropriated techniques from traditional Japanese theater, such as displaying a single red cloth to indicate a bloody massacre, incorporating the *hanamichi* (the long, raised platform that extends through the audience), and using black-clad stagehands that recall the *kurogo* of Kabuki and Bunraku puppeteers (though, unlike his Japanese peers, he wanted his audiences to notice them).[10]

But perhaps the most intriguing connection between Zeami and Meyerhold can be found in the theory and practice of *biomechanical acting*. Rejecting the focus on individual and interior psychology that prevailed at the time at Stanislavsky's Moscow Art Theatre, Meyerhold sought to "retheatricalize theatre" (in Georg Fuchs's words[11]), developing an approach to performance that focused on the motions of the actor's body, a body he considered as a kind of expressive machine, the theatrical version of an industrial worker. He positions his version of biomechanics against his mentor Stanislavsky's approach, which he believes "over-emphasized the 'spirit' and 'psychologizing'" as opposed to what he calls the "elementary laws of reflexes."[12] Additionally, Meyerhold conceptualizes the actor's body as part of the total theatrical machinery, a human element in a composite construction comprising ruthlessly simplified (and thus highly expressive) costumes and a radically different approach to stage design influenced by Constructivism and designed by Constructivist artists like Lyubov Popova.

Conventionally, historians associate Biomechanics with the industrial practices of Frederick Winslow Taylor. And while that is not an association we would disavow, we would also draw attention to Meyerhold's fascination with puppets. Though there is no direct indication that Meyerhold read Zeami, we do know that Meyerhold was fascinated by Kabuki, especially the way it externalized the emotional states of characters through bold, often highly conventional gestures. Writing in

1917, the revolutionary year that saw Russians across the nation throw off feudalism and embrace a new relationship of politics and technology, Meyerhold describes a puppeteer who tries to make his puppet as realistic as possible, rendering the artifice of the puppet and his own artistry invisible. This is an aesthetic error of the first order—and a philosophical error too. Meyerhold describes a director struggling to honor the puppeteer and the puppet in equal parts: "As soon as he tried to improve the puppet's mechanism, it lost part of its charm. It was as though the puppet were resisting such barbarous improvements with all of its being. The director came to his senses when he realized that there is a limit beyond which there is no alternative but to replace the puppet with a man."[13]

In that moment of decision, Meyerhold finds another path, a path on which both puppet and puppeteer travel together, each acknowledging the other's unique qualities: "But how could he part with the puppet which had created a world of enchantment with its incomparable movements, its expressive gestures achieved by some magic known to it alone, its angularity which reaches the heights of true plasticity?" Having acknowledged the distinct characteristics of the human and puppet bodies, Meyerhold celebrates the unique vision of nature and theater that their collaboration suggests: "On [the puppet's] stage things are not as they are because nature is like that, but because that is how the puppet wishes it—and it wished not to copy but to create." Meyerhold then extends the figure to performance more generally, writing, "The actor of today will not understand that the duty of the comedian and the mime is to transport the spectator to a world of make-believe, entertaining him on the way there with the brilliance of his technical skill."[14]

The passage closely resembles Zeami's description of the ethical relationship of puppeteers and puppets in the *Kayako* in several ways. Like Meyerhold, Zeami recognizes the relationship of the human and the mechanical as a site where the natural and the artificial work in concert while never losing their distinctiveness. Most importantly, that concert requires that the performer be mindful of all the elements of the performance—and communicate that mindfulness to the spectator. The aesthetic effect requires a conscious dialectical relationship of human and machine that is not hidden from the spectator. The performance doesn't produce a synthesis in which differences are erased or the techniques and technology of the performance are disguised. The dialectical relationship of theatrical artifice and emotional depth is affirmed in the performance, displayed consciously to the spectator. The spectator is both moved and impressed.

Though oriented toward distinct philosophical ends (i.e., the utopian possibilities of the Soviet), Meyerhold's theory of biomechanical performance can be understood as a modernist version of sokyokuchi. The similarities are further evident when we consider the ways Meyerhold explicitly links the dialectic of performer and technology to what he calls an actor's "complete self-awareness": "The whole biomechanical system, the entire process of our movements, is dictated by one basic principle—our capacity for thought, the human brain, the rational apparatus. . . . Not only movements, not only words, but also the brain . . . the brain must occupy the primary position, because it is the brain that initiates the given task, that gives orientation, that determines the sequence of movements, the accent, and so on."[15]

Though Meyerhold's rhetoric is Constructivist in tone and terminology, if we read the passage with sokyokuchi in mind, it communicates something more than utopian technophilia. Like Zeami's performer, Meyerhold's Biomechanic performer does not allow themselves to become subsumed by overwhelming emotion (which is not to say they do not feel or communicate emotion), but rather maintains an awareness of their position as part of a larger system composed of other performers, the multiple systems of the stage, the dramatic narrative, and the spectators—what he called the "industrial situation."[16]

Highlighting the conceptual and practical similarities between Zeami's writings and Meyerhold's theories of biomechanical performance potentially recasts the history of twentieth-century European modernism and, more generally, the way we think about media and performance. Meyerhold is already recognized as one of the pioneers of new media dramaturgy, particularly by way of his influence on Sergei Eisenstein, who worked with Meyerhold as a designer in the 1920s and learned from him the ways an artist might apply industrial techniques to artistic means. But if we think of Meyerhold as a dramaturg of *systems* rather than just technology, as a dramaturg of techne, not just an innovative user of machines and electric media, then the story of theater and technology changes in two ways. First, the story of new media can be expanded to include artists whose work has been generally considered at worst antitechnological, at best atechnological. We think here of the Living Theatre, Grotowski, and Schechner, all of whom cite Meyerhold as a preeminent influence. They are usually not included in histories of theater and technology despite their abiding interest in the mechanics of the human body, the ethical and moral questions of the emerging technoculture, their incisive criticisms of how theater shapes perception and emotion, and their holistic approaches to theater that apprehend simultaneously its aesthetic, ethical, and technical dimensions.

Second, by affirming the link between the preindustrial Zeami and the industrial Meyerhold, we can recast the history of digital performance, new media dramaturgy, cyborg performance, and other late twentieth-century technodramaturgies as recent moments in a centuries-long global history of dramaturgy's relationship to technology. In so doing, we access a dramaturgy that is fundamentally concerned with the relationship of technology and performance but understands that relationship within a much broader conceptual framework, one that considers not just technology but techne. Systemic dramaturgy, we argue, provides a historically deeper, multicultural context for thinking about how theater and performance respond to emergent technologies and to the impact of those technologies on artistic practice.

Even this broadly sketched and by no means complete genealogy—taking us from Zeami to Meyerhold to the Living Theatre, Grotowski, and Schechner to our present moment—suggests that the question of technology's relationship to theater has been asked and answered in more ways and in more places than many historians of digital performance have acknowledged. However, it would be naive to argue that all technologies are essentially alike—that the challenges and opportunities raised by puppets are the same as those raised by gaslight or by video recording. And it would be equally naive, if not dangerous, to ignore the fact that certain technologies have indeed radically altered how human beings perceive, communicate, and perform. Again, we must work *systemically* and try to theorize how much vaster social movements impact and are impacted by this relationship between performance and technology.

As a case in point, we might turn to the argument of Peggy Phelan, who, in her 1993 book *Unmarked* assessed the boundary between live and artificial performance as not only unmistakable but also critical to the very nature of performance itself. In fact, the impermanence and nonreproducibility of the performance is fundamental to its nature. She writes, "The disappearance of the object is fundamental to performance; it rehearses and repeats the disappearance of the subject who longs always to be remembered."[17] It's tempting to dismiss Phelan's argument out of hand. In the quarter century since Phelan wrote her book, we have undeniably expanded our understanding of what it is to perform. The performing self includes a virtual self, a self that extends from our bodies into virtual spaces and into states of consciousness determined by the interaction of our imagination within parameters defined by algorithms and maintained by computers. For many people, life is conducted substantially in virtual performance spaces where we share pictures, play games, buy and sell, care for ourselves and others, learn, and engage in any number of activities that only a few years ago were possible only in physical proximity. We form communities, engage in political action, and make art. We make mistakes, suffer shame and humiliation, behave offensively, commit crimes, and even engage in behaviors that can be threatening to our own or others' lives. Every tweet and Facebook post further complicates the definitive division Phelan marked between the corporeal and the virtual.

Neither Zeami nor Meyerhold nor Grotowski could have foreseen the total impact of social media technology on the way we understand presence, liveness, proximity, and consciousness, much less devised a correlative dramaturgy. However, they were each fully aware of and enthusiastic about the ways that subjectivity could be enriched through creative engagement with technology—and how technology could be enriched by the subjects who played with it. Indeed, they would probably be sympathetic with those theorists of performance and technology who ask not "Is the technological at war with the authentically human?" but "In what ways has technoculture changed our very experience of being authentically

> Performance's only life is in the present. Performance cannot be saved, recorded, documented, or otherwise participate in the circulation of representations of representations: once it does so, it becomes something other than performance. To the degree that performance attempts to enter the economy of reproduction it betrays and lessens the promise of its own ontology. Performance's being . . . becomes itself through disappearance.
>
> —Peggy Phelan, *Unmarked*, 146

human?" From a certain perspective, theater artists have been "post-human" for centuries, and liveness itself is and has always been, as Auslander argues, less a historically transcendent experience than a moving target for those who seek to define it—a value-laden abstraction subject to the same social and historical pressures as any other.[18]

And yet in the third decade of the 2000s, we find ourselves still helplessly in love with live performance. For Zeami's puppeteer, the liveness of performance was potent with promise and pleasure. So, too, the spectator, who revels not only in the immense skill and intensity of the performer but also in the absolute precarity, the possibility that a string will break and the puppet's *other* existence (as an unliving, obdurate, opaque bundle of stuff) and the performer's *other* existence (as simply one body among others) will be utterly, embarrassingly exposed. As historians, dramaturgs are no less enamored of liveness. As we pore over photos, friezes, murals, programs, scripts, and all the tantalizing ephemera of theater history, we can't stop thinking about—feeling for—that rare and wonderful sensation of being there. As we work with directors, designers, and actors, we seek connection of present to past, to infuse both with a vitality neither would have in the other's absence. If technology *isn't* a problem, then maybe concerns with the preservation of liveness aren't quite as dire as we have believed.

SOKYOKUCHI AND NEW MEDIA

So what, exactly, does this examination of Zeami through the lens of Meyerhold and his aesthetic descendants tell us about dramaturgy in the digital age? Though there are occasional outcries about singers using prerecorded voice tracks or audiences watching shows through the cameras of their phones, the fact of the matter is that the argument about liveness is literally academic. Most theater makers and lovers assimilate new technologies so quickly that they are largely unconscious of ever having witnessed or experienced any transition. A century ago, the presence of film projectors was a thrill for most theatergoers and a thrilling possibility to most theater makers; the same can be said about augmented reality and motion capture performance. Anyone who's visited the Disney or Universal theme parks is familiar with the fun that can be had with augmented reality, robotics, and digitally mediated performance—and how fun it is to actually be *there* when the performance is happening. Artists and audiences have never been that discouraged by academic arguments as they find new ways to incorporate emergent technologies into live performances, drawing in new audiences and exploring new themes.

But as much as we enjoy the pleasures of theme parks or playing virtual reality videogames, as academics and as individuals concerned with the political and ethical questions raised by technoculture, we find even greater pleasures in the work of the Wooster Group, Robert Lepage, Troika Ranch, Blast Theory, and dumb type, to name only a few—work that not only incorporates new technology but fosters thinking and feeling about that very incorporation. The Builders Association is exemplary of the new sokyokuchi.

Consider *Super Vision*, a production developed in collaboration with the graphic design company DBOX and first presented in 2005 at the Walker Art Center in Minneapolis. The play weaves three stories of identity theft: a Muslim traveler's humanity is gradually stripped away by electronic government surveillance; a young woman makes an electronic database of her dying grandmother's life; and a man sacrifices his son's digital data to support his suburban lifestyle, with catastrophic results for his family. As with many of the Builders Association's performances, *Super Vision* is presented so that live action interacts smoothly with digital projections, some of which include video close-ups of actors while they're performing so that the spectator can see how the characters are presenting through laptops, phones, and surveillance cameras. While the audience is watching the actors, they are being watched too. At the start of the show, a performer welcomes the spectators and shares with them data, some of it surprisingly personal, culled from demographic analysis of easily accessed credit card information. *Super Vision* is designed to call attention to that portion of the audience's life that is lived online and how vulnerable that existence renders them to disaster at the hands of unscrupulous or ignorant operators.[19] And while the audience's experience is thoroughly mediated, the experience is intensely affecting because the audience shares with the characters the experience of mediation.

The Builders Association is an excellent example of the sokyokuchi ethos applied to new media. Prostheses, motion capture, mechanical or computational augmentation, wearables, implants, and genetic incursions are all examples of machine-human blending, but as *Super Vision* demonstrates, we now live in a world populated by complicated and above all *interactive* machine systems composed entirely of information—and we are part of those systems, for better or worse. On the one hand, this incorporation of the human is unprecedented. People have little experience with and often struggle to find the language to talk about our relationship to what Salter calls our "mediated double"—those other versions of ourselves that exist on social media, within electronic medical record systems, in our credit ratings, and in the many other places where versions of ourselves composed entirely of data.[20] On the other hand, the experience of machine-human blending is as old as puppets and the deus ex machina, and the wisdom of the ancients can provide entirely pertinent lessons to the denizens of the digital age.

But whether we consider the challenge of new technologies to be new, old, or something in between, those of us with the privilege of working in the theater must commit ourselves to the cause of understanding technology. And we must studiously avoid buying into the kinds of dire prophecies cried by cinemaphobes and their descendants. For the fact is that the notion that computers, robotics, and digital media would irrevocably damage theater's ability to represent what it is to be human has not come true. Neither has the second dire prophecy: that the infection of digital tech would erase nondigital theater. Long-term financial studies show that theater profits in the United States continue to rise even as profits from videogames do the same (though at a far greater rate), indicating that each has found its own reliable economic niche.

How might dramaturgs, with their specific, time-tested perspectives and skills, further develop the theoretical foundations for a diagnostic and creative process that addresses the relationship of technology and theater? How can we help address not just the immediate questions raised by the dramatic text and the needs of our creative team, but do so in a fashion that engages the political, social, technological, and psychological dimensions of the text and the creative process too? In other words, how can a systems-oriented dramaturg help directors, designers, and audiences think and feel about technologies both old and new? How can we facilitate creation and collaboration by those who want to make those kinds of experiences?

Matthew Causey argues that one of the most powerful capacities of new media is their ability to reveal the limits of traditional ways of defining the human experience vis-à-vis the putatively nonhuman; specifically, new media have a unique capacity to represent that experience not as *either* natural *or* technological but instead as a consequence of a tension between them. This is something Zeami, Meyerhold, Schechner, and the Builders Association would find completely familiar and deeply appealing. We do too. This dramaturgy, Causey argues, "should explore new territory, focusing on performing, not representing, constructing a reality whose virtuality will expand cognition of reality itself as an increasingly complex metaphor for what one experiences as the real, inaccessible as that may be."[21] Causey's notion that *reality* is a metaphor for (rather than the substance of) human experience is, frankly, unsettling. But the confidence he demonstrates in the powers of theater and performance to shape reality and, even better, to show how that reality is shaped for us by others, is bracing.

For a dramaturg interested in the long history of theater and technology, Causey's claim is an invitation to explore. It invites us to consider conceptions of technology that extend beyond those of the European Industrial Revolution and its aftermath, to consider techne not simply in its European—and Eurocentric—dimensions. It invites us to consider technological innovators like Zeami who see performance as always and already an interplay of different systems—the corporeal and virtual, the philosophical and material, the subjective and the technological, the soulful and the illusory—seeking not dominion of one over the other but instead striving for sokyokuchi. After all, hasn't theater always engaged in creating metaphoric versions of reality, palpably artificial, if utterly convincing territories of imagination that lead audiences into new forms of consciousness, new ways of being human?

It comes as no surprise to us that, in a more recent essay, Causey calls for theorists and makers of theater to move beyond binary conceptions of theater and technology, to eschew antiquated notions of multi-, inter-, or transmedia and the false paths they intrude into thinking and making (including getting caught up in anxieties about liveness). Within our contemporary, postdigital context, identity, the body, and community "are experienced as less uncanny and more familiar, less discrete and autonomous phenomena, and understood as a flow, a becoming, and always in process." In response, artists and theorists have advocated "an internet state of mind—to think in the fashion of the network." We find quite attractive the idea of a dramaturgy that "incorporates the discourse and ideologies of the digital, and questions the significant issues involved in negotiating between being in a postdigital culture while working toward effective political engagements." Perhaps most exciting is Causey's recognition that a postdigital dramaturgy allows us to consider an expanded conception of theater that includes "immersive theatre, augmented realities, pervasive games, and new models of spectatorships in streaming and we-based media."[22]

But if, as Causey argues, the kinds of thinking about and making with digital technologies that have occurred over the last two decades should push us to reconsider the relevance of the questions that theorists like Phelan and Auslander asked, we would add that it has also pushed us to reconsider the historical presumptions of the entire debate. Yes, it's important for us to consider the undeniably unprecedented effects of digital technology. We are deeply concerned that the benefits of such technologies have not fallen equally on all. We feel that, as dramaturgs, we can foster conversations about these concerns and others. Phelan's point is well taken that art that incorporates high tech runs the risk of eliding the stories of marginalized people who are not included in the vision of a fully mediated theater.

But a systemic dramaturgy cannot simply dismiss technology. It must be attentive to the histories—plural—of those technologies. As Salter points out, using electronic tech in art as a tool for liberation of audiences is "ironic, considering that it was mainly United States and European military systems of command and control that drove research into man-machine interaction in order to develop the battlefield of the future."[23] And there is no denying the detrimental social impact of digital media, also forecast by Phelan, exemplified by the revolting phenomenon known as Gamergate, when social media was weaponized against those who advocated feminist, queer, and critical-race readings of videogames and videogame culture. Finally, we note that new tech is leading to new social problems that are as much the purview of the dramaturg as they are of the social scientist. In light of the performative and pervasive practice of using mobile phones to document and upload our everyday lives onto the internet for widespread public consumption,

Salter wonders, "Could it be that our greatest fear is not the collapse of economies or the pulverization of the glaciers but the sudden loss of connectedness to the exploding digital repositories that store our endless, everyday routines?"[24] Digital connectedness itself is a type of performance—as is the tendency of humans to look for simulated worlds into which to escape from, and therefore avoid, the labor of solving real-world problems.

THE SYSTEMIC SOLUTION

Our examination of Zeami's relationship to theatrical modernism and postmodernism is intended to make two related points: first, that the dramaturgical problems of advanced technology in performance are not in any way new; and second, that they might not really even be problems. A systemic approach to dramaturgy incites a turning away from the facile but unproductive reification of false binaries—in this case, those between the natural and the artificial, the mind and the body, the psychological and the material—and instead looks for the fundamental imbrications that relate them. This inquiry into the history and permutations of sokyokuchi establishes a historiographic basis for our ongoing research establishing the foundational assumptions of systemic dramaturgy, one that understands the dramaturg's mission to be the understanding of performance as a set of interactive conceptual and procedural systems which act and react to many other sets of interactive conceptual and procedural systems. In so doing, we can begin to answer the call of Eckersall, Grehan, and Scheer for a "new, collaborative dramaturgical model" that is "inquiring and provisional," rather than hegemonic and static, and emphasizes the "ceaseless dialogue" that performance always engages between text, convention, movement, bodies, light, duration, context, and stage materials.[25]

Systemic dramaturgy answers the Three Big Questions, then, like so:

1. Although dramaturgical theories emerge from historical understandings of performance and the technologies that determined them, dramaturgy is not in any way beholden to those understandings. Not only *can* they be adapted to new historical circumstances, but when they do, they reveal that modern problems have extant rich and exciting, sometimes ancient, solutions. Far from being rendered

obsolete, traditional dramaturgies can provide powerful insights into theory and practice. It is the responsibility of dramaturgs to seek out all possible ways of approaching problems. It is their responsibility to be aware of the history of dramaturgy itself, including the ideological conceptions—the techne—that governs understandings of technology then and now.

2. The emergence of new performance technologies does not antiquate traditional forms of performance, but rather alters them. This is nothing new. History shows that innovations in performance technology inspire new kinds of performance but do not erase older ones. The duty of dramaturgs is to be aware of how technologies alter performance and deploy that awareness to enable their team to better do its job, whether that job involves conserving older forms or guiding their transformation.

3. The incorporation of digital media, robotics, artificial intelligence, social media, and cybernetic systems into performance is only the latest chapter in the extension of human experience into new imaginative, aesthetic, and entertainment territories and an affirmation of a history of the incorporation and extension of technologies across cultures and taste hierarchies. And as those very advances in digital technology expand the experience of human subjectivity, they alert us to a history of technology that complicates the very notion of technology itself. The systemic dramaturg should remain alert to this dialectic of technology and historiography, for it is a wellspring of theory and practice.

In the chapters that follow, we demonstrate several methods for putting this dynamic mindset into play to improve our thinking as dramaturgs and, more importantly, to enable our creative teams to accomplish their objectives. For among the most important responsibilities of any dramaturg is the mandate to advocate for and create theater—for systemic dramaturgs, this means systemic advocacy and systemic creation!

INTERVIEW 2

LAYERS OF MEDIATION

MARIANNE WEEMS ON THE DRAMATURGY OF THE DIGITAL

Marianne Weems is the artistic director of the Builders Association and, over the past twenty years, has directed all of its productions. Previously, she worked as a dramaturg and assistant director with Susan Sontag, Richard Foreman, and Jan Cohen-Cruz, among other artists, and from 1988 to 1994, she was assistant director and dramaturg for the Wooster Group. She was a member of the performance ensemble the V-Girls, who performed and published from 1986 to 1995. She coedited the book *Art Matters: How the Culture Wars Changed America* (NYU Press, 2000) and coauthored *The Builder's Association* with Shannon Jackson (MIT Press, 2015). The Builders Association is a New York–based award-winning performance and media ensemble whose productions have brought together media, sound, architecture, text, and stage performance to tell stories drawn from contemporary life. Since 1994, they have toured extensively internationally to venues including London's Barbican Theater, the Melbourne International Arts Festival, RomaEuropa Festival, Singapore Arts Festival and Festival Iberoamericano de Bogota.

For a full history of The Builders Association, see their website, https://new.thebuildersassociation.org/.

Interview 2: *Layers of Mediation*

MICHAEL CHEMERS: What's happening now that you're interested in?

MARIANNE WEEMS: I'm so glad you asked. I'm interested in doing something with machine learning and theater. But the interesting thing, as usual, is the proscenium theater is kind of the last guest to the party. And so there's been a lot of work certainly with machine learning, installations, art environments, and galleries. And, you know, there's not really a lot of theater work that starts with machine learning as a point of departure. One thing that I looked at yesterday is this little company in Europe called Improbot, and they built a machine that looked at about five hundred films, looked at the subtitles themselves enough to start to learn how to provide language and improvise. And then they started doing live actor improv with the machine. And this is the part that interests me: it was completely ineffectual because there were all these pauses, and the machine was a terrible scene partner. They put in an actor with an in-ear mic and they performed the machine's part. So there was this kind of like triangulation, an uncanny valley moment, where the audience was asking about each line, "Did that come from the machine? Did that come from the actor offstage? How are they staging this so that it works as theater?" So I think there's a lot in there that could be unpacked in a more stylized, perhaps more produced way. But I haven't really seen that anywhere else.

MIKE SELL: However, you still hold tightly to a couple of old technologies, and a physical theater space is one of those, right?

WEEMS: I think that we are sort of bound by the economy and our labor. The way that we [the Builders Association] have figured out how to survive as a company is to create work in a theater that can tour to different festivals and theaters around the world. There is sort of an extant market, for lack of a better term, for this kind of work. So I've tried many times to try to do things in other contexts, to create installations or more site-specific work, for instance, but our presenters are looking for a specific kind of project. That's very quotidian to say, but essentially, we're doing something that is the only way to survive, which is to create actual theater pieces in a theater space. But beyond that, I must say this yet again: we are not really technologists. I've never started out thinking, "We're going to try this new gimmick because it's so cool." We ended up incorporating augmented reality into the project we did about *The Wizard of Oz*, but it came from wanting to do *Oz* and then finding that there was this, you know, antecedent in the digital world that we could use to expand the content. And so that is always what happens . . . we start with the content, and then it finds a form that inevitably intersects with some new technology. But it's not actually about that technology.

Interview 2: *Layers of Mediation*

SELL: Is that because you have the right people in the room?

WEEMS: There are a lot of people at the table, and it's a big mélange of different minds. But nobody in that room is so firmly embedded in traditional theater that they want to stay within a classical text. On one hand, we've worked with Jennifer Tipton our entire career, and when she's lighting the actors, she says, "I'm not looking at the screens; I'm only looking at the bodies on stage." So that's one end of the spectrum: somebody who adamantly insists that they're not going to deal with the technology. The rest of us are more interested in incorporating tools, but they're from our everyday lives. I don't think there's anybody who's come in there and said, "Let me introduce you to this piece of tech that none of you have ever thought about before." You know, it is kind of like a dramaturgy of everyday technology.

That's why I cannot abide kitchen-sink drama or anything where I have to just sit there and watch people onstage without any contemporary life around them. To me, that's intensely artificial and sort of one-dimensional. Our idea is, instead of having cuts of meat onstage, to have the tools that are, you know, the tools to which we are teleprosthetically attached.

CHEMERS: So when you talk about wanting to put machine learning on stage, is it just to put machine learning on stage?

WEEMS: I generally try to come at it from both ends of the spectrum. I have this thing in my mind that is "Machine learning is a hotbed of contemporary ideas." But then I also am looking for a story and content. Not necessarily like a canonical text, for sure. And then, weirdly, they always kind of like start to intersect. You have to hold both things in your mind at the same time. When we were doing *Alladeen*, we wanted to do a whole thing around outsourcing and fiber optic cables turning another continent into our back office, ventriloquizing another culture, and the fact that South Asian workers were rehearsing at night to impersonate Americans in order to serve American customers during the day. But then I happened to be at IBM, and I looked over someone's shoulder and saw this really primitive kind of surveillance system that had a weird ghosting effect. And that was a moment where I thought, "That would be perfect for this idea of the faces floating over the cultural and digital masking." So those two things kind of happened simultaneously.

SELL: That feels like old-fashioned dramaturgy.

WEEMS: Does it? In what way?

SELL: In the sense that you're in the world and you want to put on a show that's meaningful, about something that matters to you. And meanwhile, you're living

Interview 2: *Layers of Mediation*

in the world, and one day, you see an effective light, or you're visiting a museum and see something you love, and it clicks for you.

WEEMS: The tricky thing about dramaturgy is that you're the ones who are looking for the container for the content, right? And that's sort of like what's being expressed onstage. The form and the content are married at that point, so like in *Super Vision* or in *Continuous City*, to have the screens that open and close all over is about creating a constellation around each of the characters and having it be able to change and express a network (fig. i2.1).

CHEMERS: In your most recent piece, *Strange Window*, one of the things that affected me profoundly when I was watching it was that there's an element in the

Fig. i2.1. A performer in *Super Vision* surrounded by a constellation of screens. *Photo by James Gibbs and dbox, courtesy of Marianne Weems.*

original Henry James story "The Turn of the Screw" where the ghost of Quint is constantly surveilling the governess, and since your whole show is about digital surveillance, and the ghost appears partially modified through screens, it's very effective. This is not the nineteenth-century story about a haunted governess. It's about me. I'm being surveilled by ghosts in my culture all the time, probably even now, as we do this with my camera, and Siri is listening to every word I say!

WEEMS: Oh my god! So true.

CHEMERS: So one of the things that this new technology does is it enables us to sort of break down this boundary between now and then. When you do that, that's when ghosts show up.

WEEMS: And I think that also we just want the audience to lift the veil for a moment, feel the water that we're swimming in, or showing the nuts and bolts and then, if you're fast enough, getting a wrench in there. I like to evoke the sensation rather than just observe it.

CHEMERS: Yes, and as a dramaturg, I still have to argue that theater, however broadly defined, is more effective at that evocative process than other cultural forms.

WEEMS: I think that's right, Michael; that is really true. That's why it's alive.

CHEMERS: Then between, say, what you're doing with the incorporation of computational media into live theater, which is very *present*, and what our colleagues here at UCSC are doing with tabletop games or videogames or creating online performance communities, where is the overlap?

WEEMS: Well, I liked what Mike said yesterday—that this is like an oscilloscope. What we're all occupying and oscillating through is that gray area between mediated reality and "meat" reality. The pleasure of occupying that liminal space is, I think, the thing that we're all after. We just state it in a more framed, more explicit way, because we have live performers onstage in mediated performance. But don't you think that that's also what's happening when you play those games? We keep circling back to discussing not just the structure and mechanics of a game, but their emotional content and their stories.

CHEMERS: You are reminding me of the work I did with social robotics at Carnegie Mellon. Initially, they were trying to figure out how a robot processes emotional information, and I kind of shook them up when I said that's not important. What's important is how the audience or the user *believes* that emotional information has been processed. There doesn't need to be a ghost in the machine. There just needs to be the appearance of one that simulates emotional intelligence. My argument was that a traditional theater play is an analog, hand-operated artificial intelligence, with its own methods and systems of understanding and

Interview 2: *Layers of Mediation*

processing emotional information that it gets from the audience and reacts to that audience.

WEEMS: But just to push back on that, I do think that early on, this was always an issue for us. What's the difference between creating an extremely complex infrared triggered machine that you can see the actor interacting with and having the stage manager offstage pressing a button? What I've come to after years of tussle and turmoil is that the audience can tell when it's live; they can actually tell when it's working, when there's a live connection between the actor and the live machine, and you can tell when somebody's pressing a button offstage. You ultimately can, if you're looking carefully enough, detect a kind of deadness to it.

SELL: One of the things that makes theater different than most videogame experiences, for example, is that you're aware that you're in a room with people, and there are systems of behavior that define how you sit next to somebody, how you behave in the presence of another person who's doing something risky and beautiful and precarious and live. There's a difference between that and playing with virtual avatars on the screen or with other people whom you're only able to interact with through text or chat and through the digital avatars you are running. Is that at play in your work?

WEEMS: Absolutely. I think that that's the main thing that I was trying to tease out in *Elements of Oz*, which was complicated, because there were all these layers of mediation and remediation (fig. i2.2). There was the good old actor standing in front of the audience talking about the Wizard of Oz, then there was our attempt to remake the movie of *The Wizard of Oz*, which involved a huge amount of labor and was extremely complex. Since we were using the shooting script, we would take a scene and shoot it out of order, do the lines out of order, and the actors were dressed like the Tin Man, or Glinda with an IKEA wastebasket on her head. It was like passionate, amateurish filmmaking. We shot it out of order, and then mixed it live and replayed it in the right order. So the audience would have this experience of seeing the film assembled.

And then on top of that, we had the augmented reality, so people had an app that they could download (ideally before they were at the theater), and at certain points in the show they were cued to pick it up and look at a digital effect that would be all over the theater. So they were encouraged to turn away from the stage and look up and behind them and all around, and it produced so much anxiety in different members of the audience and people onstage. I mean, a huge amount of pleasure, especially for younger people, but for older people, or a more traditional theater-going audience, it feels impolite to hold a phone up between

Interview 2: *Layers of Mediation*

Fig. i2.2. Actors in costume in *Elements of Oz*, peering into an orb into which is projected a video recording of several other actors. The Builders Association constructed the theatrical image to show multiple forms of mediated representation and those who are creating them. A performer with a video camera is shooting a close-up of the orb, and that picture is being cast onto a large screen. A second performer is managing these various images at a multimedia station visible to the audience. *Photo by Gennadi Novash, courtesy of Peak Performances@Montclair State University.*

you and the actor. The technique was meant to be a kind of double-edged sword and a provocation: something happening onstage, and you can augment it with this fucking Technicolor door that you're carrying around all the time, and not really consciously thinking, "This is how I escape into Oz." But it was hard for the actors because all of a sudden, everyone in the audience would have their phone in front of their face.

But the other thing I wanted to say is that the audience really got into sharing their devices because not everybody had uploaded the app. And lots of people brought their iPads, which look much better than a phone. So people were looking over each other's shoulders and passing them around. What we thought might have been an isolating experience was communal, ultimately. It created a kind of weird little carnival atmosphere in the theater.

69

Interview 2: *Layers of Mediation*

CHEMERS: I was interviewed by *LA Weekly* once to talk about people taking out their cell phones and tweeting about the experience of watching the show while they were watching the show. The interviewer wanted to know how, as a dramaturg, I felt about that. And I said, I think that's horrifying because it's isolating. I said that not only is it disruptive for you and your relationship to the art object, but for everybody around you, who now has to look at your little screen, which attracts their attention. But what you're saying is that the technology had the exact opposite effect and it created a community.

WEEMS: Mm-hmm. Very effectively, almost immediately.

SELL: So many of the works of the Builders Association are about history, looking back at older texts and asking how might we adapt or alter these texts, but always in light of a profound concern with the contemporary moment. What's the Builders Association's interest in history? And why does it matter to be doing things "historically"?

WEEMS: I think dramaturgs are creating the system around any production, right? That's what we're sort of trying to do.

CHEMERS: A system of meaning?

WEEMS: Exactly, and you're constructing the vocabulary and holding everyone accountable to it. That's certainly what I try to do. As we stepped through the last twenty years, we were interested in outsourcing and dataveillance and connectivity and the 2008 mortgage meltdown. All those things are contemporary moments. They're all kind of zeitgeist moments. But what takes so much labor is to come up with a dramatic system that is particular to that content. We are staging that history, but with a sort of specific and iconoclastic vocabulary for each production. It was like we had to reinvent the wheel for every fucking show, because we weren't talking about the same content and the same history. It was always about trying to find a new expression of that moment.

CHEMERS: One of the functions of the dramaturg is to teach. When you're an arts educator, you have a level of responsibility to your students that's different from the responsibility of the artist to their audience. I'm curious as to whether you feel that your work as a professor and educator has informed your work as a maker.

WEEMS: If anything, I would say it's the other way around. I don't know how to say this without sounding incredibly selfish. The thing about being an artist, really, ultimately, especially in this, like, nonprofit world, where you're not doing it for any commercial reason at all, is to pay yourself first, right? It's really about making something for your own pleasure. And so that doesn't sound very share-y or very empathic. But the pleasure comes from the group making a space where you

Interview 2: *Layers of Mediation*

can do that, really pay yourself, and I think in the best of all possible worlds, you would be doing that in the classroom; you would be on this kind of like one-to-one journey where you are trying to get the students to enter to be in that same space where they're really getting pleasure out of it for themselves.

CHEMERS: Yeah. I see teaching as a performance art and interactive medium. I find it very enjoyable and I take a lot of personal pleasure out of it.

WEEMS: I like to create a space where that can happen. I'm not necessarily the one to occupy it.

SELL: As an artist and as an educator, you are able to do some really interesting things in spaces that aren't completely, fully, or consistently governed by the profit motive.

WEEMS: Very much so, unfortunately even to the point where I often fear that I'm teaching my students to steer clear of that. People I taught at Carnegie Mellon, whom I mentored and I'm very proud of, are working with their own experimental theater companies in New York and are not crossing into the commercial realm by any stretch of the imagination. So it is kind of a set of tools and a way of seeing that allow for analysis and a kind of freedom in terms of not capitulating to the market, but you aren't necessarily teaching people how to go out and make a great living.

CHEMERS: There's this popular notion that our job as educators is to be vocational trainers in the arts, but this is not quite the way we see what we do. And at the risk of seeming to be prejudiced against a particular type of performance, there are performances that need dramaturgs more than others. A performance designed to capitulate to market forces is not one that particularly needs a dramaturg.

WEEMS: Right, exactly. You're not going to do anything usually groundbreaking there.

CHEMERS: Although occasionally you do get something that is both very commercial *and* very good.

SELL: I think *The Lion King* would be a perfect example of that. Julie Taymor created something that spoke powerfully to audience experience in ways that required a finely honed dramaturgical eye to dislocate that production from the Disney animation aesthetic, taking advantage of traditions of puppetry, performance, display, and, to a certain degree, environmental design.

CHEMERS: I'd also think about something like *Hamilton*, which is immensely popular but is also quite revolutionary and in many ways is a deep reconditioning of our shared histories.

WEEMS: Yeah, very much so.

SELL: But is that any different than dramaturgy in a nondigital, more traditional theater space?

Interview 2: *Layers of Mediation*

WEEMS: At least half of my company at any one time were people who were trained outside the theater. Whether they've been architects, very early media artists, sound designers, or people who have never thought about theater, it's always been about sort of extending the umbrella of what can happen in a performance space and trying to bring new folks into the fold.

SELL: Historically, the most interesting innovation in the theatrical process comes from the one who says, "Let's not just limit ourselves to the people who have always worked in this venue. Let's always be looking at where and how we make theater." Is that the right way to think about it?

WEEMS: Absolutely. I mean, when we started *Master Builder*, we had Ben Rubin, who was one of the first MIT graduates to think about interactive performance, way before it was called anything like that. We said, "Goddamn, we need this sort of sound. I need somebody's voice to sound very intimate, like whispering in your ear, but also a little bit echoey." So Ben cut open a plastic bottle and stuck a mic inside, and it really was this hilarious, beautiful moment. He also lined the whole house with triggers and much more elaborate things, but the bottle is the thing that stands out in my memory. Old school, but nobody in the theater would have thought of that.

CHEMERS: Does this reflect back on what you were saying earlier about the difference between a live effect and a recorded one?

WEEMS: Yes. We did a project called *Sontag: Reborn*, which was a one-person performance by Moe Angelos, based on the fact that Susan Sontag used to reread and edit her old journals. The set was divided between Moe live-playing a young, passionate, fourteen-year-old Sontag against an older version of Sontag who appeared like a kind of homunculus on a screen. The old Sontag at one point wrote, "Childhood was a terrible waste of time." We knew that if we just projected Moe doing a prerecording of the old Sontag, it would be terrible and deadly. So Jesse Garrison, one of our video guys, made this joystick system we called the Sontagulator 3000, which enabled a real dialogue and dance. People thought there was an actor offstage, but it was Jesse slowing down and speeding up the recording, cued to the microsecond. Jesse would never consider himself an actor. In this, he was more like a musician.

SELL: One of the things that we value about dramaturgy is collaboration. Has your sense of the dramaturg's role in that process changed over the years?

WEEMS: Not at all. I'm terribly sorry to say it does not get any easier. Really, about eighty percent of my job as the director-creator-dramaturg is to keep reminding people of what the mantra is: "First we set up the system and the rules, and then you have to keep bringing people back to it." Especially in devised, time-based work where you're working over a period of two years or more, you have to keep bringing the company back to what the show is about: "This falls within that circle, and those things fall outside of it, so kill your darlings and stop talking about that." It's a kind of negotiation to exhort them to come back to the original idea and make sure that it's expressed in all these different ways. So whether it's building the website or, for me, talking to the video designer, it's a lot about just holding on to that seed idea and continuing to kind of build layers around that.

PLAYING WITH PLAY

If there's one thing theater artists know how to do well, it's *play*. Whether we're talking the director, the lighting technician, the stage manager, the usher, the costume designer, the actor—the whole lot do what they do because they love to play, and because they know there is nothing more important than play when it's done thoughtfully, beautifully, expertly, and passionately.

The play's the thing, we're told, whether one is keeping a bead on the conscience of the local hegemon or providing the career opportunity of a lifetime to a small company of players inclined to "bellow and strut about like weird animals that were made to look like men, but very badly." Hamlet understands the productive slipperiness of that word *play*. It's the word he appends variously to the entertainment he has planned for dear mother and not-so-dear stepfather; to the script with its juicy, too-close-for-comfort details about poor, doomed Gonzago, suspicious that he's being set up by his skeezy schoolmates; and to the labor of the actors who have arrived at Elsinore on the heels of said skeezy classmates. He understands the *power* of play, its ability to rattle a ruler and conceal a wavering conscience from the capricious whims of authority.

Hamlet's creator had an even more expansive conception of play. As Jaques puts it in *As You Like It*, "All the world's a stage," predicting the work of twentieth-century performance theorists like Erving Goffman and Judith Butler, particularly the idea that public identity is mutative and motile, and that "one man in his time plays many parts." And, of course, Shakespeare adored playing with words. His extravagant puns, knee-shivering insults, serpentine sentences, and delicious bon mots open the prison house of language and let loose imagination, desire, and laughter. What's more, Shakespeare clearly understood the pleasures of "sitting pastimes," as Gina Bloom calls the many tabletop and sporting games referenced in early modern drama.[1] We might recall the chess game that unveils Prospero's scheme in *The Tempest*, Petruchio's wager in *The Taming of the Shrew*, Cleopatra's brave effort to mitigate her melancholy with a bit of billiards. And we recall that though the dauphin of France intended to cow the young Henry V with that crate full of tennis balls, Henry was up for it: "When we have marched our rackets to these balls, / We will in France, by God's grace, play a set / Shall strike his father's crown into the hazard."[2] Henry proved he had a wicked backhand.

We might imagine a twenty-first-century update to that oh-so-playful insult and riposte. In this version, the dauphin sends his rival not tennis gear, but rather a super-deluxe collector's edition of the videogame *Call of Duty: Advanced Warfare*. In turn, Henry's response trades iambic pentameter for the cadences of chat-channel leet trash talk: "ZOMG Christopher Columbus has better map awareness than u! JK! Id ask u 2 shoot yrself, but ud probably miss!"

A cheap laugh, yes, but a serious point. Digital technologies, including videogames, have enabled innovative, exciting, memorable theater, dance, performance art, installation art, and augmented reality experiences. The work of dramaturgy is made all the more exciting and important in these media. They've enabled the script analyst to realize dimensions of the dramatic text—character, conflict, theme, tone, and setting—that might otherwise have been hidden from view. They've provided the historian with new tools, methods, and paradigms to document, preserve, and disseminate information about theater, whether antique (e.g., Richard Beacham's virtual-reality reconstruction of the Theatre of Dionysus) or newly minted (e.g., Barry Smith and Steve Dixon's Digital Performance Archive, which documents works from the 1990s). They've inspired new approaches to audience outreach too. For example, as part of their publicity campaign for Kristoffer Diaz's *The Elaborate Entrance of Chad Deity*, Woolly Mammoth Theatre Company and the Black Women Playwrights' Group's Cyber Narrative Project collaborated with Diaz to create a videogame that introduced players to the themes of the production (and rewarded them with a discount ticket if they won).

Finally, digital technologies and techniques have empowered dramaturgs to be even more effective as public intellectuals. Dramaturgs who think systemically about digital technology can provide unique insight into the dynamics of online performance, enabling critical perspectives on, for example, the performance of trollish whiteness on social media, the impersonation and harassment campaigns of the alt-right, or the construction of gender by queer players of live-stream videogames on Twitch. All of these are proper fields of inquiry for dramaturgs (and we dive deeper into videogames in chapter 4).

Thinking systemically about play is all the more vital in terms of the increasing integration of our lives into technological systems and algorithmic processes. In "Manifesto for a Ludic Century," game designer Eric Zimmerman argues that our relationship to media and culture—and, by extension, information and power—is "increasingly systemic, modular, customizable, and participatory." In other words, power is in play. As Zimmerman goes on to say, "It is not enough to merely be a systems-literate person, to understand systems in an analytic sense. We also must learn to be playful in them. A playful system is a human system, a social system rife with contradictions and with possibility."[3] As theater artists have long known, being playful is an engine of innovation, creativity, and critical understanding. As concerned individuals, public humanists, and innovative dramaturgs, it is vital that we understand play, our attention focused equally on the antique and the innovative. Play is both one of the oldest forms of human activity and a driver of the emerging technoculture.

However, thinking systemically about play is not just a matter of being comprehensive—what we call systemic. No doubt it's important that as dramaturgs, we challenge ourselves and our collaborators to thoroughly explore the who, what, when, where, and how of our projects. As Zeami argues, the systemic dramaturg must always consider with meticulous care the particular relationship of tool to user. To achieve sokyokuchi, we must first consider both all the possible ways we might use a given tool and, if you will, all the possible ways that the tool uses us. Abraham Maslow's "law of the instrument" teaches us that if your toolbox contains only a hammer, everything will start to look a lot like a nail. On the flip side, if you see everything in the world as nails, then all the other tools you have besides hammers are going to gather dust.

In the spirit of comprehensive exploration of both tool and techne, we offer this survey of play and playfulness. The play's the thing, no doubt—but undoubtedly, there are many more playful things than have been dreamt of so far in our dramaturgical philosophy. That said, we should note that while we consider critical play to be an important, if not fundamental, dimension of systemic dramaturgy, there are many other dimensions of theater and performance that can be considered systemically, many other ways that the ethos of sokyokuchi might be explored and achieved.

A *BESTIARUM VOCABULUM* OF PLAY

To comprehend the varieties of play (and players!), we must consult both the *Oxford English Dictionary (OED)* and the *Urban Dictionary*, attending at once to the etymological *longue durée* and the ephemera of everyday use, to the arcana of scholars and the pricks and kicks of social media. The term *play* and its cognates are notoriously multiplex and mutative. This is due in part to play's ubiquity as a human activity and the many forms it takes. It is due as well to the fascination play incites across academic disciplines from psychology to ethnography to architecture to educational theory. Certainly, the challenge of defining play is the consequence of so many kinds of things counting as play. Toys, games, animals, words, roles, and other people are only a few of the things with which we might play. But are we really doing the same kind of thing when we lay down two pairs in a game of poker and when we gently lay down the body of an actor playing Cordelia?

Not only is play difficult to stabilize terminologically, but any effort to define it is inevitably entangled in social, ethical, economic, and moral quandaries. Schechner ponders whether "scholars should declare a moratorium on defining play." As his friend, anthropologist Victor Turner, might put it, "Play is an activity—or a set of activities—that are categorically uncategorizable, the 'anti' by which all other categories are destabilized." Inevitably, observes Schechner, in the search for an understanding of what play *is*, the definer risks misunderstanding what play *does*: "the ongoing, underlying process of off-balancing, loosening, bending, twisting, reconfiguring, and transforming—the permeating, eruptive/disruptive energy and mood below, behind, and to the sides of focused attention."[4]

Playing with Play

That's one of the things that makes it such an attractive topic for the systemic dramaturg. Being authentically playful is a difficult task in societies defined by strict distinctions between things that are adult and things that are childlike, things that are work and things that are fun, things that are productive and things that are not, things that are valuable learning experiences and things that distract, things that are meaningful and things that are frivolous wastes of time. Though as theater scholars and artists, we have learned a healthy disrespect for such distinctions, we understand how they have been used to harass and oppress those who insist on the right to play a role (for instance, a racialized, gendered, political, or sexual role) other than the one assigned to them by authorities. We understand the anxiety caused by those who revel in "portentous masquerade," to recall the sixteenth-century British priest Thomas Becon, who challenge the principalities of the natural order with a bit of face paint and wit.[5] When we play, we play in and across a dense and well-guarded matrix of customs and conventions. Play has its dangers.

However we approach it, we agree with psychologist Jean Piaget that play is "difficult to understand" which is part of what makes the attempt so much fun! Yes, even scholarship can be playful. Fortunately, unlike conventional scholars, whose duty is to simplify and clarify, the systemic dramaturg revels in complexity and multiplicity and, like their fellow theater artists, has no obligation to respect the distinctions laid down by philosophers, doctors, sheriffs, and parent-teacher associations. Thus, rather than attempt to define once and for all our key term and its cognates, we thought we'd assemble something akin to the medieval *bestiarum vocabulum*, an attempt to collect and taxonomize the known beasts of the world, each illustrated and accompanied by a useful lesson. We organize this bestiary in three genera: *play* as doing; *play* as thing; and *player*.

In the end, we hope this etymological menagerie provides the reader with

> The many theories of play expounded in the past are clear proof that the phenomenon is difficult to understand. But the reason for the difficulty lies perhaps in the fact that there has been a tendency to consider play as an isolated function (as has been the case with "imagination") and therefore to see particular solutions to the problem, whereas play is in reality one of the aspects of any activity (like imagination in respect to thought).
>
> —Jean Piaget, *Play, Dreams, and Imitation in Childhood*, 147

a rich set of conceptual and practical frameworks, a systematic way to consider the activities that constitute theater as both art form and cultural event.

PLAY AS DOING

We begin with *play* as action. Under one popular definition, *play* means to pursue an activity for its own sake, existing in a kind of pleasurable purity outside the mundane demands of room, board, and wallet. Johan Huizinga defines it in this fashion in his influential 1938 study, *Homo Ludens*: "a free activity standing quite consciously outside 'ordinary' life as being 'not serious' but at the same time absorbing the player intensely and utterly. It is an activity connected with no material interest, and no profit can be gained by it. It proceeds within its own proper boundaries of time and space according to fixed rules and in an orderly manner."[6] While there is something undeniably vital, if not downright moral, in the desire to defend playing against the voracious appetite of duty and commodity, for those who play in the theater, the idea that one can authentically play only in the absence of interest and profit is, as they say, a rule honored more often in the breach than in the observance.

When we consult the etymology of the term provided by the *OED*, we find conceptions of play more miscellaneous and mischievous than those of Huizinga and his strait-laced disciples. We find beings both human and non- that "strut, dance, or engage in other forms of sexual display," that "bubble up like a boiling liquid," that wander freely within their designated spaces as a ship might around its anchor or a faithful worker within the scope of their duties, that dance across a surface in irregular but pleasing fashion, as the late afternoon light might on the surface of a lake. One cannot watch two friendly dogs meeting at a park and deny that playing is limited to humans. This unexpected diversity is a wellspring for the systemic dramaturg—a source for innovative practice and critical questioning.

We play to exhaust (as with a fish on a line), to keep in motion, to carry out an action of prestidigitous humor. We can play artillery, a jet of water, a political issue (e.g., "play the race card"). Milton reminds us that we play amorously too. "Now let us play . . . ," he writes. "For never did thy Beautie / . . . so enflame my sense / With ardor to enjoy thee."[7]

One might play to express one's joy in the presence of one's deity, to revel in their divinity. Or alternatively, we might play to mock and ridicule, trifle and jest. We might play along with a joke or a con game. When we agree to pitch in with a criminal plot, we are said to "play ball." To play is to participate, either in accordance with the rules or in studious and demonstrative rejection of them. And we rarely mean or do just one variety of play at a time. This is evident in a memorable moment from the 1995 movie *Friday*, when Smokey (played by Chris Tucker) and Craig Jones (Ice Cube) ponder the hazards of owing money to Big Worm, the neighborhood's violent but emotionally sensitive ice cream man and drug dealer:

> SMOKEY: Man, that fool just playin' man. I ain't trippin'.
> CRAIG: That's yo problem. Ain't nobody playin' but you. You walk up and down the street all day playin'. He ain't playin'! You think he playin' 'bout his money? He know where my momma stay, know where you momma stay. You say he had a gun when you seen him, right?
> SMOKEY: Yeah.
> CRAIG: Well name one person in the hood play like that![8]

Like Hamlet contemplating his theatrical mousetrap, Smokey and Craig understand the vicissitudes of play: when we enter the field of play, we enter a field governed by multiple and competing forces: attitude, desire, display, memory, authenticity, experience, status, pride, competition, affiliation, community, and ownership.

And finally, there is the definition of *play* near and dear to the dramaturg: to play a role onstage, whether that role is a fictional character, a stereotype, or a slightly heightened version of our everyday selves; whether the stage is framed by a gilded proscenium, wheeled about on a pageant wagon, or just a momentary clearing in a bustling piazza; whether that stage earns a profit, is subsidized by the state, or just leaves a negative balance on a half dozen credit cards.

Play rarely abides by categorical and ethical boundaries. But there remains something undeniably alluring about the idea that play is bound in some essential way to freedom, that play acquires a unique power when sundered from the bonds of bottom-line assessment and political security. Perhaps we should frame play in terms more patient with compromise; terms no less idealistic, but more willing to negotiate. Or perhaps the opposite. Richard Schechner coined the term "dark play" to describe activities that involve "fantasy, risk, luck, daring, invention, and deception," but also an element of real danger to self and others. He cites the example of a woman who rushes out to the end of a perilous cliff to dance, frightening her father and expressing her feelings of frustration at his inability to recognize that she is an adult. Often, those involved in dark play don't know they're playing because, "unlike carnivals or ritual clowns whose inversions of established order is sanctioned by the authorities, dark play is subversive, its agendas always hidden."[9] Online trolls are experts at dark play, luring the unknowing into verbal games whose aim is anything but clarity or consensus. If play is always, in some way, about power, dark play is a way of playing with power that can result in real-life damage to body, mind, and spirit. When Hamlet stages *The Mousetrap*, he plays darkly. No one but he knows the stakes or the rules of his audacious, cruel game, not least, poor Ophelia.

On the lighter side, there is the "playful pedagogy" proposed by Mark Sample, which recalls in many respects the process-oriented approach of devised and environmental theater. Sample identifies six principles of playful pedagogy:

o Process over product
o Low stakes over high stakes
o Mistakes over success
o Ambiguity over certainty
o Discovery over objectives
o Divergent thinking over convergent thinking

He suggests a variety of entertaining projects to enact these principles, including transforming literary texts into games; glitching music and image files; transposing poems into interactive, gloriously dysfunctional artifacts; and "breaking" productivity software to introduce new ways of organizing information.[10]

Not surprisingly, what Sample calls "playful pedagogy" aligns with our vision of playful dramaturgy: it emphasizes process, works to reduce the stakes of decision-making to enable flexibility and creativity, tolerates and values mistakes, is comfortable with ambiguity, aims toward discovery rather than rigid objectives, and facilitates divergent thinking. But what about a pedagogy of dark play? Is it legal, ethical, or appropriate to put learners—including those learners we call "spectators"—into playful situations that involve substantial emotional and physical risks without their full and consenting knowledge of those risks? That's a difficult question to answer, frankly, and depends entirely on the situation. However, the history of avant-garde performance shows that it has been done, sometimes to stunning effect. Proceed with caution.

PLAY AS THING

We turn now to the "thinginess" of play—to the material stuff that mediates our playfulness and the nouns that name them. In theater, what we call "a play" is not one but two things: the thing we read and the thing we watch and hear. The blurred etymological line between text and theater reflects an intimate supplementarity—the ways that one presumes and depends on the other. Both are associated with a kind of artfulness or evident formality. While today we might say that an event of unusual portent is "like a movie," in the precinematic era, witnesses of things larger than life would say they were "as good as a play." At the same time, we associate both the dramatic and staged text with a certain quality of openness, spontaneity, and liveliness; indeed, that's what makes them more compelling to watch than, say, a congressional budget hearing. To read a play well requires one to imagine the joyous possibilities of theatrical space, theater technology, and the capacities of those who create in that space. To watch a play well requires one to commit time and attention to an activity that is inherently precarious.

The nouns of play generally denote forms of exercise and movement, usually within a bounded space or with some kind of tool or object in hand—swordplay, for example. When we perceive someone acting with a certain kind of mirthful and motile artfulness, we might say that what they do is done "in a spirit of play." When we take humorous advantage of the accidents in language, we make a "play on words." It is the name we give to forms of action of a particular quality. The *Oxford English Dictionary* cites British statesman Benjamin Disraeli writing of the "enchanting play of fancy"; cultural critic F. R. Leavis, of the "play of intellect"; dance scholars R. Singha and R. Massey, of dance as the "*lila* or play of cosmic forces"—each of them attempting to capture a quality of motility, rapidity, and litheness, of something flitting and forming, bringing some larger, imperceptible force to the fore, giving practical being to it through felicitous, situated movement.

There are the many meanings of *play* associated with games, sport, and warfare. To put something "into play" means to move something from a state of potential use into actual use: to bring it onto the game board, for example, or onto the field of play or battle. When that something is in play, it is in a state of strategic assessment. Those involved in the activity judge the quality of that something's position, whether and to what extent that something is in play, the quality and quantity of its motility, either as it occurred, occurs, or might occur. And when that something loses the capacity for action, whether because it has been rendered moot by other agents or moved outside the defined boundaries, we say that it is "out of play": a chess piece that has been eliminated, a ball kicked over the touchline, a secret agent arrested. It is the name we give to discrete actions within that field of play: a defensive play, for example, or a play for affection. We might congratulate a teammate for a "good play." And we might characterize that teammate as having a quality of play, admiring the aggressiveness or intelligence they demonstrate and thus some quality of their character. In French, this connection is even more clearly drawn in the word *jeu*, which means all at once play, game, and theatrical event.

Gina Bloom expresses regret that we no longer honor the synonymy "between games and theatrical plays [that] was a foregone conclusion for premodern people." She reminds us, "Medieval writers used the term *ludus* for both games and plays. And the earliest commercial theaters of Shakespeare's era, known as 'playhouses,' were built right next to gaming establishments; some of these theaters even doubled as blood-sport venues."[11] As a consequence, theater is not "an obvious or even likely reference point for most gamers and theorists of gaming," and scholars and practitioners of theater are losing an opportunity to make a difference in an age characterized by Zimmerman as "the ludic century."[12] That forgetting is the unfortunate consequence of our endemic historical shortsightedness, persistent elitism, and widespread anxieties about fun. But if we look back to the early modern period, Bloom avers, we will find much to learn about "the history of games, . . . the history of theater, and thus . . . the relationship between these media forms."[13] For playful dramaturgs, the lure of this kind of historical research is hard to resist, not only for what it might contribute to productions of Kālidāsa, Behn, and de la Barca, but also for the insight it might provide into our own historical moment, which, like the early modern period in London, is characterized by a pervasiveness of games and play. Beyond the fence line of "serious theater," there are forms of theatrical play that are worth the time and attention of even the most ardent lover of modernist drama, limelight and flat, and the well-behaved audience.

The "thinginess" of play has perhaps never been more evident than now. Consumers spend billions of dollars on toys, board games, videogames, sports equipment, and backyard swing sets. Nations, states, and cities spend billions on playful spaces, ranging from soccer fields wedged between high-rise apartment buildings in the dense urban spaces of Rio de Janeiro and Bangkok to Hokkaido's four-hundred-acre Moerenuma Park, designed by modernist sculptor Isamu Noguchi. There is a thriving business around the collecting of playful things, too, from *Star Wars* action figures to antique board games. Some collectors build a library so they can play with friends and family ("retro-gaming"); others, to await the moment when a profit can be turned or, if the collector is a scholar and historian, to answer the call for evidence of what and how we once played.

The inextricability of play and the things we play with is especially evident in games. Board game designer extraordinaire Wolfgang Kramer reminds us that the games we play are governed not only by rules but also by components. "The components are the hardware," he writes, meaning the board, the game pieces, the cards, all the stuff that goes with a given game. "The rules are the software. Both define the game. Both can exist independently from each other, but separately are not a game."[14] Indeed, archaeologists have unearthed boards and pieces and play fields of various kinds, but in the absence of a document delimiting their rules, we can only speculate how they were played. And though it is relatively easier to reconstruct a game if we have the rules, though not the components, the game so reconstructed will necessarily be an historiographical interpretation, a more or less educated guess.

Theater historians are entirely familiar with the challenge of restoring the playfulness to the things that have been played. Examining archival documents—scripts, props, architectural drawings, programs, reviews, and the other doughty survivors of history's trials and tribulations—one finds that the liveness of the performance event is tantalizingly close, yet just beyond grasp. Or perhaps it is all too close, all around us, but invisible, illegible, or indecipherable due to the limits of our imagination and methods. Marvin Carlson scries such fugitive moments among the recycled matériel of theater—scripts haunted by other scripts, bodies of actors haunted by previous roles and celebrity, props and sets used and reused, and the theaters themselves where, with eyes properly focused, one can see spectators arrayed, stagehands laboring, actors walking the boards, voices echoing in the rafters.[15]

Joseph Roach alerts us to the "social processes of memory and forgetting, familiarly known as culture." He attends to a congeries of things that might not seem particularly "thingy" at first glance—the way a word is pronounced, a gesture performed, a costume worn, a parade route traveled, an exchange of goods completed—but that with the right historical and critical tools, reveal the dance of the ephemeral and the durable, of "performative practices that maintain (and invent) human continuities, leaving their traces in diversified media, including the living bodies of the successive generations that sustain different social and cultural identities."[16] Such performances, such as the Corpus Christi celebrations that occur annually across the Americas, "function as vital acts of transfer, transmitting social knowledge, memory, and a sense of identity" in contexts where such cultural continuities are subject to violent attack and repression.[17]

How might a better understanding of playful things help us better comprehend theater history—and vice versa? Bloom explores precisely this rich intersection of games and theater in *Gaming the Stage*. "Game rules," she writes, "are to gameplay as dramatic texts are to theatrical plays." Both, she avers, are "systems of information" that provide opportunities for playful interaction.[18] In a fashion similar to the way a theater historian enriches our understanding of a dramatic text by reconstructing its social, cultural, and institutional contexts, a historian of play can enrich our understanding of a game's text—its rules—by reconstructing the "conventions of gameplay" that surrounded its play. In the case of card games, as an example, that might include the conventions of "shuffling, dealing, revealing, bluffing, table talk, and so forth" that are typically not described in rule books.[19] Bloom demonstrates that understanding the rules and conventions of game play can provide useful insight into centuries-old dramatic texts, as she shows in her examination of the early English comedy *Gammer Gurton's Needle*, in which characters use the terminology of gaming and a climactic scene revolves around characters playing a game of cards. Deploying her detailed understanding of the rules and repertoires of fifteenth- and sixteenth-century card games, Bloom sheds light on the text's exploration of friendship and refines our understanding of how it reveals and hides crucial information. And vice versa! Through careful analysis of the play's representation of game play, she is able to add details to our understanding of how early modern Brits played the games they played.

The motile materiality and mercurial performativity of gamified things are aspects that make defining what a game is so challenging—and perhaps futile. Pat Harrigan and Noah Wardrip-Fruin suggest the term "playable media," highlighting the fact that games "invite and structure play" in a fashion that troubles distinctions between rules, components, and milieu—and sometimes our very sense of self.[20] Players of tabletop roleplaying games like *Dungeons & Dragons* are familiar with the way a character constructed out of randomly generated numbers, warmed-over fantasy tropes, and statistical tables can become something as attractive, memorable, and complex as anything invented by Marí Irene Fornés or Jean Racine. In a similar vein, when videogame players discuss their experiences, they inevitably speak in the first person: "I climbed up the cliff face. I fell in love with the prince. I achieved a higher level." Videogame scholars have long recognized "that audiences use . . . media as a vehicle for exploring alternate self-concepts or personality concepts."[21] But because videogames provide an energetically and multilayered interactive experience nested within multiple kinds of gamelike challenges, videogame players arguably experience a unique and uniquely vivid sense of becoming the character. As Casey Hart puts it, "Avatars are not just digital dolls for the player to

> For me, this phrase ["playable media"] shifts my thinking from a question I've found only temporarily useful ("Is this a game?") to one I have found rewards sustained attention ("How is this played?").
> —Noah Wardrip-Fruin, "Playable Media and Textual Instruments"

interact with in electronic space, but rather cultivated projections of the user."[22]

But as appealing as it may be to seek the nuances of human action and feeling in the things with which we play, we must not forget dramaturg Marianne van Kerkhoven's call to "listen to the bloody machine."[23] The field of "new media dramaturgy," which we discussed in the introduction, is premised on the notion that technology isn't simply a tool to be used to communicate ideas, emotions, and experience, but rather is an entity with a "voice" all its own. As Eckersall, Grehan, and Scheer explain, new media dramaturgy deploys the technical elements of theater to foreground the "tension between new media as an enabling part of everyday life and culture, and as something that threatens it."[24]

In new media dramaturgy, machines are often the dramatic focus of performance—reversing Hamlet, the *thing* is the play. For example, dumb type's *pH* (1990) featured enormous mechanical armatures that periodically swept the stage area, forcing the human performers to quickly shift their position. In A Two Dogs Company's production of Kris Verdonck's *Box* (2005), spectators stood in a small space at the center of which was positioned a clear glass box with a light inside. As an offstage voice intoned a text by Heiner Müller, the light within the box grew in intensity, eventually reaching a level of brightness intolerable to the human eye, compelling the spectators to don protective goggles. "To experience this work," Eckersall, Grehan, and Scheer write, "is to feel super-saturated with light, overwhelmed by it, your existence threatened by it. Nothing else exists." Exemplary of new media dramaturgy, *Box* points to "the importance of objects in performance for their own sake, their materiality, and their spectrum of performance parameters."[25]

The distinction between play as doing and play as thing is perhaps nowhere more thrillingly uncertain than in what Jennifer Parker-Starbuck calls "cyborg theatre." Exploring the multimedia theater of George Coates, the Wooster Group, the Builders Association, Cathy Weis, and others, she unfolds the recent history of the "intertwinement and negotiation between organic and non-organic materials, the body and technology." Among her many fascinating discoveries are the connections she unearths between contemporary "fear and fascination with technologies" and older myths, including Jewish golem stories and Mary Shelley's *Frankenstein*. Further, by attending to the theatrical and dramatic dimensions of theatrical work in which performers and technologies are merged, she not only draws attention to the ideological and political dimensions of our own technological moment but also strengthens the argument—so crucial to systemic dramaturgy—that the history of theater is the history of technology as "co-author with the living performer" and always, inevitably "a space for trying things out."[26]

PLAYER (NOUN)

And now to perhaps the most intriguing denizen of our *bestiarum vocabulum*, the one who tries things out. The question of how and what we play can inspire intense feelings, particularly among moral authorities, but that hardly compares with the feelings aroused by those who do the playing. Those who play artfully and well have inspired intense, sometimes inflammatory passions, from the philosopher justifying the exclusion of actors from the perfect society to the church father inveighing with spit-flecked hatred against theater, gambling, and prostitution as the same thing; from the child weeping at the sight of her favorite team failing to win the league championship to the community theater director struggling to rein in a ham; from the wallflower marveling at the alacrity with which their charismatic classmate makes romantic friends to the audience rising to their feet, enraptured, clashing their palms together in tribute to a perfected moment of voice, body, and spirit.

The denotation of *player* most familiar to the dramaturg is "one who acts a role on stage." One of the dramaturg's duties is therefore to thoroughly understand the powers of the player, whether in terms of the vast repertoire of theatrical techniques performers have used around the world and across the centuries or the diverse cultural assumptions about what performers are and do or what this particular performer, with this body and this voice, might achieve. This duty is all the more pressing when we work with writers who like to play with matters of widespread moral or political concern: Antonin Artaud, Bertolt Brecht, or Split Britches, for example. Or when we work with plays that self-consciously use roleplaying and acting to explore larger themes: Shakespeare's *Hamlet* and *Twelfth Night*, Griselda Gambaro's *Strip* and *Information for Foreigners*, Pedro Calderón de la Barca's *Life Is a Dream*, Dion Boucicault's *The Octoroon*, Lanford Wilson's *The Madness of Lady Bright*, and Alice Childress's *Trouble in Mind*, to name but a few.

The *OED* says that the original, now obsolete meaning of *player* is "a reveller, a merrymaker," and all the best Christians from Rome to the Renaissance avoided players like the plague (indeed, in Elizabethan England, the theater was thought to be a great place to catch the plague, and the master of the revels could close the playhouses at a moment's notice, citing plague as the cause). That sense of the term—of one who seeks fun at the expense of good, old hard work—lost favor after 1600, we are told, but was revived by Huizinga in *Homo Ludens*, where we discover a most audacious attempt to redefine the human being not as "one who thinks," but as "one who plays." And to top that off, he defines play not as an escape from the work of culture, but as its antecedent. For Huizinga, players are the unacknowledged inventors of all that so many of us hold dear: freedom, order, extraordinary experience, the humanist ideals that bind us beyond concerns of profit and utility.[27] No wonder so many cultures tell stories about tricksters, those puckish creators who know how to play with power, who know the rules and how to bend them, who know how to wear a mask and how to take it off—the Signifying Monkey, Coyote, Wakdjunga, Anansi, Joha, Mbeku, Kumiho, Amaguq, and Prometheus.

Indeed, what makes a player a player is their willingness to play in *systems*, which are usually defined by rules of some kind. According to the *OED*, the second-oldest denotation of *player* is "a person who takes part in a sport or game," a "pleyar at the bal," to recall Geoffrey the Grammarian's *Promptorium Parvulorum* of 1440. To play ball, you have to know the rules of the game: the arcana of baseball's balk or soccer's offside rule, whether one should roll a Wisdom or Intelligence check in *Dungeons & Dragons*, the laws governing foreign contributions to a U.S. presidential campaign, whether the playground bully will target you for wearing a T-shirt with your favorite anime character on it. The knowledgeable player actually revels in the constraints of the rulebook, since the rules define the parameters of the game. Bernard Suits defines games as a form of goal-oriented play whose participants must use "less efficient means" to reach a goal that might be achieved more easily.[28] The great players (and the vilest cheaters) know that rules are the mother of invention. That is certainly true of theater, where cheating is often valorized, for better or worse. One of the singular pleasures of the art is when a production or performer finds within the constraints of a script—whether intrinsic to the text or accreted by tradition—something new and surprising.

A systemic dramaturg is a technologically mindful dramaturg, as we've argued, but a systemic dramaturg is also a collaborative thinker. And among the most interesting thinkers are the players themselves. A player, after all, is one who plays an instrument. Thus the player must know the mechanics of how to interact with that tool—how to blow properly, how moist to render the reed, how to accommodate the latency in a server when readying a computer command. This playful consciousness can extend beyond the tool to the larger systems in which their play occurs. A good player of Texas hold 'em continually calculates the odds of cards appearing in the next draw and continually monitors their opponents for tells. The financier doesn't just know the laws that govern the movement of wealth but also the people in the profession, those who pull the strings and whose strings can be pulled. Speaking of strings, there is speculation that the thirty-four-match winning streak of Serena Williams in 2012–13 was enabled in part by a midseason change in the kind of tennis string she used, enabling her to exert just a little bit more control and significantly diminish the number of unforced errors she committed.[29] The player doesn't just know how to play their chosen instrument; the player is often an inventor.

Who better to improve on the tools of play than those who play with them, whether the tool is an algorithm that can detect and exploit subtle fluctuations in pork futures, a putter that diminishes inconsistencies of posture and swing, or a mechanism to make one's wig flip up at the sight of the ghost of Hamlet's father, as was the case with eighteenth-century actor David Garrick. And the player is often a faithful friend and thus someone who can help the systemic dramaturg understand the intimacy that exists between human beings and the instruments with which they play. Musicians can be wedded to their instruments with a degree of fealty they might not show to the humans in their lives: John Coltrane's 1965 Mark VI tenor saxophone, the Gibson ES-345–355 model

> To play a game is to attempt to achieve a specific state of affairs, using only means permitted by rules, where the rules prohibit use of more efficient in favor of less efficient means, and where the rules are accepted just because they make possible such activity.
>
> —Bernard Suits,
> *The Grasshopper*, 54–55

guitars that B. B. King named "Lucille," Kim Chee-Yun's Francesco Ruggieri violin.

But not all instruments require a human player, and the systemic dramaturg should be cognizant of the kinds of instruments that play independently of human heart and hand. We might think of the Aeolian harp, an instrument whose sound is produced by wind blowing across strings. Such harps inspired melancholy in Samuel Taylor Coleridge's "Dejection: An Ode," childish fear in Ian Fleming's *Chitty-Chitty-Bang-Bang*, and lines of tourist buses for the twenty-foot-tall harp created by Giuseppe Ferlenga in 2015 for the Sports and Cultural Group of Mazzano, Italy. There are the exquisite automatons of Swiss watchmaker Pierre Jaquet-Droz (fig. 2.1). One of them, "The Musician," plays lovely melodies on a miniature harmonium. Jaquet-Droz's automatons (he and his team constructed three between 1767 and 1774) are widely recognized as early computers. As systemic dramaturgs, we find this kind

Fig. 2.1. Two automatons designed and constructed by Pierre Jaquet-Droz, Henri-Louis Droz, and Jean-Frédéric Leschot in the late 1800s. *Photograph by Rama. Wikimedia Commons.*

Playing with Play

of inventiveness not only delightful but fascinating. After all, systemic dramaturgy is premised on the notion that our understanding of and relationship to technology is vastly improved when we think beyond European modernism. "The Musician" and her sibling computers are decidedly (and charmingly) anthropocentric precursors to the "autonomous objects, instruments that play themselves, exploding engines," swinging robot arms, and blinding light boxes one encounters in the works of dumb type and Kris Verdonck.[30] And they might offer new ways of thinking about and creating with new media dramaturgy.

But there's little doubt that when most people think of players, they think of human beings. There are, for example, those players who combine know-how and glamour. In Black American vernacular, we find "players" admired for their successful and multifarious pursuit of sexual conquest. Similarly, there are the players who are the movers and shakers in their chosen craft. The term is especially common among those who play in the financial markets—hedge funds and the like—and not surprisingly, those are the kinds of players portrayed in movies and advertisements as attractive, equipped with long legs, firm jaws, and profit-seeking mid-distance gazes. These players are trendsetters, followed avidly by those who one day hope to play with the big guns—or at least to look like they do. David Mamet's *Glengarry Glen Ross* is a play about such players and a lesson to players that one should be wary of whom and how one plays, lest one be played. Coffee, after all, is only for closers.

Sarah DeLappe's 2016 play *The Wolves*, crystallizes the multiple meanings of *player* in captivating style—and presents an equally captivating set of challenges to the dramaturg. *The Wolves* tells the story of an under-eighteen girls soccer club whose members gather weekly to warm up for matches and, while doing so, talk about contemporary events, school, their bodies, their passions, their fears. *The Wolves* is rather unconventional in form—episodic, elliptical—and in action, as the performers are tasked with a double challenge: to convincingly portray a group of highly competitive, funny, fractious young women and to display the kinds of soccer skills typical of high school athletes who have entirely realistic aspirations of competing at the college and national levels. It is a highly physical work, the drama unfolding as the women stretch and run and kick and dribble.

DeLappe's text poses multiple challenges for the dramaturg. First, they need to know soccer as both game and culture—the rules, the repertoire of skilled players, the demands placed on those players by coaches and parents. They need to know the kinds of warm-up drills that would be typical of this age group. They need to know that a striker thinks and moves differently than a defensive back does. *The Wolves* is, in some respects, a dance drama—the warm-up drills should be designed so that each scene possesses a different tone, a distinct kinesthetic tension among the players. The dramaturg for this play must understand that soccer is a global multiculture. One of the central dramatic conflicts concerns the arrival of a new player, the daughter of a globe-hopping travel writer. The conflict between her and the others is, in many ways, a conflict of play styles. The new girl, known as #46, learned soccer playing pickup games on streets and vacant lots as she followed her mother around the world. But the other girls learned within the rigid, drill-oriented model of U.S. soccer training. The tension between these styles should be visible to audiences in #46's unfamiliarity with the warm-up drills and when, in an act intended to both show off her superior skills and knock the other plays down a peg, she executes an astonishing feat of ball juggling and trash-talking.

The dramaturg may need to work with the director while casting the show. It is unlikely that more than a few actors will be found with requisite soccer skills or soccer players with requisite acting skills. Thus *The Wolves* obligates the dramaturg to coordinate with people not typically found in their iPhone contacts: sports trainers and soccer coaches. Less fit or skilled players need to be provided with expert advice to avoid and mitigate injury and acquire the kinds of ball skills they need so that this play about players is played by players who can play.

WHAT IS NEW IS OLD AGAIN

Having assembled our *bestiarum vocabulum*, we turn now to the question of the old and the new. At the crux of systemic dramaturgy is an understanding of play that encompasses with equal brio both the time-tested and the emergent, both the pleasures of the proscenium and the computer roleplaying game, both the cultivation of a subscription audience and the identification of fake social media followers, both Zeami and *The Legend of Zelda*. This capacious understanding reflects our desire to empower theater artists to more effectively comprehend and deploy the textual, historical, theoretical, technical, and social dimensions of theater in all its forms; to unlock the unprecedented aesthetic, critical, and social potential of theater in a digital age; and most importantly, to serve as an effective team member. In other words, we want to help dramaturgs play well with others.

LaRonika Thomas is an excellent example of a new generation of "digital dramaturgs" and the broadened conception of play we're advocating. In her essay "Digital Dramaturgy and Digital Dramaturgs," Thomas affirms the importance of the conventional locations of dramaturgical labor—the rehearsal hall and the library—but adds a third location, what she calls "virtual space." She urges dramaturgs to take an ambitious position "on the digital terrain, . . . plotting the frontier of where we may be headed," and identifies four roles for the digital dramaturg:[31]

o Creative collaborator. In this role, the dramaturg uses online research, software and interactive platforms, and other digital media and technologies to improve teamwork, ask useful questions about a production in process, and find answers to enable their team to achieve production goals.

o Promoter. In this role, the dramaturg uses social media, web design, and online databases to provide audiences with information, to promote the production, and to educate and excite the audience.

o Archivist. The dramaturg is a historian, too, whether developing an archive for a small regional theater, for a library, or for international organizations like the American Society for Theatre Research or the International Federation for Theatre Research. In this role, they create archival materials using digital technologies and platforms and pay attention to issues concerning access, degradation of records, and so on.

o Experience designer. In this role, the dramaturg helps develop theatrical experiences beyond the usual spaces of theater. Northwestern University's Fabula(b), for example, developed a side-scrolling 2D combat videogame that captures the visceral violence of the Norwegian invasion scene in *Macbeth* and highlights the symbolic role of blood in the play. And there is Kris Verdonck, "who creates wordless performances involving interactions between human performers, machines, and digital video, often in collaboration with a dramaturg."[32]

Though they may be playing with new tools, Thomas's digital dramaturg isn't all that different from dramaturgs of yore. The digital dramaturg is still a jack of all trades, a scholar-practitioner who reads the dramatic text with an incisive eye, who asks unexpected questions about the production design, whose contact list includes both teachers and merchants, who understands the difference between limelight and gaslight, and who loves nothing more than wandering the stacks of the university library, except maybe helping actors learn how to dance a pavane. The digital dramaturg might ponder what that pavane would look like in a massively multiplayer online roleplaying game. When we play across historical reference and technology, we are playing like systemic dramaturgs.

The contemporary dramaturg has a diverse collection of tools at their disposal and more tasks that can benefit from their versatility, adaptability, and willingness to go where no theater geek has gone before. The dramaturg who aspires to the systemic follows in the footsteps of historians like Steve Dixon, whose book on digital performance attempts to encompass its histories, theories, contexts, and primary modes. Like Dixon, we hope to be conscious of historical precedents, skeptical about claims of the unprecedented, and enthusiastic about the diversity of methods and contexts that he calls "digital performance" but we might call "digital play." Indeed, we embrace in a playful way the tendency to use terms like "digital" and "performance" in an expansive, if not all-encompassing, fashion. But we diverge in one important respect from Dixon. He seeks to "provide a history of the fascinating development of digital performance, but also to identify and evaluate the degree to which the use of new media in the performance arts has brought about new paradigms, genres, aesthetics, and interactive experiences."[33] In contrast, we hope to turn those historical and analytical tools to practical use, to use that history to guide the systemic dramaturg in their efforts to negotiate the thrilling, sometimes daunting tensions between old and new.

But if we embrace an expansive, playful conception of dramaturgy, we do not intend to ride roughshod over what Sarah Bay-Cheng, Jennifer Parker-Starbuck, and David Z. Saltz have identified as the "subtle but significant differences in how critics and practitioners delineate the parameters of [performances] with an integral reliance upon, and relationship to, forms of media that surpass traditional uses of lighting, sound, and scenic effects." The systemic dramaturg doesn't forget that technologies and practices are continually "expanding and changing," and thus "necessitate a constant renewal of techniques."[34] We must attend with care to what artists do and what they intend, as well as the intrinsic characteristics of the media they use. A "new media dramaturgy," to recall Eckersall, Grehan, and Scheer again, doesn't treat technology "simply as scenographic elements or techniques," but as "core components of the dramaturgy of the production." This is not to say that we don't celebrate the traditional scenographic use of new technologies, but we recognize the potential of a dramaturgy that approaches technologies in a way that honors "their own modes of existence," recognizing them not simply as tools for performers, designers, and directors, but as, potentially, "key *players* in each work's dramaturgy."[35]

Like Bay-Cheng, Eckersall, and their coresearchers, as well as other scholars who have explored the interface between theater and technology, we seek to conceive a dramaturgy that is "provisional and conceptual," that "enables the discussion of a dramaturgy of various mediated and material properties in terms of their thingly influence on the 'soul' and 'structure' of productions."[36] To play with the digital is therefore not to lose sight of the histories that brought these technologies into our hands or the social, economic, and political forces that allow some to play while denying others anything but immiseration. The ethos of sokyokuchi demands this attention. That said, if it works, it works. The play's the thing.

Being playful does not mean being naive about the hazards posed by the technologies of performance, surveillance, and data processing. We envision systemic dramaturgy, like all dramaturgy, as an essentially ethical practice. History has taught us difficult lessons about flash pot igniters, white lead makeup, poorly maintained rigging, inadequate ventilation, and power saws. Likewise, Jon McKenzie argues, scholars, critics, and practitioners of performance must remain alert to the ways that new technologies and paradigms of performance mortgage our minds, bodies, and imaginations to regimes of "social efficacy," "organizational efficiency," and "technological effectiveness."[37] We are well aware of how culture and technology have been employed by those who control them to weaken and assault those who do not. These matrices of technology, ideology, and social convention, he continues, force us all to constantly perform, whether under the watchful eye of employers, the law, or marketers.

Theorists and practitioners of performance must be vigilant about the ways our putatively "critical" forms of play can serve unwittingly to obscure or innovate the very technologies, ideologies, and conventions we thought we were playing against. It can be easy to think of a moment of theatrical power as existing essentially beyond everyday life and politics, as the apotheosis of what Johan Huizinga called the "magic circle" of play, a "temporary worl[d] within the ordinary world, . . . an act apart."[38] No doubt there is something undeniably powerful and empowering about that notion of play—and not just in our imagination. Most of us have sat around a table with friends playing some game or another and experienced the unique pleasures that come with the temporary suspension of the rules, mores, and hierarchies that govern every other moment of our lives. And all of us have had an experience in a theater that was transcendent, that launched us out of our

> The fields of organizational, cultural, and technological performance, when taken together, form an immense performance site, one that potentially encompasses the spheres of human labor and leisure activities and the behaviors of all industrially and electronically produced technologies. As extensive as these combined fields might be, the paradigms of Performance Management, Performance Studies, and Techno-Performance do not exhaust the performance research now operating in the United States. In linguistics and philosophy, the concept of "performative" has been employed to theorize utterances that constitute rather than represent social actions. In the health sciences, performance has emerged as a field studying the effects of pharmacological and physical therapies on activities such as work, sports, and everyday life. And in the realm of finance, individual stocks and bonds, mutual funds and pension investments, and even entire markets are daily, if not hourly, analyzed in terms of their short- and long-term performance. These and other paradigms deserve study in their own right.
>
> —Jon McKenzie, *Perform or Else*, 12–13

Playing with Play

threadbare chairs to somewhere . . . else, somewhere resplendent, sobering, shocking, moving. But as Mia Consalvo reminds us, there really is no such thing as a magic circle, at least not in the way Huizinga conceives it. Speaking to the forms of play specific to games, she writes, "Players never play a new game or fail to bring outside knowledge about games and gameplay into their gaming situations. . . . Structures may be necessary to begin gameplay, but we cannot stop at structures as a way of understanding the gameplay experience."[39] The magic circle is always fictive, always compromised.

So does that mean the systemic dramaturg can't be a utopian? Precisely the opposite! As Consalvo explains, the rules of play that enable the magic circle "apply, but in addition to, in competition with, other rules and in relation to multiple contexts, across varying cultures, and into different groups, legal situations, and homes."[40] And it is precisely in that space, in that tension, that the imagination finds its purpose and purchase. Play teaches us that we can always find time and space for "freedom dreams," to borrow a phrase from Robin D. G. Kelley.[41]

Those dreams can be about bodies finding new beauty in old and practiced movements, of voices finding new emotion through electronic amplification, of new visions of space and time created with scenographic tricks both tried and true and just invented and untested. Those dreams can be about social justice, about moments of possibility retrieved from the past, about moving an audience to action. Those dreams can be about beauty and fun: the thrills of a well-staged sword fight, a perfectly tuned duet, or the embrace of long-lost lovers happening onstage and on video screen simultaneously. What matters is that those dreams are, as Kelley puts it, "dreams of a new world," "poetic and prophetic" insight into the "richness of our daily lives" and the transformative power of what the surrealists call "the marvelous."[42]

A systemic dramaturgy embraces all forms of play and therefore all forms of freedom. After all, the best social critics know how to play. Mexican performance artist, telenovela star, historian, and cultural gadfly Astrid Hadad mischievously mixes and matches visual, sonic, and gestural elements from Mexican visual culture, music, street theater, cabaret, and movies. Her elaborate costumes mix and match Catholic iconography, popular political symbols, folk costumes, flea market ephemera, and the paintings of Diego Rivera and Frida Kahlo. And her voice is itself a vehicle of cultural criticism. Hadad rejects the traditional dulcet tones of the *ranchera*, favoring instead what she calls a *canto bravío* style: deeper, breathier, centered in the chest and grounded in the feet. As Roselyn Costantino sums up, in her performances, Hadad "strikes a chord in the illusive concept of *ser mexicano* or Mexicanness by, without falling into nostalgia, underscoring those sights, smells, traditions, and historical realities that . . . create a common bond within a shared geographic space." And not only that, "it is obvious she thoroughly enjoys the process."[43]

Though Hadad might not consider herself a systemic dramaturg, we do. She embodies the playful spirit of systemic dramaturgy. She is at once historian, flea market picker, stage designer, choreographer, conscious and charismatic performer, public intellectual, and savvy negotiator of her media ecology. She not only dreams dreams of a new world, to recall Kelley again, but she dances them, she sings them, she gathers them with a gesture, and sends them on their way with a triumphant laugh and a ringing stamp of her foot.

GAMING THE SYSTEM

Let's return to that medieval assumption admired by Gina Bloom that the synonymity "between games and theatrical plays was a foregone conclusion for premodern people."[44] How might we revive that commonsense connection for a systemic dramaturgy? Certainly, the need for such a revival is self-evident, particularly when we look at the ways that play, theatricality, and performance infuse our daily lives. Indeed, marketers, social media makers, and critics now speak of "gamification," a process by which the performative pleasures of play—overcoming challenges, achieving goals, having fun, striving in front of our peers, cheering together—are designed into aspects of our lives that we wouldn't typically understand or experience as playful in any fashion: advertisement, self-care, labor output, educational testing, political campaigning, industrial design, and so on.

Eric Zimmerman argues that we live in a moment when "information has been put at play," when "game-like experiences replace linear media," and when "the ways that people spend their leisure time and consume art, design, and entertainment will be games—or experiences very much like games."[45] However, as dance scholar Kiri Miller points out, this places all of us in a dangerous contradiction. We may well revel in the way these games and gamified systems spice up the banality of applying for insurance or taking a standardized test. We might cherish the possibility that a machine might allow us to ask, "Tell me something I didn't know about myself." But we may fail to ask other questions: "What might this machine know and not tell? What might it conceal from me but sell to someone else?"[46] This places a special responsibility on those who have unique insight into play and players.

Among those shouldering that responsibility is Blast Theory, an artist group that uses multiple media—most notably, performance, video, social media, videogames, and installations—to playfully explore the evolution of technology and its impact on social relations and the exercise of political power. A good example of its work is the 2001 augmented reality game *Can You See Me Now?* created in collaboration with the University of Nottingham's Mixed Reality Lab and performed in Sheffield, Rotterdam, Barcelona, Banff, Chicago, Amsterdam, Belo Horizonte, Madrid, and Tokyo. In this performance, a team of Blast Theory performers, called runners, who wear GPS receivers (which allow them to be tracked by satellite) and hand-held computers, move through an actual city space, trying to catch audience members. These, in turn, are scattered across the world, playing in a virtual re-creation of the city, communicating with each other online and listening in on the communications of the runners.

Beyond its obvious concern with satellite surveillance and the differences between mapped and lived spaces (underlined by the photographs the runners take of the sites where they caught audience members), *Can You See Me Now?* also asks more subtle questions about electronically mediated, gamified social relationships. When audience members register, they are asked to respond to a question: "Is there someone you haven't seen for a long time that you still think of?" That person's name is said by the runner when they catch the one who named them. Thus a person from the player's past is suddenly brought into the present and "forever linked to this anonymous square of the cityscape."[47] Further, as they play, the audience members become aware of the existential difference between themselves, seated comfortably in front of a personal computer, and the runners, who must contend with the challenges of the built environment with its weather, traffic, and hazards. When games, the internet, and mobile phones converge, what new possibilities arise? That question means something different when asked in terms of theater and performance.

For the systemic dramaturg, the work of Blast Theory and other performance and theater groups exploring the technologies of contemporary play suggest ways to reinvigorate the dialogue about how, where, when, and why we play and what it means to be a player. And given the rapid pace of gamification, the size of the videogame industry, the resurgence of board and roleplaying games, and the dizzying expansion of the media of social performance, that reinvigorated dialogue must necessarily concern not just the nature and purpose of play but also its entanglement with technology, to recall Salter once more. The systemic dramaturg must work to understand the technology of theater as it "reveals itself not only in the machines that descend from the heavens by their own will, but also in how—through craft, skill, construction, or making (what the Greeks call *techne*)—it orders the world."[48] The systemic dramaturg puts that knowledge into play. Ultimately, we understand play as a mode of pleasurable, imaginative, critical comprehension and creation, an inherently dramaturgical practice that explores the crux between technology and techne, between clever technical solution and emerging technical hegemony again. That understanding is not just an appropriate but a necessary response to our moment, a moment described by Zimmerman as "the ludic century," a moment when digital technologies and emergent forms of creative activity, social expression, and political hegemony are reshaping both how we imagine play and what it means to put on a play. Systemic dramaturgy affirms the power of plays, players, and playing.

INTERVIEW 3

PLAY MATTERS

ELIZABETH SWENSEN ON THE THEATRICALITY OF GAMES

Elizabeth Swensen is an assistant professor of Art & Design: Games & Playable Media at the University of California–Santa Cruz. She holds an MFA in interactive media from the University of Southern California. As a game designer, Swensen's research has focused on metacognitive development outcomes and strategy-based learning in games, taking advantage of the medium's strength in establishing learning through systems thinking and social interaction. Her artistic focus is on exploring issues of imposed identity and on the powerful role language plays in enforcing that identity. Her work has been shown at the Independent Games Festival, IndieCade Festival, and Games for Change Festival.

MIKE SELL: Why do you think play matters? And what's the difference between play and games?

ELIZABETH SWENSEN: Ah, that is strikingly broad.

SELL: Narrowing the question is almost as interesting as any answer you might give.

SWENSEN: No, it's fair, and many people in my field spend a lot of time thinking about the difference between or where play intersects with games. I tend to be less of a stickler for those distinctions. I tend to define *game* very broadly. That certainly incorporates play, where some might draw a division and say, "This is a playful behavior, but it is not a game." While I don't do a lot of study into the cultural

Interview 3: *Play Matters*

benefits of play, there is a lot of work already underway in that area. "Play is the child's work" is a famous quote. We do a lot of study on health and children and play, but there isn't a lot of study on the benefit of play in adult life, and that might be specifically cultural, and it might be different in different cultural contexts. But I think it's something that we should invest in, as a culture, because certainly as a practitioner of play and someone who invests in play personally, I can say that is a deeply enriching part of culture. Also, media literacy is an essential part of a healthy adult life as well as of the healthy learning life of a child.

So again, not being a cultural anthropologist or having any kind of claims on the sociology or psychology of play, but to speak instead in terms of understanding recreation and entertainment, I think play often gets a bad rap in that we see it as a child's pursuit, and yet the creative and proactive aspects of play I think can be really healthy. We somehow accept that adults can consume entertainment and media, but the idea of participating in the creative process if you aren't being paid for it is somehow "childish." Yet engaging that creativity, even in games we might not typically think of as being creative but which engage our ability to make choices, to invent personas, and to practice critical thinking in a safer environment, isn't childish. It's never a safe environment, because all play requires putting yourself out there in a certain way. It is a way to explore different ways of thinking, of decision making, of engaging with others socially, and of enacting different parts of your own persona. I think it's as important to adults as it is to children.

MICHAEL CHEMERS: I am thinking about the notion that the main cultural product of a theater culture is a "play." We don't think of it as a "game," although in French the word is *jeu*, which also means "game." Perhaps one of the reasons why theater is not as respected historically as other art forms is because there's a sense of this playfulness that goes along with it. It's not really serious. It's just grown-ups doing pretend.

SWENSEN: Well, I think less the medium, but more the makers. You notice there that consuming or participating in watching a play can be considered high culture. Sure, being an actor is the butt of jokes, maybe because the creation of this fantastical thing is considered the work of children, whereas watching, imbibing, reading, and thinking about something that's created by others is considered participating in the culture of art.

SELL: How do you imagine yourself helping to break down those value hierarchies?

SWENSEN: I find that I'm teaching and practicing in a time when this is easier than it's ever been. Part of this is the resurgence of digital games and the changing demographic of the players of those games. I believe that the average age of someone who identifies as a gamer or someone who plays digital games is now the late thirties. I believe that will go higher. I believe that players won't, at the age of thirty-seven, suddenly say, "Oh no, no more games for me." And I think that as digital play becomes accepted as an adult activity, the same will happen with some other forms of play. There's been a resurgence in board games over the last decade, and now college students play *Settlers of Catan*. That hasn't always been true. I think part of that has to do with digital games and the growing number of people who are now aging with them.

SELL: Is the rise of interest in board games a kind of backlash against the hegemony of digital games?

SWENSEN: I don't know that I buy it as a backlash. But I will say that physical games fulfill a need that, for a brief moment, digital games began to forget. Speaking as someone living through those times and watching design practices during those times, there was a period where we did a lot of playing in the same room in digital games, especially in early multiplayer, through LAN, just due to the limits of technology. We couldn't get speeds fast enough; we could only network so many machines at a time. Internet was terrible. Internet still is terrible, but it's much better, and when the internet got faster and technologies changed because we could connect a bunch of strangers, that's what people did. But there has always been that desire for the fun of having these competitive or cooperative experiences with people you know and people in the same room so you can have that emotional and verbal presence.

Now there is also a sort of response to perhaps several of these things in concert, a number of more independently developed videogames that are interested in the "couch competitive" or the "couch co-op," as it's called. People are saying, "Oh yeah, no, the thing that we loved about playing against each other has been lost in some of these games. We want both kinds of experiences." Those preferences rubber-band as we recognize what we love about games, so I wouldn't say that the popularity of tabletop games is a refusal of the digital or somehow a direct response to the digital. But it might be a direct response to people's awareness of the enjoyment of playing with the same people looking at their faces.

SELL: Perhaps play is becoming a dominant way of relating to one another socially?

SWENSEN: I think the moment that you say, "Play is an acceptable form of recreation for adults," you need play that's appropriate for adults. You need a variety of experiences. There is a place and a time for something chance-based, but oftentimes the expansion or the maturity of content that you might want to see includes

Interview 3: *Play Matters*

mature narrative, interesting characters, paid writers—especially in pieces that employ linear narrative. All of this comes from the understanding that if games are going to be played by adults, then maybe there should be games designed for adults. Typically, the term "adult game," at least from the 1980s and '90s, meant "pornographic."

CHEMERS: The videogame *Leisure Suit Larry*, for example.

SWENSEN: Exactly, and a number of arcade traditions. But when I say "adult games," I mean games that are designed for an adult mind.

SELL: Do we still define an adult game in terms of its content, themes, characters, subject matter?

SWENSEN: I don't think there are any hard lines there. Games have had ratings that tried to suggest age appropriateness for a long time, but I think that's a separate discussion. I don't think that there is a specific set of qualities that I could put together to say, "This makes a game for adults," but I can say broadly that when I observe someone trying to speak to adults, they're speaking to adult experience and using narrative and character to relate to experiences that adults have. Sometimes it's around complexity of motivation, or narrative style, or subtlety. Sometimes it's around complexity of interaction, strategy, and engagement with critical thought, with the content itself. And that doesn't mean that a young person couldn't play these games. They often do.

SELL: That doesn't feel like it's a boundary line between children and adults, but more about the capacity of the individual player and the community in which they're playing.

SWENSEN: At least in the same way that a novel or a play can be enjoyed within certain contexts by both adults and young people. But certainly, if I'm designing a game for someone who's five years old, I'm going to have some thoughts about what might be accessible, what other game literacy they may have. And I'm going to be testing with that audience exclusively, if that's my target. That's not to say that it might not become a breakout hit among a different audience or it might not be enjoyed by an older audience. As a child, I loved reading books that I was maybe not the right age to be reading. I would read adult books as a child, and they were not catering to me, they were not thinking of me, but that doesn't mean I can't enjoy them and appreciate them. I'm just going to enjoy them a little differently until I come back and read that same novel when I'm older.

CHEMERS: I think this is true of most cultural products. I think about those *Looney Tunes* cartoons that we used to watch when we were kids and then we outgrew them. But now if you watch them again in your forties, you see all this stuff in there that you never saw before. But in terms of the explosion in popularity of games in the past twenty years, there was a transformation, right? What was "geek culture" in the 1970s and '80s is now just "pop culture." It used to be that comic book superheroes represented a niche market, Tolkien-style fantasy was a niche market, *Dungeons & Dragons* was a niche market. But this is all very mainstream right now. *Black Panther* is up for seven Oscars [and would go on to win three]. It's not just a comic book story—it's about race and politics and dealing with global realities.

SELL: And it is a comic book story with explosions and punches and all the good stuff, right?

CHEMERS: The geeks who designed the cell phone also designed the content on the cell phone, and that's what everybody who bought a cell phone was exposed to. Everybody became a geek. But maybe it's also because people like Mike and me, who in the 1970s and '80s were kids who now have the purchasing power of middle-age white men in our society, we want to buy stuff that we thought was cool in our childhood, which has matured along with us. So that culture expands. I think there are a lot of factors at play here.

SWENSEN: There are a lot of factors. But to go back to the *Looney Tunes* analogy, it's not to say that any particular content is just for one age group. But for a while, games were thought of as all *Looney Tunes*—childish and silly—and now people are trying to make something that isn't *Looney Tunes* and everything in between. They're making *The Handmaid's Tale* and *Game of Thrones* or a quiet detective story. So while anyone can enjoy *Looney Tunes*, and anyone can enjoy *The Handmaid's Tale* with a little bit of supervision, the notion is that there is a broad series of experiences and interest that people might invest in by playing.

CHEMERS: Why do you feel the need to say that there needs to be a broad inclusivity about what games are? Are you responding to a resistance against that?

SWENSEN: I think I'm responding to a critical conversation that was going on while I was still in graduate school that worked hard to define what a game was. I would direct you to that scholarly conversation rather than put my flag into it, other than to say that while I think that there is a good argument toward creating structure and definition, oftentimes those same tools are used to push people out of the game-making community, and that was never the intent, or at least I would hope not, of people interested in that conversation. It's still a crunchy, fun conversation for someone who loves systems. I love talking about what falls into which different systems and categories, but when it comes to a maker community, I'm loose with that particular kind of language. For me, a game is partially an

Interview 3: *Play Matters*

invitation to play. I typically would say that there are some rules or constraints that help guide that play. But beyond that, I don't put much definition.

While I'm someone who loves designing systems, I would say that that same kind of conversation about the pleasure of games doesn't apply to something like *That Dragon Cancer.* What is the strategy of *That Dragon Cancer?* How do you win *That Dragon Cancer?* I can tell you, you do not. But I would still call it a game and consider it part of games culture. So while I think of games in play sometimes from a simulationist or systems-based approach, I also acknowledge that there are a lot of narrativist pieces that are interactive, that ask for your participation, and that play with this idea of agency and storytelling. I would also call those games. Not everyone would.

SELL: I understand the stakes of your desire to have *That Dragon Cancer* and other games like it categorized as games. But the characteristics that you just laid out could apply to many different kinds of texts that wouldn't by any stretch of the imagination be considered games. You've also described what it means to put on a play in the theatrical sense.

CHEMERS: When electricity-powered media started to find its way into live performance more than a century ago, a conversation began about what liveness is, and what presence is, and the impact of mechanical reproduction on the authenticity of art, what's a play versus what's a film, and so on. Some critics argued, and some still do, that the most important part of a theater piece is that the audience participates fairly directly in the creation of meaning, as opposed to a film where the creation of meaning is already done and you just let it wash over you. I'm wondering if you think this idea of presence, actual or virtual, is what links our notion of theater to your notion of games.

SWENSEN: I think so. I look at the agency of a piece or at least try to be conscious of agency or the lack of agency. Some of my favorite games remove agency in very strategic ways. The difference to me between, let's say, a recipe and a game is around the authorial intent of the experience. A game designer has an idea to generate a set of emotional content that, one could argue, a recipe book writer does as well. The recipe book writer may be aware of the emotional intent of the work. But a game designer has in mind a series of emotions they want you to feel. They're building a structure for those emotions, and then deciding how much reach they give you within that emotional structure. Some games benefit from giving you many choices within certain frameworks and within a responsive system. But some of those designers restrict that sort of communication between the designer and the player.

CHEMERS: This is also true of theater. The playwrights have the same authorial intent toward creating emotional experiences around which they build a structure, and that structure can be more or less elastic and more or less interactive with the audience.

SWENSEN: But the difference between writing a play and putting on a play might reveal some differences. Some might argue that reading a mystery novel is not too different from a game, in that it is a communication between the reader actively trying to guess "who done it" and an author who's trying to lead and sort of piece together information.

SELL: You seem to be avoiding the ontological question of what is and is not a game in favor of the expectations, mindsets, conventions, and histories that come into play when we sit down to play.

SWENSEN: Some designers and some games play with the magic circle or the idea of a magic circle in order to problematize it or expose how much it exists or doesn't exist. I use it, certainly, within my classes to talk about some of the behaviors that we engage in. We certainly separate from ourselves and our real lives when we play. For instance, we're willing to lie when we play games that involve bluffing, or we're willing to make someone else lose and do things that within the context of the game hurt their feelings, but they have a level of acceptability because we have agreed to the set of rules and we've agreed to a number of metaunderstandings. We say, "Okay, it doesn't explicitly say I can't punch you in the face when we're playing *Diplomacy*, but we understand at this table we're not going to do that." And yet people have real emotional reactions to games within that magic circle that bleed outside of it. And I think many scholars now will talk about the magic circle and how permeable it is, but in terms of how it is a conceit that we sometimes use to frame when we are playing and when we are not.

SELL: It feels like a useful conceit.

SWENSEN: Absolutely. I don't believe it doesn't exist, but it certainly isn't a solid wall. We move as through a permeable membrane, in and out of it, and should acknowledge, as many others have done, that there are people at the table, and people are affected by what we do, even if we have an understanding that it's acceptable to violate certain social norms in the context of games.

CHEMERS: Could you talk a little bit about the relationship between game content and operational dynamics, the mechanics of the game? I was thinking back to the question of the adultness of a game. One of the ironic things about an adult game like, say, *Arkham Asylum* is that it is so complicated that I literally don't have time to play it because I'm an adult and I have a job. Whereas I love to play

Interview 3: *Play Matters*

Qwirkle, which is a game only about one step up in complexity over *Candy Land*, and you couldn't force me to play *Candy Land* if you put a gun to my head.

SWENSEN: It's very depressing.

SELL: *Candy Land* taught me to cheat.

SWENSEN: *Candy Land* taught me to cheat as a child. But as an adult, the game taught me about determinism. You shuffle the deck at the start of the game, and the game is done. The game is decided. You're just going to play out what has been prewritten. Many games play with agency in a really fun way. *Candy Land* for me does not play with agency in a fun way.

CHEMERS: All right. None of us is ever going to play *Candy Land* again. But *Qwirkle* . . .

SELL: Well, but we might play *Candy Land* because the act of gameplay sometimes includes making a commitment less to the game than to the people we are playing with. I have played with any number of young people who are totally into *Candy Land*.

SWENSEN: The stakes are high when you're young.

CHEMERS: Absolutely right. But my point is that *Qwirkle* is a game whose mechanics are nearly as basic as *Candy Land*, and I will play that all night long with the right people.

SWENSEN: To speak to your point, one of my many loves about the sort of explosion of indie game content, especially in the digital realm, is that design constraint leads to some magical experiences that are four hours or less. When I think about playing as an adult, I do think about time. There are some sixty-hour console games out there. They're complex, they're narratively rich, and you have time for them before you are in high school in a way that is much more difficult in adulthood. Now I'm looking for the next perfect two-hour game. And luckily, there are a lot of them out there.

Part of the reason for this is the small teams and small budgets of indie developers, but part of it is also thinking about games in a world of other forms of entertainment. We go to a play, we go to a movie, we expect to spend two to three hours there. I think that sometimes adult games are not more complex. Instead, what makes them adult is that they're thinking about adult lives. They're either easy to pick up and play on a phone or they're contained. You're going to start and you're going to finish, and it's going to be lovely.

SELL: Throughout your responses, I hear an implicit understanding of where play is happening. Can you speak to that location in more specific terms?

SWENSEN: Within the MDA [mechanics-dynamics-aesthetics] framework, which we use often at Santa Cruz, that falls under mechanics, which is not the way we use mechanics colloquially. Oftentimes when we talk about mechanics, we talk about more formal rules or structures, but within the MDA framework, mechanics includes everything you need to play, which includes space and also includes some thought of who is playing and what are their interests and capacities. Not everyone wants to or can play tag as it's traditionally played. This is something that students struggle with. When I ask, "What are the mechanics of hide-and-seek?" they say, "Well, one person counts and they have to close their eyes for a predetermined number of seconds, and everyone else finds a hiding place and waits to be tagged, depending on the variant . . ." But no one talks about where hide-and-seek must be played, which is a place with a lot of really interesting hiding places. You can't play hide and seek in an open field.

When we think about physical space in terms of physical practice, there are a number of designers who work specifically in installation spaces, as with escape rooms. How can you prepare someone to set the table, as it were, for what they need to play? Being a designer for a roleplaying game, you not only are teaching someone the pieces, the steps, the rules, and systems of how to play, but you're creating a guidebook for someone else to create an atmosphere of play within the desired aesthetic tone. I'm talking about emotional tone in that respect, as well as maybe some actual physical staging as you might think of in theater games that are played in the dark and games that are played with candles. Thinking as a designer in guiding someone else to stage a narrative, improvisational experience, I imagine there's some connection to playwriting, insofar as the playwright knows that there are going to be more productions of the play after the first one.

CHEMERS: You're right. The assumption is that the playwright is not present.

Mechanics-Dynamics-Aesthetics (MDA) Framework

Mechanics describes the particular components of the game, at the level of data representation and algorithms. Dynamics describes the run-time behavior of the mechanics acting on player inputs and each other's outputs over time. Aesthetics describes the desirable emotional responses evoked in the player, when she interacts with the game system. Aesthetics are further delineated in terms of eight subcategories: sensation, fantasy, narrative, challenge, fellowship, discovery, expression, and submission.

—Robin Hunicke, Marc LeBlanc, and Robert Zubek, "MDA: A Formal Approach to Game Design and Game Research"

Interview 3: *Play Matters*

SWENSEN: Yes. Similarly, in a tabletop roleplaying game, you're guiding a production that involves quite a bit of performance as well as rules learning, and the game document has to tell them how to do that. And I think there's an assumption by a playwright that the people who are going to take that document have that training to put on a play.

CHEMERS: Yes, plays are written in a code that can be adequately interpreted only by people who know how to read the code. What Mike and I are exploring is exactly what that code is.

SWENSEN: There are some designers that are writing for people who've played *Dungeons & Dragons* and they're going to use the shorthand. But more modern tabletop RPG [roleplaying game] designers are trying to create a document that can guide the uninitiated, so that someone who has heard of tabletop RPGs but has never played one could take this document and have everything they need to lead this experience. And sometimes it's beyond narrative techniques or tools or ways of thinking. Sometimes it goes even further into outside readings, recommended music selections—they're really thinking about how to help someone who's maybe never staged anything within this context and guiding them through that work. And so that work is done over and over and over again, in all these books and guides, because there isn't an assumption that someone has the library.

CHEMERS: What's interesting about that is the intersection with what scholars in our field call *performativity*. Gary Gygax, creator of *Dungeons & Dragons*, called his game "the theater of the mind." But in the original *Dungeons & Dragons* edition, there were no instructions for creating the proper atmosphere for a compelling improvisational experience.

SWENSEN: Well, the mechanics of *Dungeons & Dragons* are not geared toward that aspect of play. But most people who play *Dungeons & Dragons* adore that aspect and don't mind the fact that the system doesn't support it. A more charitable way to think about it is that the system says, "Let us handle this part, the part that you might fight over, or where we can provide a sense of fairness, but then we'll step back and say, let humans do the human thing.'" I think that there are systems that better serve some of this generative social interaction, but I like to think that the continued popularity of *D&D* is the understanding that the system trusts you with the story.

SELL: That's an intriguing point. As a person interested in digital games, I think that probably the most important technological advancement in digital games has nothing to do with processor power. It has everything to do with the emergence

Interview 3: *Play Matters*

of vast narratives, multiplatform play, and a collaborative fan community. When we look back at the first iterations of *D&D*, it's evident that Gygax and his designers assumed a deep knowledge of fantasy literature, mythology, and comics. They were familiar with the tradition of dysfunctional superhero teams, and they assumed the players were attracted to the game because they also had that knowledge, so it never had to be made explicit. Everyone understood exactly what was implied when you were playing a dwarven warrior versus a human wizard. I think this was an early form of what Henry Jenkins calls "convergence culture."

SWENSEN: I was hoping you were going to say Jenkins. There's a strong corporate interest in transplatform work and how these stories that people fall in love with can be a part of different aspects of their life in different contexts, both social and personal.

SELL: Creating different product lines.

SWENSEN: Oh gosh, different product lines, different forms of interaction. You know, you can do the *Guardians of the Galaxy* off-brand escape rooms. There are certainly RPGs that are interested in that kind of dynamic. There are digital games in addition to social media and I don't know what else. That's very interesting from a product perspective. But I think it's also inherently interesting to the audience that if they embed themselves in a particular fiction that they love, they'll have different opportunities to express that fandom.

SELL: And to understand the mechanics, procedures, and importance of games. When we are playing *Super Mario Bros.*, that's a very different experience than *Braid*, despite the fact that they're more or less exactly the same game. But there's a different fiction surrounding those actions.

SWENSEN: Yes. A *Mario* jump is not a *Braid* jump, and a *Braid* jump is not a *Last of Us* jump. These things are using the same verb, and we think about it in terms of movement through space. But the feel embedded in the calculations of how far, how responsive, and to what sort of consequence these actions are made is precise and would constitute a very different kind of mechanics.

SELL: That sounds like what, from a dramaturgical perspective, we would consider the "staging" of an action or word or emotional turn.

SWENSEN: Well, it depends on how you're using the word *staging*. This gets crunchy, but the difference between the velocity, the height, and the physics of the other objects in that system—these are different jumps, and people will live and die by the perfection of a *Mario* jump. To give an example, *The Last of Us* is a game that mostly uses verbs that other games use and is differentiated largely, critically, by its narrative content, which would fit into what you were talking about just now about staging. You occasionally jump over things, you occasionally jump to get to a higher platform, but my visual input and audio input around *jump* with the character—Joel, for example, is a tired old man—tell me a lot about the game. The game is limiting my ability to jump, so I cannot jump over buildings in the way that I can in other games. I do not stick on buildings like Mega Man. The mechanics around that jump tell me not only something about the story but also something about my relationship with the physical reality, or the metaphor of physical reality.

The Last of Us does not look like real life. It has a flavor that suggests that realism, but everything in that game is telling me something about my relationship to the other mechanics, as well as to the story. This is conveyed not only by the animation, the height, and the sound telling me narratively that Joel is a grizzled guy who is good at combat, but he's not eighteen anymore. So the difference between a *Braid* jump and a *Mario* jump might be a little thinner, but even within that language, a game designer is thinking about the kind of jump we want, and it might take months to get it right.

SELL: Does that mean we should get away from this broad notion of the staging of a mechanic and think instead about the granular details of how something is staged?

SWENSEN: Exactly. If in the script the playwright says, "This character wears a dress," I have a lot of questions. As an actor, that's not enough information for me. The same with a jump.

CHEMERS: When we talk about the scenography of a piece of live theater, we talk about the full range of semiotic signals: what kind of dress, how long it is, what color it is, how heavy it is, and how that interacts with the much broader semiotic matrix of the performance, including the lighting, set design, and so on. It's interesting to think about the history of these things, these verbs. In *Donkey Kong*, you play a plumber named Mario, and the fact that he is a plumber is totally incidental and makes zero difference to anything. You have to climb a broken tower to rescue a princess from a giant ape. And in order to do this, you have to jump. In all the *Mario* games since then, I've never seen one where you didn't jump. Even the *Mario Kart* games, right?

SWENSEN: Got a little hop.

CHEMERS: Yeah. Why? Why would you jump? Go-karts don't jump. But perhaps it's impossible to be in a *Mario* world in which you cannot jump.

SWENSEN: Sure. Part of Mario's identity is around the verb of jumping.

CHEMERS: The verb of jumping. He's a jumper.

Interview 3: *Play Matters*

SWENSEN: And is that Mario if he doesn't jump? Marios jump.

SELL: For me, the classic example of this historical persistence is less *Mario* than *Zelda*. One of the great pleasures for me as a player of *Zelda* games is the moment when I recognize a verb that I have played many times before, but in different technological and narrative contexts. And I think, that's the verb! That's the thing I shoot across a space to grab something. Oh, this is this game's version of the monster that shoots the rocks at me.

SWENSEN: This is where we talk about game *feel*: the small calculations you make with, for instance, gravity, time, distance. All of this is guided by authorial intent to create emotional response. I think you'll find that even though the difference in platform on the *Zelda* game is vast in terms of sort of the literal animation or button response, those blocks will likely *feel* very similar from an experiential perspective. That sort of continuity across brand, or across character, or across narrative is important to a lot of folks. Not that it can't be broken.

SELL: There's a kind of haptic nostalgia?

SWENSEN: But consciously maintained. There are so many different ways to make a jump feel, you could absolutely innovate there. And there are changes like the gravity systems in *Mario Galaxy* that affect that, but Mario's jump will always be bouncy and fun and energetic.

CHEMERS: And with the same "Boing."

SWENSEN: That's part of its identity.

CHEMERS: All the way back to *Donkey Kong*. "WUH wuh WUH wuh WUH wuh WUH wuh BOING."

THE EMPATHY MACHINE

Titan! to thee the strife was given
   Between the suffering and the will,
   Which torture where they cannot kill;
And the inexorable Heaven,
And the deaf tyranny of Fate,
The ruling principle of Hate,
Which for its pleasure doth create
The things it may annihilate,
Refus'd thee even the boon to die.
          —Lord Byron, *Prometheus* (1813)

THE ANTIDOTE TO BARBARISM

One of the most important concepts in the long, broad, and deep conversation about dramaturgy is *empathy*. In ancient Greece, Aristotle spoke of tragedy's mimetic, instructive power to elicit *eleos* (pity). In classical India, Bharatamuni wrote that the god Brahma created dramatic performance to provide

> right for the people going wrong; enjoyment for those who are pleasure-seekers; restraint of the ill-behaved or tolerance of the well-behaved; putting courage into cowards or the exploits of the brave; knowledge for the un-knowing or the wisdom of the wise; enjoyments of the rich or fortitude of the grief-stricken; money for those who want to make a living and stability to disturbed minds. . . . It gives you peace, entertainment and happiness, as well

as beneficial advice based on the actions of high, low, and middle people. It brings rest and peace to persons afflicted by sorrow or fatigue or grief or helplessness. There is no art, no knowledge, no yoga, no action that is not found in *natya*.[1]

No small promise. In Rome, Horace wrote that poetry was the medium for teaching proper thought and action, an antidote to barbarism. In the fourth century, Donatus wrote that theater "teaches us what is harmonious in life and, on the contrary, what is to be avoided." In the seventh century, Isidore of Seville, one of the early fathers of the Christian church, wrote that pagan theater could be a tool for teaching Christian wisdom and love, and the tenth-century literary giant Hrosvitha of Gandersheim put those ideas into action in her plays. In similar fashion, in the fourteenth century, Zeami reconciled performing arts with Buddhism as a means of teaching the Noble Truths and the Eightfold Path. Lodovico Castelvetro in the 1500s tried to harness theater's empathic power in the cause of humanism by making it follow strict rules. In the 1700s, Pierre Beaumarchais was deeply concerned with the power of theater to teach moral lessons, and G. E. Lessing devoted all his considerable brainpower to this notion, arguing that "the most compassionate person is the best person" before going on to demonstrate theater's facility for increasing empathy in the viewer (and thus establishing the basis for modern dramaturgy).

Following suit, Enlightenment dramaturgs thereby extolled theater's power as a weapon against tyranny and injustice. In the ensuing centuries, Karl Marx, Henrik Ibsen, George Bernard Shaw, Susan Glaspell, Bertolt Brecht, Hallie Flanagan, Seiko Sano, Jacob Moreno, Arthur Miller, Caryl Churchill, Amiri Baraka, Wole Soyinka, Luis Valdez, and August Wilson, among many, many others, wrote forcefully about the power and the responsibility of theater makers to make society more compassionate, and therefore a more harmonious and politically stable place to live.[2] For modern dramaturgs, despite their diverse goals and challenges, considerations of empathy and theater's power to elicit it remain at the forefront.

But dramaturgs interested in becoming part of, say, digital game development or game developers interested in broadening and deepening the emotional impact of their art cannot ignore a simple fact: as dramatic, action-based art forms go, games are far more popular than theater. U.S. professional theater netted about $3 billion in 2017–18, while the U.S. game market brought in $36 billion, and the market is growing about 20 percent every year. Setting aside Edwin Zeydel's admonition about dramaturgs rashly interfering with theater's goal of making money, we conclude that digital games have a much broader audience than theater—and a look into the recent history of videogames demonstrates that a good segment of this audience is quite as fanatic and dedicated as die-hard playgoers. However, digital gaming culture, both its makers and audiences, has demonstrated a serious empathy problem.

In the previous chapter, we demonstrated that games, digital and otherwise, share many salient dramaturgical qualities with theater, and that the analytical, creative, and collaborative skills that dramaturgs develop have tremendous potential for the enrichment of content in games and other playable media. In this chapter, we situate the recent history of digital game culture into dialogue with the centuries-long effort to understand the powers and responsibilities of artists. Here we ask how a systemic approach to play can transform the empathic structures of games and game culture, particularly as concerns a recent crisis in that culture known as Gamergate.

THE DRAMATURGY OF EMPATHY

What do dramaturgs mean when they talk about *eleos*, *Mitleid*, decorum, *itihasa*, love, or any of the other terms in the constellation of ideas that refer to the phenomenon of human compassion? For our purpose, we define *empathy* as a value-neutral term referring to *an individual's capacity to consider matters from a point of view not their own*. We know that dramaturgs from diverse historical periods across time and diverse places across the planet agree on several key points about empathy and its relationship to performance and to individual and social moral development. Reviewing this global discourse of dramaturgical empathy as a whole, we can come up with a sort of manifesto about those relationships that seem especially and enduringly pertinent to the work of systemic dramaturgy:

o   Dramaturgs believe that in order for a performance to be moving and relevant to a viewer, the viewer must *identify* in some way

The Empathy Machine

with the characters of the performance as they undergo their actions.

o Dramaturgs believe that because of its immense facility for establishing such personal identification, performance is a highly effective tool for the deepening of empathy in its audiences.

o Dramaturgs believe that this deepening leads to prosocial sentiments from which prosocial politics will naturally follow, resulting in general amelioration of social ills.

These principles are useful when considering what dramaturgy has meant, means, and might mean in the future, particularly when we approach it in systematic fashion.

But *empathy* remains a rather slippery term, even if dramaturgs generally agree on its significance to the form. Psychologists, social scientists, ethicists, philosophers, and artists have tackled this topic from multiple perspectives and from many disciplines, and unsurprisingly, there are many sophisticated ways of discussing the phenomenon. In the social sciences, empathy is usually broken down into two categories: *cognitive* (when a person specifically attempts to see matters from another point of view, as they might while studying a foreign culture) and *emotional* (when the experience of someone else's distress elicits an emotional response in the viewer, either by experiencing the other's distress as if it were the viewer's own [*parallel empathy*] or feeling pity for the distressed person [*reactive empathy*]). Aristotle's *eleos* seems to be describing *reactive* empathy, while Lessing's *Mitleid* appears to be referring to *parallel* empathy, and Horace's *decorum* is likely akin to *cognitive* empathy.

> *Cognitive empathy*: The intentional consideration of a subject from another being's point of view.
>
> *Emotional empathy*: The feelings caused by witnessing another being's experience.
>
> *Parallel empathy*: Feelings that align with another's as a result of identification.
>
> *Reactive empathy*: Feelings caused by witnessing the experience of another without a sense of identification (for example, pity or disdain).

Social science researchers generally agree that empathy is strongly correlated with certain widely valued human behaviors. People who are highly empathic tend to evince concern about other people's feelings, respect for their experiences, and motivation to ameliorate the suffering of others, especially those in stigmatized groups. They also tend to exhibit aptitude for conflict resolution. In contrast, low levels of empathy tend to correlate with a lack of conflict resolution skills, hostility toward stigmatized groups, and negative behaviors like child abuse, sexual aggression, and alcohol-related aggression. However, research has found that bullies, demagogues, and other ill-intentioned manipulators may also exhibit highly empathic qualities, which ironically enables them to predict their victims' emotional responses, and thus ensure the negative effects of their behavior have even more impact.[3] This should alert us to the fact that empathy is not an intrinsically moral or ethical experience, but rather the foundation for moral and ethical experience. We are reminded of Nazi-era theater, film, radio, and other performance spectacles that employed "Reich dramaturgy." These were highly effective at generating empathy for individuals understood to be members of the community and just as effective at denying empathy for those who were not.

And we should note that empathy is not always desired. As micha cárdenas explores in our interview with her, for some marginalized groups, the facility of performance to generate empathy for stigmatized outgroups (say, generating empathy for queer people from straight audiences) is not a desirable goal. For creators like cárdenas, empathic game design is not about appealing to the oppressor, but rather about generating solidarity and community with those who have been excluded and oppressed, for sharing important information among members of the outgroups, for creating social sites where safety and healing can occur. This is why we insist that empathy be considered as a value-neutral concept. A heightened capacity to identify with others or respond to suffering does not necessarily result in an increase in ethical moral behavior. And the structures of empathy can be deployed for multiple purposes.

Furthermore, different kinds of empathy have been shown to have different levels of effectiveness in eliciting ethical behavior. Cognitive empathy has been observed, for instance, to have little impact on changing the behaviors or attitudes of people with deeply held prejudices toward certain groups. This is likely because prejudiced people would have to consciously set aside their prejudices in order to learn the perspectives and struggles of the groups they hate, which they tend to be disinclined to do, since prejudice obviates the need to do that kind of inquiry in the first place. In practical terms, programs that teach schoolchildren that racism is bad have proven ineffective in the long-term reduction of stereotyping or marginalizing behavior.[4]

Emotional empathy, in contrast, whether parallel or reactive, relies on a visceral, almost subconscious response and a simpler, more fundamental dynamic within the psyche. It does not require the self-conscious suspension of a deeply entrenched set of beliefs; rather, it bypasses this kind of socially generated, consciously held ideology and strikes at the core of a shared, embodied human experience. An emotionally empathic experience is one in which the viewer experiences a profound emotional reaction to pain that is not their own. And this appears to provide a sense of deep connection to the subject that feels far more personal and important than the intellectual exercise of cognitive empathy ever can.[5]

With these considerations in mind, we would like to consider how dramaturgs in the digital age might design into their and their teams' projects structures of empathy that promote a positive collective experience, even when the project in question engages with subject matter that is controversial or elicits strong ideological responses from the audience. From our point of view, a deep and systems-oriented dive into dramaturgical theories of empathy can help us better understand these dynamic, difficult factors and the many situations in which they play. Fundamental to our approach is the question of performance. Dramaturgy, both dramaturgy in general and systemic dramaturgy in particular, takes a critical departure from social science precisely around *performance*, the real-time, real-space social rituals governed by written and unwritten rules. But we depart from conventional dramaturgical understandings of empathy by distinguishing between affect and structure. When a dramaturg discusses empathy, they may have a particular feeling and social good in mind, but ultimately, they are identifying and creating a *structure* (for example, a particular combination of words, movement, lighting, and music) and an *affect* (a particular emotion intended to be produced by the structure), which are distinct analytically but inseparable one from another in practice.

Taking the parts of this system individually, we understand the *structure* of empathy as the thing social scientists tend to be more interested in—for example, the neurological capacity to read a person's face, body, voice, verbiage, and other sources of emotional information to glean

The Empathy Machine

their mental and emotional condition. However, as dramaturgs, we emphasize the performativity of these processes. As we know, the production and reception of this emotional information are difficult to control. We're all familiar with those moments when we laugh when we should be serious or when someone takes our remarks the wrong way. The information can be evidently contradictory, too, as the minds that generate and receive this information are often divided against themselves. Much of a theater artist's training focuses on how to manage this complexity. Actors spend an inordinate amount of time refining their ability to take advantage of the structural character of empathy in widely differing performance contexts. It can take a lifetime to master that skill, and many actors never do. The same can be said of directors and designers. The complexity of human feeling is one reason the structured, repeatable, polymorphous mimetic art of theater is so useful to help humans be better at understanding what's going on inside the minds and hearts of others. And if we are to believe the researchers and trust the playwrights and actors and directors and crews that create theater, it all comes down to one thing: the character and intensity of our identification with the characters who strut the stage in front of us.

But it is not enough to talk about the *structure* of the empathy-building experience, which is where the second element, *affect*, comes into play. For our purposes, we can define *affect* as the *dramaturgical intent of a performance to activate the devised empathic structure*. According to Aristotle, Greek theater culture was singularly and explicitly focused on the construction of effective empathic structure, which he felt was best expressed by tragic dramas performed at certain times of the year in huge auditoriums with extravagant costumes, unworldly masks, and actors booming out their innermost feelings to an audience composed of select members of Greek society sharing a specific set of common experiences and values.

By comparison, Susan Glaspell felt that the travails of a married woman in 1916 rural America were best expressed in a far more intimate theater, where the audience could see the subtle movements of the actors' faces and hear the nuances of their voices, to be close enough to witness the subtle visual and sonic signs of the struggle to *not* express some inner truth out of fear of, or for, the other person in the room. In the case of the premier production of her play *Trifles*, which was staged at the intimate, drafty Wharf Theatre in Provincetown, Massachusetts, Glaspell and her team could count on the fact that the audience was close enough to see the tiny expressions on the actors' faces. (Glaspell played the role of Mrs. Hale in that first production.) These expressions were an effective way to activate the empathic structures of the script. However, let us be cautious in this territory. Scholars and theater artists alike have tended to make broad generalizations about techniques. But the intimate realism presumed by the script of *Trifles* works quite differently from the intimate realism of *Miss Julie* or *Hedda Gabler*. And all three scripts will have their empathic structures modified by the empathic structures of the specific production.

We must avoid what Mike Sell has called the "technical fallacy": the tendency to conflate the effects of a particular technique or technology in a given place or time with the technique or technology itself.[6] Theater history, particularly recent theater history, is strewn with examples of artists finding their work appropriated for purposes entirely unlike their own, most infamously when the left-wing director Erwin Piscator was approached by the Nazis to run the propaganda theaters in Germany. The relative autonomy of empathic structure and empathic affect, the situational nature of their conjuncture, and the varied ways in which audience members might receive and process all this information—all of this should be kept in mind when we attempt to adjudicate the particular character of a particular performance text or performance of that text.

Imagine, for instance, a situation in which a racist finds himself in the audience of a very good production of *Othello*. The producers of the play have chosen not to underline the explicit and implicit racism of the text. It merely displays it as a given circumstance and a dramatic obstacle that Othello must navigate, no different than, say, the machinations designed against Hamlet by Claudius. There is therefore no intentional challenge to the beliefs of this racist audience member, and thus no need for him to put up any emotional or logical barriers to protect his beliefs. However, the producers of the play do aim to make the experiences of the characters believable, Iago's malignity properly motiveless, Othello's suffering properly tragic. As the play proceeds in front of the racist's eyes in real time and in the presence of live performers and a community of viewers who communicate in small and larger ways their growing identification with the protagonist, the racist begins to identify more and more with Othello's own struggles and insecurities. Othello experiences betrayal that reminds the racist of betrayals he has experienced. Othello's complex relationships remind the racist of his own. Once the process of identification with the character is complete, the racist has come to accept Othello's humanity because it reminds him of his own. He is invited to see the world from Othello's perspective, and he does because he believes it mirrors his own.

Before the play is over, the hypothetical racist has no choice but to understand the racism in which Othello lives as irrational, because it denies the humanity of this obviously human person and, by association, the racist's own felt humanity. The racist now harbors the notion, however dimly, that racism itself is a threat to his own sense of dignity and right to live. An empathic connection has been elicited, and if it is reinforced and repeated by other experiences, this empathy may over time (or perhaps quite rapidly) erode the viewer's racism from within. Yes, this is a helplessly optimistic hypothetical situation, but many of us can recall moments in our own artistic lives when we either witnessed or experienced something like this.

As naive as it may be, it is the tale favored by most dramaturgs of empathy. It is not the tale we tell here, at least not the whole tale. After all, dramaturgs have chipped away for millennia to explain how empathy might make the world a better place, starting first in the theater and then extending to other performative storytelling media such as radio, film, television, comic books, and videogames. Since Lessing, the mainstream of dramaturgy has been unwaveringly devoted to these lofty social aspirations—never mind the fact that it has served the crassest commercial interests or the most brutal political movements. But because it has proven so useful to interests that would seem opposed to the betterment of society, and because that sense of emotional movement is desired so strongly by audiences around the world, the dramaturgy of empathy cannot be avoided—and why would we? While plenty of market space remains for theatrical experiences—whether in actual theaters or on screens or on handheld computational devices—that are merely diverting, there is still a widespread desire for something *meaningful*, something that expands the human capacity for belonging and becoming, something that challenges the mind and moves the heart. That's what we want too.

The Empathy Machine

But we maintain that challenging the mind and moving the heart is not an essentially moral goal or act. Again, we assert that empathy is a technological function, a conjunction of structure and affect that can be tuned to whatever purposes its user might desire. Indeed, to characterize a theatrical experience as "merely diverting" is not to say that it fails to promote empathy. That is categorically impossible. The evaluation of a theatrical experience as "merely diverting" should be understood as saying it promotes an experience of empathy that we find uninteresting, insignificant, or familiar. We understand performative empathy as a heuristic system that invites both identification and social bonding to a greater or lesser degree and to whatever ends, intentional or otherwise, desired by those who deploy it.

Finally, we assert that the history of theatrical theory and practice affords creators and critics in other media useful ways to think about how they design the interface of structure, affect, and audience. Consider, for example, videogames. Like other forms of performative art, videogames are dramatic, occur in real time and virtual space, involve communities of shared experience, and require at least some level, however rudimentary, of identification between the user and the action of the game. This is true of even the most abstract games, but is especially evident in games that aim to challenge and move their players. And as the recent history of videogames and the culture of those who play them demonstrates, the need for a systemic understanding of how performance produces and strengthens identification and social bonds has never been more necessary.

GAMERGATE

The perfect case to illustrate this dynamic can be found in the recent history of videogames, videogame players, and videogame culture. While we have a general interest in how a systemic approach to dramaturgy can help videogame designers be more conscious of empathic structures and the ends toward making the world a better place, we are also interested in moments when just the opposite happened—when videogame players designed structures of empathy to foment a culture of intolerance, hatred, and violence against those who were designing structures of empathy to promote a more diverse, humane, and creative community.

Though the story of this clash of empathic structures is almost as old as the videogame itself, we'll begin in February 2013, when a small team led by game developer Zoë Quinn released a single-player, interactive fiction game called *Depression Quest*. At the time, the game was unusual in terms of the story it tells and how it plays. It puts the player into the position of a protagonist dealing with severe depression. Over the course of play, we encounter various situations in their everyday life that are affected by their illness. The player makes choices—for example, whether to continue taking an antidepressant medication or whether to stay home from work rather than go to the office—that alter the game's plotline in terms of the protagonist's mental health, their social well-being, and their employment status.

However, the game is quite frank and clever about the limits of the player-character's agency. To begin with, the game's design is simple in terms of what we do as players. Most of what we do as we play is read and click on hyperlinks—evidence of Quinn's desire to make the game as accessible as possible. But sometimes even that small amount of agency, of player and player-character choice, is strategically limited. The player often discovers that links that describe choices are disabled. For example, our mother comes to visit us and asks, "So what's going on with you lately?" The text tells us that we want to share with her what's going on, that we're trying hard to be positive, but we fear she won't understand. We are provided with four choices, but two of them, the ones that would allow us to share with our mother what is happening and how we are feeling, are disabled. The choice is there, we can see it, we can ponder it, but it is not a choice we can actually make (fig. 3.1).

Depression Quest is a perfect example of how game designers can use the empathic affordances of digital game design for a greater good. Indeed, Quinn explicitly designed the game to raise awareness about depression for both educational and therapeutic purposes. Our experience as both players of the game and teachers who have assigned it to our students is that it works marvelously. As a game designed to generate empathy, it's unmatched. We also admire its simple game design, which bucks many of the narrative and gameplay conventions of mainstream videogames.

But that combination of progressive empathy design and accessible gameplay proved volatile for a small but vocal and technically adept

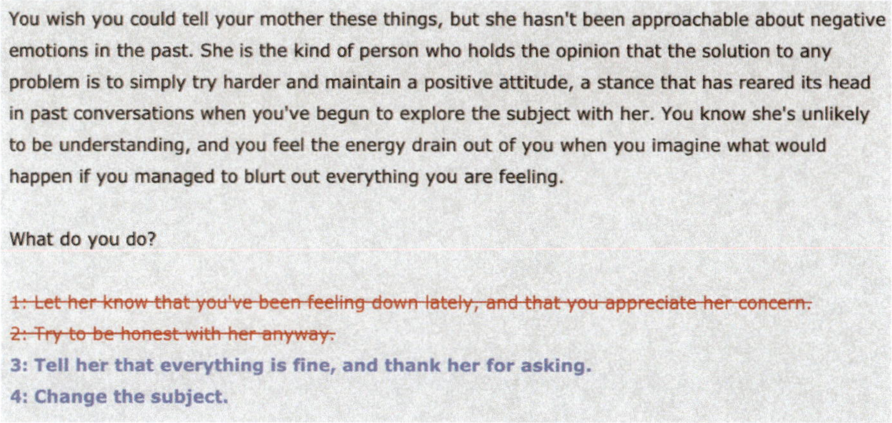

> You wish you could tell your mother these things, but she hasn't been approachable about negative emotions in the past. She is the kind of person who holds the opinion that the solution to any problem is to simply try harder and maintain a positive attitude, a stance that has reared its head in past conversations when you've begun to explore the subject with her. You know she's unlikely to be understanding, and you feel the energy drain out of you when you imagine what would happen if you managed to blurt out everything you are feeling.
>
> What do you do?
>
> ~~1: Let her know that you've been feeling down lately, and that you appreciate her concern.~~
> ~~2: Try to be honest with her anyway.~~
> 3: Tell her that everything is fine, and thank her for asking.
> 4: Change the subject.

Fig. 3.1. Screenshot from *Depression Quest* showing a set of links that represent different possible choices a player might make for the game's protagonist. Two of these are disabled, representing the idea that a person suffering from depression may recognize a decision but be unable to make it. *Courtesy of Zöe Quinn.*

group of videogame players in a video-gaming community that was experiencing rapid change. Initially released as a free web browser game (though it offered a "pay what you wish" option to raise funds for the National Suicide Prevention Hotline), *Depression Quest* was picked up by the popular gaming platform Steam through its Greenlight program, introducing it to a far wider audience than would be typical for a game focusing on serious content and lacking the kinds of videogame mechanics characteristic of mainstream games. While its presence on Steam raised the profile of the game, Quinn's personal safety became increasingly precarious. Vicious criticism from subscribers and a rape threat mailed to her home address prompted Quinn to withdraw the game. However, an invitation from IndieCade, an international juried festival of independent games, convinced Quinn that she should rerelease the game, despite the personal risk that would entail. "I thought, honestly, I could take the hate if it meant the game could reach somebody who would get something out of it, feel less alone," she later told an interviewer.

Steam released the game on August 11, 2014, coincidentally the day that beloved comedian (and enthusiastic player of digital games) Robin Williams committed suicide after a lifelong struggle with depression. Though Quinn once again considered withdrawing the game, knowing that it would intensify the threats and harassment they were suffering, she decided, "I would rather have those people hate me than [to have] the people who are currently quietly suffering with this illness sit at their dinner tables tonight and . . . hear people not understand how someone who had so much could kill themselves, and lack a resource they could have needed right then to point to and say, 'This is why.'" Meanwhile, *Depression Quest* began to receive attention from another sector of the videogame community: journalists and reviewers. Which led to even greater danger for Quinn.

The events that we know as Gamergate are in part the story of changes in the ecosystem of games journalism and the increasing access of consumers to creators by way of social media. In early 2014, Quinn's ex-boyfriend posted a blog that described their relationship and breakup in extensive detail, including personal communications between them. What became known as the Zoë Post also included details about Quinn's relationship with Nathan Grayson, a reporter for the website Kotaku, which had given *Depression Quest* a positive review. Quinn, it was implied, had exchanged sex for the review. This was categorically untrue. However, users of the controversial 4chan website got hold of the blog, amplifying the rumor, and actor Adam Baldwin further amplified it on Twitter, coining the hashtag #Gamergate to describe what he felt was an example of unethical journalism. Again, this was categorically untrue, but the appeal to "ethical journalism" provided cover to an increasingly coordinated campaign of harassment that included releasing personal information and hacking Quinn's Tumblr, Dropbox, Skype, and Twitter accounts. Quinn and her family received thousands of threats.

Though noteworthy for its intensity and the fact that it was acknowledged outside the traditionally insular videogame community, the kind of harassment that Quinn suffered was not at all unique. Two years earlier, Aris Bakhtanians and members of the competitive fighting game team Tekken were recorded on video aggressively harassing the team's sole female member, forcing her to withdraw from the competition. Though he eventually apologized, Bakhtanians initially defended their actions: "The sexual harassment is part of [the] culture. And if you remove that from the fighting game community, it's not the fighting game community." Less than a year later, Jennifer Hepler quit her job as a writer at the game company BioWare after receiving threats to her family and children for remarks she had made years earlier about wishing she could skip the combat sections of a popular videogame. What made Gamergate different, therefore, was not that women and queer creators were being harassed and threatened, but that the conflict was being staged in an entirely new way. As Joan Donovan notes, the kinds of disinformation and harassment campaigns deployed against Quinn and others were pioneered in 2013 to undermine the growing presence of Black women on Twitter and hashtag-led movements like #solidarityisforwhitewomen. Not only were the manipulation tactics developed to harass women of color "a blueprint for running larger harassment and disinformation campaigns," but the failure of Twitter and other social media platforms to do anything about such campaigns enabled them to persist and find new targets.[7]

One such target was Anita Sarkeesian. While a student at York University in 2009, Sarkeesian launched a website she called Feminist Frequency, which featured feminist criticism of popular culture texts—for example, the way LEGO toys reinforce conventional gender roles. In 2011, she partnered with *Bitch* magazine and tightened the focus of the website to the analysis of common tropes that governed depiction of women, at first focusing on their presence in speculative fiction texts. The success of this and other ventures brought her to the attention of the videogame developer Bungie, which invited her to speak at its headquarters. Pleased by the response, she launched a Kickstarter campaign to fund the production of a series of videos focusing on sexist tropes in videogames. The harassment and threats she suffered immediately afterward only hinted at what was to come, but it also inspired the large community that would emerge to support her, as she raised more than twenty times her original fundraising goal of $6,000. She released the first video on March 7, 2013.

The *Tropes vs Women* videos called attention to the decades-long practice of systematic derogatory and retrograde depictions of women in videogames. Female characters, Sarkeesian argued, regularly appeared in videogames within clichéd narratives and visual devices such as the "Damsel in Distress," "Ms. Male Character," or "Women as Background Decoration." These devices, she continued, propagated harmful misogynist stereotypes, made even more pernicious via their ubiquity and repetition, that reinforced larger cultural patterns. The *New York Times* went so far as to call the series "essential viewing for anyone interested in videogames."[8] We would agree. Indeed, we consider these videos a groundbreaking criticism of the empathic structures of videogames and an affirmation of a different way of making and playing them.

The harassment that Sarkeesian suffered became, as she put it, "the background radiation" of her life. Like Quinn, Sarkeesian was subjected to an organized campaign of racist and misogynist harassment from individuals and groups who identified themselves as true videogame players and fans, or "gamers." Other female and queer game journalists, critics, and developers suffered, and continue to suffer, similar treatment, including game developer Brianna Wu, who publicly confronted Gamergate advocates and monitored their posts on the social media website 8chan. The content of much of the abuse and harassment is too vile to reproduce. But it was so widespread and severe that the United Nations Broadband Commission for Digital Development released a report by its Working Group on Broadband and Gender in September 2015, after Sarkeesian and Quinn testified at the UN, calling for a "worldwide wake-up call" regarding cyberviolence toward women and girls and for radical policy changes by governments to ensure that the rights of internet users are better protected.[9] Authorities in the United States were far less responsive. After the FBI obtained confessions from two men who sent threats to Wu and her family, the U.S. attorney for the District of Massachusetts refused to prosecute.

The events of Gamergate represent how the design and deployment of structures of affect within a digital environment can be used to both promote and diminish critical thinking and progressive forms of empathy. And not surprising, given that the clash between progressives and reactionaries was about games, the attack on the former took the form of a game, or as Stephanie Boluk and Patrick LeMieux would put it, a metagame—in other words, a game about games:

> From trash talking to verbal abuse in arcades; griefing to cyberbullying in online games; trolling to hate speech on web forums; and from pizza bombing to DDoSing, doxxing, swatting, and stalking through locative, biometric, and other forms of identifying media, the metagames that both emerge from and envelop

videogames contain varying amounts of toxicity, sometimes reaching pH levels so high that they become uninhabitable. If media . . . constitute an "environment for life" and metagames function as an environment for games, what happens when the environment becomes unlivable?[10]

Sarkeesian sees quite clearly how that metagame framed her and the other critics and creators who were insisting that videogames, videogame players, and the videogame community be better. As she puts it, she was the victim "of men who turned their misogyny into a game, in which gendered slurs, death and rape threats are weapons used to take down the big bad villain (which in this case is me)." As Boluk and LeMieux note, "The game Sarkeesian referenced didn't come in a box. It wasn't on sale at some electronics superstore or available for download on digital distribution services. Her harassment wasn't protected by any intellectual property laws, end user license agreements, or digital rights management."[11] It was, nevertheless, a game—a game that deployed the same strategy that videogame writers and designers had used to deny women characters an opportunity to generate forms of empathy that would affirm their agency and individuality. But instead of the "Sexy Sidekick" or "Fighting Fuck Toy," they were the "Feminist Spoilsport."

Thus when we consider Gamergate from within the framework of systemic dramaturgy, we must do more than describe the words and actions that put Quinn, Sarkeesian, Wu, and others in danger. We must understand it as a designed and deployed set of technological, narratological, and social systems, systems designed and deployed to frame their object as abject other, unworthy of empathy, deserving of contempt. The questions for us, then, are how this particular set of systems was created and why it proved so effective at victimizing others. (Indeed, it was so effective that it was deployed by the alt-right to support the political campaign of Donald Trump.)

THE DRAMATURGY OF GEEK TRIUMPHALISM

There are certain humans who find themselves drawn to social fringes where they can indulge deep and abiding fascinations and find those who share those fascinations. Members of these groups are sometimes called "geeks."[12] The geek is a stereotype, of course, but a stereotype that is grounded in a truth. Typically, geeks struggle with conventional social norms, as their passions set them apart, but they are also adept at carving out cultural space to explore and experiment with their passion in relative peace. Like monasteries, artist colonies, guilds, and universities, geek spaces are designed partially to keep them cloistered away from the teasing and bullying that is too often the cost of their specialized passions, partially to foster an insular culture of appreciation and expertise, partially to indulge the fantasy that what they love has a unique value to the greater society—a fantasy that occasionally comes true, as the ascendancy of the comic book superhero movie in the Hollywood economy demonstrates. But even when that fantasy comes true—when the mainstream embraces the fringe—they often respond in a defensive fashion. Adrienne Massanari helps us understand this paradox: "Geeks valorize expertise and specialized knowledge and geek culture often revolves around the acquisition, sharing and distribution of this knowledge with others. They often value wit, cleverness, and craft, negotiating a sense of collectivism and individualism within the communities of which they are a part."[13]

Geek cultures, then, are often initially formed as communities of sharing and learning, a place where social norms more amenable can be formed and sustained in the service of greater knowledge and aptitude. Not surprisingly, the internet has been a welcoming space for geek culture since its inception, in no small part because it required, and continues to require, geeks of various kinds for its conception, growth, and utility. But the advent (and explosive proliferation) of internet technology, and access to that technology, has facilitated something of a grand paradigm shift in geek culture. In many ways, geek culture is the only culture. Many factors are at play here: the invention of portable computers, the fragmentation of the media landscape and the niche marketing that developed in response to it, the lionization of tech pioneers who changed modern life and made fortunes doing it, and the showcasing of digital media spectacle in immensely popular big-budget fantasy and science fiction offerings. But the speed and access that the internet provides to its users have changed the social ecosystems of geekery perhaps most significantly, largely by removing geeks from their erstwhile social isolation without putting at risk the loneliness that often rules their lives on a day-to-day basis.

Though the contemporary Poindexter may still be bullied and disdained by jocks, bullies, and other agents of conformist tyranny, they neither suffer alone nor go unappreciated. Thanks to online communities, supported by platforms dedicated solely to their passions or online forums such as Reddit, 4chan, Twitter, and other platforms that foster highly specialized interests and discourses, the twenty-first-century nerd can swiftly find a strong and supportive community. Coming together, geeks have awakened to one another and found themselves powerful. Indeed, as Adrienne Shaw has demonstrated, there is powerful social capital to be garnered as media makers both cater to and are catered by formerly marginalized consumer communities—a situation especially evident in the case of videogame players.[14] After all, there is no consumer more desired by media makers than a consumer who considers the product theirs by dint of authenticity, loyalty, and co-ownership.

But why has the videogame community managed to foster such a uniquely toxic brand of authenticity, loyalty, and co-ownership? And how might a systemic dramaturgical approach help us better understand and mitigate that toxicity? In line with the principles we've defined, we start first by putting that culture into historical and social context. "Despite the ways in which geek culture may welcome and promote deep engagement with niche, often unpopular interests," writes Massanari, "it often demonstrates a fraught relationship to issues of gender and race."[15] We would add queerness and disability to Massanari's list of concerns, but the issues of racism and sexism are at the core of Gamergate and the broader culture of videogames. Why is this? And why would this particular culture of geekiness be so dedicated to upholding models of white masculinity that were so often deployed against them?

There are several good explanations for the presence of this toxicity, beginning with the military-industrial origins of digital games and eventuating in the profound overrepresentation of white men in the tech industry. Silicon Valley companies like Google, Facebook, Twitter, Yahoo, and Apple released employee demographics for the first time in the summer of 2014. Over 70 percent of the workforce at these companies was male. And while Asians constituted a significant portion of employees (30–40 percent), over half were white. Nonwhite and non-Asian people accounted for less than 10 percent. Responding to these rather horrifying numbers in a contemporary blog post,

Christopher Fan concludes that the emergence of geek-authored and geek-consumed narrative, metastasized on the internet, situates modern geeks as triumphant victors of the culture wars, but also assumes and is shaped by the more or less homogenous group of white and assimilated Asian men, with the latter made to occupy a second-class "guest" position in the new order.[16]

The triumph-of-geekery encomium positions geeks as righteous but long-suffering victims of conformist thuggery finally getting their social and political due, and it is from this mythology—deeply rooted and protected by ethnic and gender homogeneity and the secretive nature of high-tech development—that much of the toxicity arguably arises. For the dramaturg interested in empathy, geek triumphalism is a model for how affective structures designed to foster passion about and loyalty to a particular cultural product or technology can translate into passion and loyalty for one group against others. Massanari notes that despite the racial and gender homogeneity of the tech industry and the immense concentration of wealth and political power therein, any critic "suggesting that geek culture can also be oppressive and marginalize certain populations may create a sense of cognitive dissonance for these individuals, who likely view themselves as perpetual outsiders and thus are unable or unwilling to recognize their own immense privilege."[17] It is in this conjunction of culture and techne that toxicity finds its perfect soil. Or to put it in terms that comport with the larger argument of this book, the *dramaturgy* of geek culture renders any critique of geek culture, however justified, from whatever quarter, as evidence not of fact but of the petty grievances of jocks, thugs, bullies, and feminist spoilsports (to recall Boluk and LeMieux once again) trying to take back what they have lost or co-opt what was never theirs to begin with.[18]

The dramaturgy of geek triumphalism has proven so potent for the videogame community precisely because cultural homogeneity was never a reality. While the gender and racial demographics of the companies that make and distribute videogames align with those of other tech industries, the players, independent designers, and hobby designer communities have always been diverse. What is changing—a change whose emergence in 2014 ignited Gamergate—is not the community itself, but the growing recognition by the industry of the facts of the matter and the development and diffusion of a discourse designed to dismantle the fantasies and privileges of a powerful minority within geek culture. If you will, a new generation of videogame dramaturgs came to the fore. At the XOXO Festival in 2014, Anita Sarkeesian observed that "gaming and gaming communities are currently undergoing a massive paradigm shift. For several decades the industry catered almost exclusively to a straight white male demographic. This is no longer the case. The new reality is that gaming is becoming a more diverse and inclusive environment for everyone. The . . . vocal, aggressive, mostly male gamers who are unwilling or unable to accept this new reality? Their reactionary response can only be described as a massive and terrifying assault directed at the female fans, developers, and critics who feel they are destroying games."[19]

Since the gaming industry has done little to diversify its internal demographics after an abortive attempt to recruit female players in the 1980s, it has tended to foster only internal dialogues regarding what kinds of games gamers would like to play and therefore a culture of development and marketing that promoted a toxic, macho culture. This echo chamber was further reinforced by websites and other news outlets that had similar biases of message and workforce.

The absence of diverse voices in the design, marketing, and reporting of games meant that dissenting viewpoints were rarely heard or taken seriously—and genres of games that explored forms of playful empathy that eschewed "militarized masculinity" tended to be designed and played by those who were not part of the mainstream, more than a few by choice. The fact that the trolls of Gamergate targeted independent game designers, university-trained critics who weren't funded by game companies, and players seeking an experience beyond running-and-gunning was no coincidence. All of these had preexisted Gamergate. But all of them had found new ways to amplify their message and get their games into the hands of players. They were geeks, too, and benefited from the same technocultural transformations that enabled the trolls.

What does this tell us from the perspective of systemic dramaturgy and, more specifically, the dramaturgy of empathy? For one, in the absence of an aggressive and sustained effort to recruit creators, marketers, and audience members, it is virtually impossible for the need for alternative structures to be recognized—let alone be implemented in the production process, the design of games, or the marketing plans. Second, the construction of privileged straight white men as authentic, righteously aggrieved caretakers of geek culture and everyone else as misguided arrivistes was precisely that—a construction, a staging. On one hand were the predominantly white, male, young, and straight culture and social media platforms of "mainstream" videogames. On the other were older and female players; the independent, queer, and hobby community; and the emergent critical discourse and social media platforms represented by Sarkeesian. Thus it is no surprise that the mere idea of a game that might challenge the status quo would be interpreted by the devotees of straight-white geek culture as a direct threat not just to their tastes but to their identities.[20] Unlike our example of the racist viewer of *Othello*, who actually sits among a diverse audience and experiences with at least a degree of commitment the art before them, the trolls of Gamergate refused to join the community. Which was precisely the goal of what might be called Gamergate Dramaturgy.

Gamergate Dramaturgy had profound effects on the social ecosystem of game players and makers. Indeed, the very notion of videogame "play" and a passionate identification with it became objects of suspicion. Robin Hunicke recalls, "One phenomenon that resulted was a change in the meaning for the term 'gamer.' This descriptor rapidly evolved from an innocuous catch-all for anyone who enjoys gaming to one that specifically describes the vocal subset of hateful, misogynist, and intolerant fans who react with violent imagery and profanity to any perceived critique of their own intolerance or misogyny."[21] And indeed, misperceptions of the player community remain widespread. Our students are routinely astonished when they learn that 46 percent of those who describe themselves as regular players are female, that in 2020 the average age of a regular videogame player was between thirty-five and forty-four years and adult women represent a higher proportion of the playing community than young men.[22] But the facts of the matter do not mean that the affective dynamics of play have changed. How could they when the dramaturgical structures remain unaltered? The Swedish YouTube star Felix Arvid Ulf Kjellberg (aka PewDiePie) repeatedly uses racist and anti-Semitic imagery and slurs in his videogaming blogs, actions his hundred million followers mostly ignore or consider insignificant—a joke, an accepted part of play, an incidental. Kjellberg, in turn, responds to his critics (including the Walt Disney Corporation, YouTube, and the *Wall Street Journal*) in a fashion that reminds one not only of the trollish disinformation strategies of Gamergate but also of others who have been accused of similar actions: "It was an attack by the media to try and discredit me, to try and decrease my influence and my economic worth."[23]

Meanwhile, female players still need to conceal their identities while playing or participating in the social media around games. The Gamergate Dramaturgy ensures that they must continue to be considered illegal aliens. Kristin Bezio writes that "narrative accounts of online gameplay from female players [are] often riddled with anecdotes about leaving microphones turned off, muting the speech of other players, a nearly endless litany of requests for 'pix or not a girl' and 'boob pix pls,' and accusations of either juvenile boyhood or being 'the real player's girlfriend.' . . . For women of color, already fraught gaming spaces are made even more intolerable by the presence of racial slurs and stereotyping."[24] Bezio goes on to note that while 45 percent of white women reported being targeted by cyberviolence, 90 percent of women of color reported such instances.

Yes, many factors fostered this culture of hatred and intolerance and enable it to persist despite widespread criticism, among them the fecklessness of corporations afraid to shed consumers. But a change in attitude is not enough, because the need to change concerns more than just individual attitudes and the employee demographics of game companies. It concerns the concrete technological, material, and social structures that shape the perception of what games are, what games mean, and whom games are for. Again, we recall Joan Donovan's contention that the playbook of Gamergate was first designed to attack Black women, "attacking the character of critics, exploiting known divisions in feminist communities, and attacking the tone and language of allies."[25] This disinformation strategy, this dramaturgy of distortion, was then repurposed for Gamergate, integrated into a strategy of physical and emotional harassment enabled by the coordination of multiple social media platforms. Though the specific systems might have evolved, the structure of affect and its designed effects remained the same: consolidate the sensibilities of the aggrieved and undermine the claims of critics by casting the former as authentic keepers of the flame and the latter as misguided arrivistes.

In sum, the attack on Black feminists in 2012 and the events of Gamergate in 2014 demonstrate not just the social power of straight white men but also their ability to successfully stage their resentment. In the same way that the technologies of the conventional stage—whether the deus ex machina of classical Greek tragedy, the *hanamachi* of Kabuki, the alienation effects of the Berliner Ensemble, or the "poor theatre" of Grotowski—stage the emotional drama of character and spectator alike, the systemic dramaturgy of straight white male resentment, Gamergate Dramaturgy, is not only effective but replicable. It is, after all, a way of using technology to structure affect. And it has proven effective in multiple contexts. The strategies employed by the Gamergaters were mimicked and generalized by the alt-right and other antidiversity cultural campaigns such as the Sad Puppies, an organization that ran a five-year campaign to undermine diverse authors nominated for the Hugo Awards for science fiction literature. One prominent Gamergater, Milo Yiannopoulos, continues to spread divisive misinformation about feminists, reaching beyond games to female critics and scholars of all kinds. One subject of this assault was the medieval historian and digital humanist Dorothy Kim, a professor at Brandeis who has made the attack on her a cornerstone of her study. And she argues that the crux of the issue concerns presence and how the rhetorical, technological, social, and media systems stage our presence:

> Without any frames of effective moderation, that is to say, ways in which the tech companies failed to make sure that interactions were not happening online, which would get you arrested if you did them face to face, Milo and others went after Black Indigenous women activists first. Gamergate was a big moment because they went after white women, and so the mainstream media finally noticed. But it was still fringe—still just "gamer people." Part of the reason why mainstream political and academic culture didn't understand how dangerously toxic things had become is that they were not actually in these digital spaces. We in the U.S. are still having a hard time understanding that that digital space is an extension of real space.[26]

Or, as we would put it, the dramaturgies of digital space are a historical and technological extension of the dramaturgies of theatrical space. If "reality" means "having real effects on real people," then nothing drives home the reality of digital spaces more than the way the Gamergate Dramaturgy staged the international social, political, and aesthetic discourses of videogames, videogame players, and videogame cultures. Specifically, the Gamergate Dramaturgy staged not only a specific dynamic of empathy but also a specific ethos of performative presence. That idea is a troubling one for dramaturgs, as the question of presence and technology has been the topic of contentious debate for several decades. But we feel a rethinking of this debate is in order, given the proliferation of the dramaturgical strategies of Gamergate and the potency of its empathetic design.

NOT UNMARKED

One of the core principles of systemic dramaturgy is avoiding any essentializing of media or the technocultures shaped by media. Doing so, we have positioned ourselves in partial opposition to Peggy Phelan's thesis in *Unmarked*, which asserts that contemporary technologies of recording and reproduction corrupt the essence of live performance. But let us revisit that thesis—and our opposition—for a moment. We should recall that Phelan's hesitancy about digital media was grounded in what she, as a theater theorist, saw as the dangers they posed to the particular situated empathic structures of performance and, by extension, to the possibility of empathic culture writ large. But how exactly does Phelan understand the way empathy is generated by structures of affect? For one, she locates the spectator of a live performance at the empowered end of an always unequal exchange of power. Following the observations of the philosopher Michel Foucault in *History of Sexuality*, in particular his concerns about the ways power are built into structures of observation, Phelan argues that the energy that enables performance to do its work of signification and representation—including significations and representations that generate strong emotional responses—is ultimately located not in the performer, who struts and frets and commands attention, but rather in the spectator, who (at least in conventional, contemporary Western theater) sits, observes, and participates in a more reactive, less visibly participatory, but sometimes intensely affective manner.

In the particular kind of theater that concerns Phelan, the spectator is a kind of judge who "dominates and controls the exchange," and it is the performer who, despite appearances of agency, actually serves the silent, typically unseen spectator's desires. By performing, the performer renders themselves visible—located in a specific architectural, theatrical, and dramatic conjuncture—to provide the spectator with "a stable point upon which to turn on the machinery of projection, identification, and (inevitable) objectification."[27] This relationship is another similarity that theater and digital games share—or at least share in terms of their most conventional forms and uses. It is the "end user" who ultimately grants or withholds approval in both the immediate existential context of artistic engagement and the larger economic context of buying the opportunity for that engagement. Both structurally and economically, the audience has a particularly privileged position in the discourse on performance.

So ingrained is this power dynamic in most mainstream, particularly commercial Western performance, Phelan argues, that it is hard to see it at all, much less to understand how deeply unfair it is, how it reinforces unequal relationships in other aspects of social interaction, and how it militates against the conception of a better system to replace it. This is particularly evident when it comes to the spectatorial structures of gender. In a comment that is all too pertinent to Gamergate, Phelan writes, "Part of the function of women's absence is to perpetuate and maintain the presence of male desire as desire—as unsatisfied quest . . . the female body and the female character cannot be 'staged' or 'seen' within representational mediums without challenging the hegemony of male desire."[28] While Phelan certainly was not thinking of videogames, the metaphor of the quest is pertinent to them.

As Anita Sarkeesian and other feminist critics have argued; as critical game designers like Zoë Quinn, Brianna Wu, Anna Anthropy, micha cárdenas, Mary Flanagan, and others have demonstrated; and as the angry trolls of Gamergate confirm, the empathic structures of performance concern far more than stage and storyline. As dramaturgs in the digital age equally concerned with the boards of the stage and the buttons of the controller, we recognize and affirm Phelan's concerns with technology and its particular relationship to gender and sexuality. But rather than treat certain media as essentially subversive of empathy, we would understand all media in systemic fashion, in this case as structures of affect within structures of affect within structures of affect.

Which, not surprisingly given her profound sensitivity to the impact of technology on affect, is exactly what Phelan argues. As she notes, "Redesigning the relationship between self and other, subject and object, sound and image, man and woman, spectator and performer, is enormously difficult."[29] What is required, she continues, is nothing less than the rejection of the binary between self and other, a binary that cannot simply be engineered by a change in attitude but has to be hard-wired into the performance experience. Theater historically has proven a perfectly untrustworthy tool for that job. As a generator of empathy, performance has the ability to muddle this binary, even if it all too often reinforces those binaries, particularly in the hands of those who fail to comprehend it as a technology. Phelan observes that "it is in the attempt to walk (and live) on the rackety bridge between self and other—and not the attempt to arrive at one side or the other—that we discover real hope."[30]

Though Phelan does not explicitly argue the point, we find in her conclusions a *systemic dramaturgical* answer to the problem she has posed. And that answer specifically concerns play—the play of the performer, the play of the audience, the play of the text, the play of the system. While she acknowledges the swiftness with which audiences tend to retreat to the "self" side of the bridge when challenged by fear, uncertainty, or confusion, that bridge is always there. It is in that *between* where there is what Derrida calls *jouissance*, room to play not only in the formal sense but also in the affective sense. In other words, the game of performance is not just in the limited sense of the play of performers within the bounded space of stage and text. The game of performance encompasses and is encompassed by other "games," other conjunctures of rules, components, goals, variability, metagaming, and play.

Understanding performance as a system that is part of other systems is not a solution to the problem. But it can guide creators toward solutions—better said, toward systems of solutions. Phelan herself imagines it: "The task, in other words, is to make counterfeit the currency of our representational economy—not by refusing to participate in it at all, but rather by making work in which the costs of women's perpetual aversion are clearly measured."[31] That kind of clear measurement is evident in the continuing development of venues for the creation and criticism of digital games that provide some degree of buffer against misogynist, racist, and queerphobic violence. We think here of academic programs that ensure that game design is understood as more than simply a formal and technical process—that embed game design within a broader humanistic context. We think here of websites that foster critical discourse. And we think here of the role that policy and polity can play in ensuring that the creation and marketing of playful media are done in an ethical and moral fashion, promoting diversity and taking seriously the experiences of those who have suffered or are vulnerable to violence.

This work is only beginning—and much work remains to be done. So, to the question. With mind and heart attuned to the discourses of dramaturgical empathy from Aristotle to Zeami to Phelan to Sarkeesian, what can the digital dramaturg do to foster positive forms of empathy within videogames, videogame players, and videogame culture? We would identify three approaches:

1. We recognize that, as in theater, the content and mechanics of games have a real influence on the culture of gamers that create, consume, and support game development. While the question of how videogames influence their audiences remains unclear—and is often treated in simplistic fashion, as has been the case with the question of how videogames inspire violence—we must continue to insist that they, like any art form, are a structure of affect and therefore an engine of empathy.
2. We recognize that, as in theater, the work game developers do is impactful and important for real people and their lives. But we don't separate that work out from the wider matrix of systems in which that work is done. The "work" of game developers concerns not just the things they make but also where and how and with whom they make it.
3. We recognize that dramaturgs have a responsibility to our community to change the currency of videogame culture. This requires personal responsibility, calling out games and players that play into

the empathy strategies of trolls. This also requires collective responsibility, promoting policies and projects that ensure that creators and critics and audiences that promote empathy strategies of tolerance, diversity, and self-reflection are given proper support and protection.

As Frank Zappa observes, information is not knowledge, knowledge is not wisdom. In *Ghost Light*, Michael Chemers explores the idea that dramaturgs are to information what metallurgs are to ore: experts in the transformation of a raw resource into something useful to those who would create something even more useful—and more beautiful. Unbound from conventional conceptions of dramaturgy to consider a broader set of questions, resources, and strategies, the systemic dramaturg can plumb new depths and networks of information, collaborate with friends new and old to devise strategies for transforming that information into useful knowledge, and bring both old and new forms of insight and self-awareness to raise critical questions about not only what *can* be done but also what *should* be done to engage positively, creatively, and most importantly, justly with the massive digital culture that constitutes so much of the modern human experience. For us, the answer is to be found in systemic understanding of play, an understanding that does not separate play from player or player from context. Dramaturgs have always had access to a particular kind of power, and while that power may concern primarily an art form that some would consider old-fashioned or elite or inconvenient, it is a power that has never been more relevant: to improve the human condition through the cultivation of empathy that cannot be turned toward hatred and violence.

INTERVIEW 4

EMPATHY FOR WHOM?

MICHA CÁRDENAS ON ACTIVISM AND DIGITAL PERFORMANCE

micha cárdenas is an assistant professor of Art & Design: Games + Playable Media at the University of California–Santa Cruz. She is writing a new algorithm for gender, race, and technology. Her book in progress, *Poetic Operations*, proposes algorithmic analysis to develop a trans of color poetics. She also coauthored two books, *The Transreal: Political Aesthetics of Crossing Realities* (2012) and *Trans Desire / Affective Cyborgs* (2010), published by Atropos Press. Her artwork has been described as "a seminal milestone for artistic engagement in VR [virtual reality]" by the *Spike* art journal in Berlin. She is a first generation Colombian American. Her articles have been published in *Transgender Studies Quarterly, GLQ: Journal of Lesbian and Gay Studies, AI & Society, Scholar & Feminist Online,* the *Ada Journal of Gender,* and *New Media and Technology,* among others.

MICHAEL CHEMERS: I'd like to open up by asking you, as a new media scholar, artist, and activist, about a key moment in recent history known as Gamergate. What is the aftermath of this event, and how does it affect your work as a scholar, artist, and teacher?

micha cárdenas: That's a big question. There's a clip with game designer Zöe Quinn on the BBC that I used to show my students a lot. Quinn says at the end of this interview that she has a folder on her desktop that contains games designed by

Interview 4: *Empathy for Whom?*

women who left gaming because of Gamergate, and she's constantly just adding things to that folder to remember those games they made. It's true that a big part of the aftermath of Gamergate is that in some sense the perpetrators of this violence were very effective, because their methods are very scary: being attacked online, being doxxed, having your personal life broadcast online, having your family attacked, having your home invaded. These things are still happening.

Brianna Wu, another targeted designer, ran for Congress and said in an interview just two months ago that, during her congressional campaign, somebody put a brick through her window. So the violence and hate are still ongoing. A lot of women I know who were game developers left, saying, "This is not what I signed up for." So that is sad. The industry is making some small changes for the better, but we also see that tactics developed during Gamergate really spread out into the rest of society. We see it with the alt-right, Trump, and online attacks against Hillary Clinton and other female politicians.

MIKE SELL: The perpetrators of the violence were able to think about social performance as a mixed-reality event. They had the idea that one could work across multiple platforms, and the most effective attacks on feminist critics and women game developers were articulated across several different kinds of mediated spaces. They then utilized that to bring those attacks into real space, whether through doxxing or showing up at events or putting bricks through windows. Is one of the focuses of your work to think across these kinds of mixed realities? Could that kind of cross-platform performance be useful in combating the alt-right as well?

cárdenas: Well, what happened with Gamergate is not new. There's a long history of women being attacked online—I think about the article "A Rape in Cyberspace" [by Julian Dibbell]. But there was another really well-publicized case of a woman in the 1990s who was an online author harassed to the point where she had to basically stop using the internet. These tactics are old and also have been used for harmful purposes as well as for better purposes. In my book *The Transreal*, I start with a quote from Karl Rove from the *New York Times*. This was around the time of the first Iraq War. I'm paraphrasing. He said, "The problem is that you all are stuck in reality. ('You all' meaning leftists, activists, journalists.) The problem is that you're all stuck in reality, and while you're busy studying reality, we're over here changing it." That really stood out to me as, wow, we really need to be thinking in terms of constructing realities and changing realities and multiple realities. The way I did that in my book was to think about artwork that makes those things visible, like mixed reality or augmented reality or virtual

Interview 4: *Empathy for Whom?*

Julian Dibbel's "A Rape in Cyberspace" was originally published in the *Village Voice* in December 1993. It describes a "cyberrape" in a Multi-User Dungeon (or MUD). A player installed a subprogram that enabled him to falsely attribute his own actions to other players, among which were sexual acts. Dibble's article not only drew attention to the particular kinds of pain that could be inflicted in online environments but also to the larger social context of such acts. Dibble revealed that the account in question "had been more or less communal property of an entire NYU dorm room floor, that the young man at the keyboard on the evening of the rape had acted not alone but surrounded by fellow students calling out suggestions and encouragement, that conceivably none of those people were speaking for [the account] when he showed up . . . [that he] in fact embodied just one member of the original mob—just one scattered piece of a self more irreparably fragmented than any [real-life] multiple personality could ever fear to be."

---

reality. But recently, I think that has a different kind of resonance when thinking about "alternative facts." These are the times that we're living in, where there are multiple ideological realities, and they oftentimes seem unbridgeable. I feel that conversations, as with my students or with people online, often happen with people who have a whole set of beliefs that are separate and incompatible with my worldview.

CHEMERS: As teachers, can we bridge that gap somehow?

cárdenas: I've tried different things over the years. What I try to do now is to say that our main goal is for the students to learn critical thinking. So everything I present as a teacher is something for the student to critically analyze, and I tell them they are welcome to disagree, in an informed, well-cited way.

SELL: But it feels to me that part of what you're doing is also critical *play*, right? You seem to have a very particular understanding of what it means to play and play critically. How is playfulness part of teaching? How are you teaching your students not just to think critically but to play critically? How are you helping them to design things that promote forms of critical play?

cárdenas: Last quarter, I taught the critical history of digital games, and I would start every class with a critical play session by projecting whatever game we were going to play that day onscreen and having one or a few volunteers come up and play it in front of everybody. Sometimes they'd get input from the audience about what choices to make in the game. And then after the play session, we'd talk about it critically: What happened? What did we feel during the game?

Interview 4: *Empathy for Whom?*

How could the way we receive the game be improved? Something I tried to do in that class was to introduce different critical thinking methods. One day, we might play a game and then talk about the racial and gender dynamics, and on another day, we talked about phenomenology. I introduced lots of different specific tools for them to play and think critically. Of course, Anita Sarkeesian starts her video ["Damsel in Distress (Part 1)"] saying, as a kind of disclaimer, "I think it's important and maybe necessary to be able to critique the things you love." I communicate multiple times to the students that when I have something that's really important to me, I try to take it further because I think that critique is a form of love. I care enough about you to have read what you wrote. I care enough about you to come back and say all things I think are wrong with it, or even to say the way that it hurt me.

SELL: This is how you teach them to play critically.

CHEMERS: And to be playful critics?

cárdenas: Yeah, totally. I had them design a "dungeon of videogame history," where you encountered characters that represented the theories that we read, and they would say things to you from their theory.

SELL: What platform did you use?

cárdenas: I let them use whatever platform they wanted. We talked about Twine and WordPress, anything with clickable links. But you know, I think that creating things always involves a multitude of critical decisions—the color and font, the platform. Every single step of the way, I feel, is a critical choice, and a choice of poetics. Oftentimes people want to make some distinction between critiquing and making—it's a commonplace misconception that you can't be making and critiquing at the same time, you just have to get in the flow, just leave all that critique behind. Maybe that's true for some people, but that's not how I think about making.

SELL: That implies that you have the ability to get into the flow, which presumes a sense of safety, presumes that one has a space and a mindset that allows flow, and I'm not sure that's necessarily available to everybody at all times.

CHEMERS: It also implies, doesn't it, the false dichotomy that critical thinking must be the enemy of creative thinking? I've never found that to be the case at all. I find that they are enriched by one another.

cárdenas: This was precisely where I had some conflict with some of my students at the end of the quarter. For their final, they tried to make the argument that game designers shouldn't have to worry about being "politically correct." That is, and these were their words, they "shouldn't have to worry about offending

Interview 4: *Empathy for Whom?*

people, or have to succumb to the demands of content from others; they should just focus on making good games, rather than safe games, out there."

SELL: Do you also concern yourself with getting students to think more diversely about what counts as a game?

cárdenas: Absolutely. Defining games narrowly is a tactic that's been used by people who want to police the boundaries of games, to keep certain communities—namely, women, queer people, trans people, and people of color—out of games. It enables the gatekeepers to say, "Oh, that's not fun, so that's not a game, so that doesn't count." I try to educate students about that tactic so they can respond and think more capaciously about games. In my class, we look at virtual and alternate reality, electronic literature, many different forms, but it's a class on digital games, so we stick to the digital format. It's come into my work. When I submitted my game *Redshift and Portalmetal* to IndieCade, one of the judges specifically said, "This is not a game," so it didn't get accepted. I got my rejection letter the day that I was presenting *Network* at the Museum of Modern Art in New York.

CHEMERS: On what grounds was it not a game?

cárdenas: That it wasn't fun, that it involved too much reading. I don't remember the exact words.

SELL: If we want to create, to reconstruct, to reclaim a history of critical game design, one of the genres that has been marginalized most frequently, and that was in many respects at the heart of that moment of Gamergate, was text-based games, like *Depression Quest*. It was a game where you had to read, and it wasn't very "fun." And when you go back and look at the history of queer games and games designed and played by people of color, text adventures have always been a big part of that history. Text-based adventure games were where women designers got their earliest and biggest opportunities, and they took games with a really heteronormative, white-centric, gendered attitude and flipped the scripts.

CHEMERS: I've been astonished by how few people who now identify as gamers are aware of this history. The very term *gamer* in 2014 had distinct antifeminist connotation, and I've heard people say, "Well, I play games, but I'm not a gamer," which was code for, "I don't identify myself so strongly with this hobby that I'm willing to behave in an abominable, indecent way towards people." That's been forgotten now too.

cárdenas: That sounds to me like progress. Perhaps a good outcome of Gamergate for queer people and people of color who are making games, and even in the face of violence, is that maybe some people have different ideas about games now. In

Interview 4: *Empathy for Whom?*

preparing this class, I talked with two hundred students, and most of them were clearly on board with the notion that games should be diverse. On the first day of class, I asked, "Why are you here?" and one person said, "Because we need more queer games." Over the quarter, we read about how women, trans women, and people of color have been excluded from design opportunities. Most of them were mortified by what I showed them, even the *Feminist Frequency* videos. The students had no idea, and they said, "Whoa, this is terrible."

CHEMERS: So perhaps it's less a problem of covering up an unpleasant history that nobody wants to deal with and more one of a falling away from the cultural consciousness. Gamergate was, after all, a very tiny percentage of the gaming community coming out and behaving like real jerks, and my understanding is that a lot of those people eventually became disgusted with themselves once they realized that it had gone beyond just plain old trolling and gotten into something really more dangerous.

cárdenas: I don't know. It's hard to identify the cause of why things are different. There is other evidence that some people involved in Gamergate moved on to bigger targets—namely, the Obama presidency and eventually organizing around white supremacy and against queers. I do see some progress around queer and trans politics. Yes, there are more murders of trans women every year, but at the same time, there's a new kind of social pressure to understand queer and trans perspectives.

CHEMERS: Yes, there's a change in the way those things are represented in popular culture as well.

cárdenas: It's complicated. I was a part of this book called *Trap Door*, and I pointed out that, in 2014, when Laverne Cox was on the cover of *Time* magazine, there was a dramatic increase in hate crimes and murder against trans women. That year, the number of hate crimes tripled, the number of murders went up by fifty percent and just keeps going. So to some degree, more visibility has meant more violence. I grew up in Miami, which was really conservative. I didn't have any friends, and no one told me what transgender meant. I thought it was like *Tootsie*—men wear dresses and everyone laughs at them. I think back now to what it was like for me thirteen years ago, when I started transitioning, what representations of trans woman or Latino trans woman were available to me. Today there's an abundance of positive powerful images, thanks to the bravery and work of people like Laverne Cox and Janet Mock and *Pose*.

SELL: What role does empathy play in your thinking about multiple realities or trans realities?

Interview 4: *Empathy for Whom?*

cárdenas: I have tried different experiments for different projects; some of them are more concerned with empathy and some are less. Mary Flanagan and Jonathan Belman have a really good essay ["Designing Games to Foster Empathy"] in which they break down different types of empathy. I often give that to my students to make them aware that empathy is not monolithic. If you have, say, a game that shows the details of somebody's life in an effort to gain empathy from the player, players who are unempathic might actually just enjoy watching this person suffer. It could backfire.

Some of my work is unconcerned with empathy. I did a project called *Pregnancy*, about my efforts to have a kid with my former partner. It's about sperm banking and hormones and stuff. I mostly made that project for other trans women to learn about my story, to get actual medical details, and to provide some steps to take if you want to be fertile. So in that case, empathy that viewers might get from that was really a secondary concern to me.

In *Redshift*, I was thinking more about empathy in terms of borders. I was living in Toronto and traveling to the U.S. a lot because I could only get my refills in the U.S. Even as a person with documents, I was terrified a lot of the time. My documents weren't exactly perfect, because I had been in Canada for too long. I wasn't really sure if they would let me back in. But as a person with white skin privilege, they always let me back in. But I still felt a lot of fear crossing the border and wondering if I was going to get home to my partner. I feel like there is a really common voyeurism that happens with cis-gendered

---

In "Designing Games to Foster Empathy," Belman and Flanagan define principles for such games, which they delineate in two categories: emotional, which occurs spontaneously in response to witnessing another person's experience; and cognitive, which is intentional in purpose. We paraphrase their principles here:

1. Games must clearly signal the need for empathy to ensure intentional effort on the part of players.
2. The consequences of empathetic (or unempathetic) action must be clearly legible to players.
3. To ensure longer-lasting shifts in a player's attitudes, a game requires both emotional and cognitive empathy.
4. While it is important to construct points of similarity between the player and those with whom they are asked to empathize, those can also provoke defensive responses that can block empathy.

Interview 4: *Empathy for Whom?*

audiences of transgender artwork, in which cis-gendered people want to know the "truth" of a trans person. Even if this comes from a kind place, it's invasive, and it enables the viewer to feel like a good, empathic person while the subject winds up feeling like a specimen.

In my *Pregancy* piece, there are no images of my body; you only see my body tissue under a microscope. I wanted to highlight that dynamic—to dramatize what it feels like to be looked at literally under a microscope. So, sometimes I'm thinking about empathy from the audience, and sometimes I'm trying to resist that closeness with the audience. Sometimes I'm thinking more about concrete, practical things. I did a project called *Hold Your Boundaries* that was mostly an Instagram feed of digital security tips for trans people, Muslims, immigrants, and everybody targeted by Trump.

SELL: I wonder if part of what's happening here is that when we talk about empathy, what we really need to talk about is ethics, because what I'm hearing you describe in part is not just what one does, or how one looks, or how one communicates. It's about reflecting and thinking about your own behavior.

cárdenas: When this discussion of empathy comes up, my initial question is, "Empathy for whom?" Mattie Brice's game *Mainichi* is about a Black trans woman trying to avoid violence while she goes through her daily life and gets coffee. She said she literally designed this game so that a friend would feel empathy for her. But that implies that the audience is not Black trans women, or maybe not even trans women. My primary audience is not always necessarily cis-gendered people, or straight white men, or straight people, or any of those people. My goal is actually safety and healing for myself and for other trans women, women, and people of color.

SELL: It seems that this work can also be about establishing certain kinds of boundaries and being comfortable, even when some people are frustrated when they are not invited.

cárdenas: A project I'm working on now is called *Sin Sol* or *No Sun*, about wildfires and climate change (fig. i4.1). The main characters in this game are a trans Latina and her dog. The dog leads her through a damaged environment, filled with smoke and through a wildfire and other things. Part of what I'm trying to encourage people to think about, inspired by Donna Haraway, is the importance not only of caring for other humans but also other species, and even for AIs, because the way we treat inanimate objects shapes who we are just as much as the way we treat animals. Perhaps what I'm trying to do is create empathy in abundance, or a global kind of ethics.

Interview 4: *Empathy for Whom?*

Fig. i4.1. A view of the augmented reality game *Sin Sol/No Sun*, by micha cárdenas. *Photo courtesy of micha cárdenas.*

CHEMERS: It's a foundational ethical premise: I don't really understand the terms of my own subjectivity, so I treat you well not because I am certain you are a person with a self like the one I feel, but because of its impact on me.

cárdenas: Yes, maybe it is more about an ethics towards the Other. It's less about how I'm going to treat you well, because you're like me or I feel your pain, but instead to say, "No, we're different. And I still care about you." Perhaps I am less concerned with empathy than with solidarity. I feel that a lot of the politics of the last five or ten years have been very much about dividing our specific, particular identity categories and then declaring that I'll only hang out with people who have these five adjectives. What we need is more connection and support across differences, support for each other across differences. I mean, I don't fit snugly into easy categories myself.

SELL: And yet, you love to play.

cárdenas: Yeah!

CHEMERS: *Solidarity* as a term implies difference, doesn't it? Rather than unity? Finding a common purpose or struggle within a diverse group?

cárdenas: There's element in solidarity in which your struggle is my struggle, but not because they're the same. Because there's a lot of people that you don't want at your table.

TOWARD A DRAMATURGY OF VIDEOGAMES

Imagine you are standing at a border. The territory before you is neither terra incognita nor imperial frontier. In fact, it's entirely familiar. Your apartment is just over there. Around the corner, your favorite place to get coffee. A little farther on, your favorite bodega. You have family there, friends, coworkers too. But the thing is, you don't typically travel there in your dramaturgical finery.

The border at which you stand is the border between what is and what isn't theater.

Unlike national or corporate borders, this one is free of guards, guns, red tape, detention cells, and security drones. But for all its openness, when we flash our dramaturgical bona fides, we tend to attract suspicion, a wary glance here, a patronizing smile there. This is especially true when the border we cross is the one that separates the Theater Department from the rest of academia. I mean, what can theater people possibly have to say about economics, politics, communication, or marketing? No doubt, part of the problem is that theater people, like most artists, aren't taken as seriously as, say, economists and bioengineers and criminologists. But another part of the problem is the way "interdisciplinary" research works in academia—or, better said, doesn't work. As Sanne Taekema and Bar van Klink note, the term "interdisciplinary" lends to research "a sophisticated and contemporary image," but a closer look reveals that much of what claims to be interdisciplinary is, when it comes right down to it, monodisciplinary.[1] Rather than submerge themselves in the conceptual, methodological, and historical particularities of a field, rather than collaborate with experts who can question their questions and challenge their interpretations, cross-field researchers tend to cherry-pick the stuff that affirms what they already know.

Dramaturgs, on the other hand, are, as Michael Chemers puts it, "the ones who question."[2] It is incumbent upon dramaturgs to cross and recross disciplinary and social boundaries, seek out whatever information and experts can help them find what they need to tackle the challenges that face them, and never let up on asking the hard questions for the creators and audiences with whom they work. In point of fact, theater people have a lot to say about economics, politics, communication, marketing—and much else. This is particularly true of the systemic dramaturg. A systemic approach has little interest in conventional distinctions between the old and the new, the human and the inhuman, the sacred and the profane, the self and the other, the analog and the digital. Like Zeami and other dramaturgs who aim for a more holistic, self-conscious understanding of the craft, we seek a dynamic relationship between the human and the technological, a relationship that can, when achieved, produce meaningful, soulful, memorable, beautiful expression. This requires a rigorously interdisciplinary approach.

Richard Schechner's "broad-spectrum" approach to performance studies offers a useful model for doing this kind of work. There are, he tells us, forms of human behavior we all commonly agree *are* performance: singing a song in a cabaret, playing Hedda Gabler onstage, juggling, doing stand-up comedy. Conversely, there are expressive behaviors that we typically wouldn't consider to be performance, but were we to adjust our perspectives and methods a tad, we might consider them *as* performance.[3] We might apply performance studies methods to, say, the chants of soccer fans or the behavior of our fellow employees at the annual office party. Doing so, we might gain useful insight into those behaviors. And if we're really lucky, we might gain insight into our own disciplinary methods, recognizing previously hidden biases, assumptions, or methodological flaws.

We can do the same with dramaturgy. On one hand, there is the historical, critical, and collaborative work that any dramaturg would agree is properly "dramaturgical." This might involve providing information about Yoruba spiritual practices to a costume designer tasked with creating the Egungun costume for a production of Wole Soyinka's *Death and the King's Horseman*. Or working with a choreographer to

Toward a Dramaturgy of Videogames

create historically accurate dances for a production of Aphra Behn's *The Emperor of the Moon*. There is, on the other hand, work that might not seem "dramaturgical" on its face but could be if we shift from the *is* to the *as*. This is border-crossing dramaturgy, a systemic application that enables us to use our skills and knowledge to better understand—and help others better understand—the things that interest and concern us beyond script, proscenium, and box office. This is work that can, with a bit of luck and sweat and, most importantly, the cooperation of experts who can help us ask the right questions, provide empowering resources for dramaturgs to innovate what they do and how they do it.

So with skeptical disciplinarians and *Bunraku* puppeteers equally in mind, we hope to demonstrate in this chapter how to apply systemic dramaturgy to something most dramaturgs wouldn't normally consider their purview: videogames. Why videogames? First and foremost, because we play them and have played them for a long time. We know how fun, how beautiful, how moving and memorable they can be. We know how troubling and frustrating—if not downright dangerous—they and those who play them can be. We've witnessed the racism, misogyny, and other vulgar evils of the medium and its culture. For those who play without the privileges and protections of straight white masculinity, videogames can be a lot less enjoyable, their pleasures much more precarious. And whether we're having fun or not, the quality of our experience playing and teaching videogames has been deeply informed by our understanding of theater not only as an aesthetic form but also as a creative practice.

Second, we've chosen videogames as a case study for border-crossing systemic dramaturgy because they are big business and global culture. In 2020, the videogame industry generated nearly $140 billion in global revenues, growing 12 percent over the previous year.[4] In the United States, three out of four households have at least one person who plays videogames, 70 percent of people under eighteen play videogames regularly, and 65 percent of people over eighteen play, with 41 percent of those being women.[5] Anything that can inspire so many people to spend so much time and money to have fun surely requires our attention. And if we can bring some useful perspectives as dramaturgs to the conversation about the videogame industry, if we can help designers, consumers, marketers, journalists, and critics better understand what they do, if we can help players have more fun, then all the better.

Third, we've chosen videogames because we believe their ubiquity is a sign of a broader shift in how culture and cultural power works. To recall, in "Manifesto for a Ludic Century," game designer Eric Zimmerman writes, "It is not enough to merely be a systems-literate person, to understand systems in an analytic sense. We also must learn to be playful in them. A playful system is a human system, a social system rife with contradictions and with possibility."[6] Being playful is the engine of innovation and creativity: as we play, we think about thinking and we learn to act in new ways. As a cultural form, games have a particularly direct connection with play. Systemic dramaturgs embrace a historically informed, multifaceted, capacious understanding of play. That puts us in a unique position to help others engage critically and consciously with the playful information systems described by Zimmerman in "Manifesto for a Ludic Century." While reading Zeami may not help us get past that tricky boss fight in *NieR: Automata*, it will help us recognize the ways our lives are increasingly gamified to ensure profitability and security. Indeed, it may be time to revise Jaques's line to read, "All the world's a videogame, and all the men and women merely players." If power is becoming increasingly gamified, then we all need to be better players.

Finally, we've chosen videogames as a case study for cross-disciplinary dramaturgy because they're already part of the theater and performance scene. Two of the earliest and most influential studies of digital interactivity used theater as their analytic paradigms. In *Computers as Theatre*, originally published in 1991, Brenda Laurel argues that the interface between human beings and computational devices is essentially dramatic: "Theatre is about interaction, about themes and conflicts, goals and approaches to those goals, frustration, success, tension, and then the resolution of that tension. Theatre is dynamic, changing, always in motion. Our modern technologies with their powerful computers, multiple sensors, communication links, and displays are also about interaction, and treating that interaction as theatre proves to be rich, enlightening, and powerful." Of special interest to dramaturgs, Laurel argues that computational processes (whether big or small) should be conceived in Aristotelian terms as "whole actions" that engage users

Toward a Dramaturgy of Videogames

in a fashion that stimulates both empathy and catharsis. Fortunately, she alerts designers to thinking beyond this one model of plot design, urging them to "extend the geometry of dramatic interaction."[7]

Janet Murray's *Hamlet on the Holodeck*, first published in 1997, focuses more exclusively on videogames, arguing it is a medium that is essentially dramatic because of its capacity for immersion, agency, and transformative action. Further, as she demonstrates in extended analyses of *Brave New World, Neuromancer, Star Trek: The Next Generation*, and other texts, the analysis of videogames benefits from being situated within a comparative multimedia humanities framework, an approach that shows its virtues when, as she puts it, we seek to better understand "our hopes and fears for richly immersive and interactive entertainment."[8]

Thus it should come as no surprise to discover that playwrights, designers, and performers have been playing with videogames too. The 1990s were a watershed. Theatrical installations featuring videogames were part of the Walker Art Center's *Beyond Interface* exhibition of 1998, and many of the games featured in Anne-Marie Schleiner's 1999 exhibition *Cracking the Maze* foregrounded the relationship among games, players, and the social spaces and roles players enact when playing games. Steve Dixon cites Tod Machover's 1996 "game-like performance" *Brain Opera* as an early, influential example of the use of software and "games paradigms." Some versions of Machover's composition featured interactive musical games that could be played by the audience either in the performance space or via internet. The performance collective Blast Theory has explored the relationship among power, interactivity, and technology for almost three decades, and videogames often feature in their productions as both subject and scenography. The 1999 virtual reality work *Desert Rain*, created in collaboration with Nottingham University's Mixed Reality Lab, combined videogames and installation art and is generally regarded as their first "videogame work" and "a seminal experimental production fusing the technological complexity of hard science skills with a truly original artistic vision."[9] A more recent creation, *Karen* (2015), is a phone-based app that morphs from a banal daily life-coaching program to a disturbing meditation on big data, the hazards of personal disclosure, and online codependency.

Videogames have been used scenographically, as with ieVR's 2000 production of *A Midsummer Night's Dream* at the University of Kent,

159

which represented the magical forest as a computer game. Videogames have been the subject of dramatic works, including David K. S. Tse and Yellow Earth Theatre's *Play to Win* (2000) and Jennifer Haley's *Neighborhood 3: Requisition of Doom* (2008) and *The Nether* (2013). Mary Flanagan's work crosses theatrical and virtual spaces to reveal the embodied, collaborative, theatrical qualities of electronically mediated play. *[domestic]* (2003) modified a first-person shooter game into a psychologically tense domestic drama. Punchdrunk's smash-hit *Sleep No More* (2011) and Justin Fix's *The Willows* (2017) deploy environmental storytelling techniques common to videogames. In the former, the audience members move through the fictional McKittrick Hotel as they desire, exploring an adaptation of *Macbeth* in a fashion familiar to players of point-and-click adventure games or narrative-centered shooters like *BioShock Infinite*. Theater has been staged in massive multiplayer online games like *World of Warcraft* and *Second Life*. EK Theater stages adaptations of Shakespeare, Yeats, and Ovid, as well as Korean, Turkish, and Japanese folktales in games like *LittleBigPlanet 3*, *Halo: Reach*, and *World of Warcraft*. Videogames have borrowed liberally from theater and performance too. Nolan Bushnell, cofounder of Atari, learned the craft of attracting players to games while working as a carnival barker. The videogame *Kentucky Route Zero* remediates the stage designs of Jo Mielziner and Beowulf Boritt to create environments that communicate themes of memory and loss.

So there are plenty of good reasons for crossing the disciplinary border and approaching videogames within the framework of systemic dramaturgy. And a perfectly useful approach is, as we've done in the previous two chapters, to think about them in terms of play and empathy. To accomplish this, we return to the *bestiarum vocabulum* of play we toured in chapter 2. The reader will recall that we divided play etymologically into (1) play as doing, (2) play as thing, and (3) those who play. These are well suited to the dramaturgical work of clarifying, complicating, and collaborating across the borderlands between videogames and theater.

WHAT IS A VIDEO GAME?

Our dramaturgical expedition begins with a question whose answer might seem rather obvious: What is a videogame? Seems like a relatively easy question, right? A videogame is a game one plays with a computer of some sort by wiggling one's thumbs and fingers while holding a controller of some sort while staring at a screen of some sort. Mostly shooting stuff. Or whacking stuff with a sword. Or doing sporty things. Or flinging emotionally unstable birds at egregiously underconstructed buildings. Or jumping and climbing.

If we're talking about the mainstream of the videogame market, that's not an altogether inappropriate answer. In 2018, the top ten best-selling games for videogame consoles globally—consoles being dedicated game machines like the Playstation 4, Xbox One, or Nintendo Wii U—included two military-themed shooters, two sports games, and five open-world adventure games that involved a lot of running, jumping, climbing, and murder. Most of these were the latest in long-lived franchises: *Grand Theft Auto, Pokémon, Call of Duty* (two games, no less!), *Super Mario* (two games too!), *The Legend of Zelda, Uncharted*, and the latest iteration of the evergreen *FIFA Soccer*.[10]

But the console market is not the only market. Mobile games—played on smartphones, tablets, or dedicated handheld devices—were the fastest-growing sector of global media and entertainment in 2017 and, for the first time, accounted for over half of global digital game revenues in 2018, a trend driven by the growing processing power of phones and tablets, but also by growing numbers of smartphone users with internet access in the Asia-Pacific region.[11] One tends to see more diversity in the mobile market in terms of game mechanics, though fantasy themes dominate. A quick glance over the list of the top ten mobile games of 2017 reveal several flavors of role-playing games (where one controls characters that grow in strength and skill over time), an online battle arena game (in which one's team fights other players' teams), two real-time strategy games, two puzzle games (including the perennial favorite *Candy Crush Saga*), and *Pokémon Go*, an augmented reality game where players walk around their neighborhoods searching for elusive creatures to collect while avoiding collisions with pedestrians and shrubbery.[12]

Back to the question of platform, we should note the personal computer market, which is its own beast. Though one will find a couple of new releases on the top ten global bestsellers list, the PC game market is dominated by antiques. According to the Steam digital distribution service, the top sellers in July 2018 included only four games released that year and one the previous. Two were released in 2015, three in 2013, and one in 2012. With the exception of the turn-based strategy game *Civilization VI*, these older games are all multiplayer games, most of them competitive games in which one plays against others in real time.[13]

But wait, weren't we answering the question, What is a videogame? Does it really matter whether we are a young African American male playing on a $300 console and a seventy-inch flat-screen television, a middle-age white woman on a reconditioned laptop, or a Japanese elementary school student on an iPhone? Does it really matter who we are, where we are, and what we've got in our hands? Aren't these games basically the same: a computer, a controller, wiggling fingers, some kind of software, a screen? The short answer is yes. But the short answer is not an especially satisfying answer, particularly from the perspective of systemic dramaturgy.

Consider how a dramaturg approaches a dramatic text. What is *A Raisin in the Sun*? The obvious answer is a play by Lorraine Hansberry about a working-class African American family struggling with the opportunities and obstacles of a racist society. It's a conventional text in terms of dramatic structure and characterization, decidedly unconventional in terms of its subject matter, particularly its focus on the struggles of black women. That's the obvious answer. However, for dramaturgs, the obvious answer is always inadequate. Dramatic texts are shaped in sometimes profound ways by the conditions in which they are staged. This is a matter of history. *Raisin* was the first play written by a black woman to be staged on Broadway, at the Shubert Organization's Ethel Barrymore Theatre. That theater is a story unto itself, though one for another time. Its success boosted the careers of a generation of black playwrights, actors, and directors, yet another story. The theater in which a play is staged affects the spectator's social and phenomenological experience of the play. Watching *Raisin* performed on a proscenium stage (which was the case for the premier production), for example, is different from what one would experience with a thrust stage (which was the case for the 2016 production at the Park Square Theatre in St. Paul, Minnesota). Watching with the donor class is a different experience from watching with the families of a high school cast and crew, or in a church basement as part of a community organizing to bring about a better political future.

This is just as true of videogames. Playing *Colossal Cave Adventure* on the original PDP-10 mainframe computer for which it was originally designed is different from playing it on an emulator on a MacBook Pro. This is not just a question of the look, sound, and feel of the game, though those factors are undeniably significant. Gaming is a contextual experience shaped by the materiality of the device in our hands, our eyes, our ears, by who and where we play, by what we bring to play, by what we take away from it. The experience of playing a videogame solo on a smartphone on the Green Line rattling toward the Bronzeville station on Chicago's South Side is different from playing with a group of friends in the bustling Jiyu Kukan internet café in Kyoto is different from playing in Rio de Janeiro's Oi Futuro NAVE high school is different from playing at a queer game jam at MIT is different from playing in Seoul's Sangam Stadium in front of forty-seven thousand roaring spectators and eleven million online viewers. Indeed, as Stephanie Boluk and Patrick LeMieux argue, to study videogames without reference to their historical and social contexts is to fundamentally misunderstand the nature of games and play. To ignore "everything occurring before, after, between, and during games as well as everything

Metagames are not just games about games. They are not simply the games we play in, on, around, and through games or before, during, and after games. From the most complex house rules, arcade cultures, competitive tournaments, and virtual economies to the simple decision to press start, pass the controller, use a player's guide, or even purchase a game in the first place, for all intents and purposes metagames are the only kind of games that we play. And even though metagames have always existed alongside games, the concept has taken on renewed importance and political urgency in a media landscape in which videogames not only colonize and enclose the very concept of games, play, and leisure but ideologically conflate the creativity, criticality, and craft of play with the act of consumption. When did the term *game* become synonymous with hardware warranties, packaged products, intellectual property, copyrighted code, end user licenses, and digital rights management? When did *rules* become conflated with the physical, mechanical, electrical, and computational operations of technical media? When did *player* become a code word for *customer*? When did we stop making metagames?

—Stephanie Boluk and
Patrick LeMieux,
Introduction to *Metagaming*

located in, on, around, and beyond games" is to divorce the game from "time and space."[14] Systemic dramaturgy is, in this perspective, a form of metagaming.

Acknowledging the diversity of identities, platforms, communities, contexts, and histories in which videogames are played is an important first step toward answering the question, What is a videogame? And it is an important first step toward developing a systemic dramaturgy of videogames. But there's also the question of genre. There are first-person shooters, puzzle games, augmented reality games, real-time strategy games, gacha games, and on and on. There are casual games, which can be played while waiting in line for a bowl of ramen and require little to no thought and effort. There are serious games, which explore significant political and social issues. There are educational games, which are designed to introduce or improve skills such as reading or math. There is gamification, a process that transforms the nonentertaining, off-putting, or obligatory into something that resembles, to some extent, fun. If you've ever taken an online quiz while browsing a website or participated in a point-earning process to earn a better insurance rate, congratulations! You've been gamified! And there are therapy games. Semi Ryu uses three-dimensional imagery, virtual puppetry, and Korean ritual and storytelling to help older people manage trauma, disability, memory loss, and other mental health issues (figs. 4.1a and 4.1b).[15]

While it is vital that dramaturgs recognize the diversity of offerings for the curious and diligent videogame player, we shouldn't limit our imagination to what has existed in the past or what exists in the present. The mission of systemic dramaturgy, while inspired by the remarkable innovations enabled by digital technology, is committed to exploring the relationship of theater and technology beyond the present moment and the usual suspects of traditional and new media dramaturgy. We are as interested in what, say, the instruments and choreography of traditional Kutiyattam theater can teach us about the application of digital projectors as what digital projectors can teach us about Kutiyattam.

This applies to videogames too. For example, let's consider one of the common material components of videogame play: the controller. In a fascinating essay on game controllers, Miguel Sicart bemoans the fact that, though there are more games about more topics made by more

Toward a Dramaturgy of Videogames

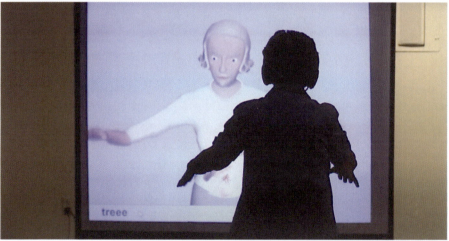

Figs. 4.1a and 4.1b. VoicingElder's digital avatars mimicking the user's gestures and lip-syncing with the user's voice, enabling users to create dramatic digital representations of their stories. Semi Ryu describes VoicingElder as a reminiscence storytelling platform for older adults. *Photos courtesy of Semi Ryu.*

people for more audiences today than ever before, "most games are either controlled by fancy typewriters or impersonal pieces of plastic with protruding sticks and more buttons than one has fingers." How does this limit our ability to conceive, build, and play? Sicart calls for "controllers for the alternative emotions, alternative bodies, and alternative experiences that games now foster." And he finds models for those in sex toys, whose "designers set off with the goal of creating pleasurable, embodied experiences, and they do so by asking users, materials, and contexts, key questions about how these devices would be used, what their users are looking for, and how they can satisfy those needs."[16] In similar spirit, Jess Marcotte surveys a variety of unconventional controllers that require players to, for example, hold hands and remain silent or manipulate handmade textile constructions or gently brush plants to provide subtle audio feedback. Thinking beyond conventional interfaces "expand[s] the definitions of what is possible not only for ourselves as designers, but also for players and for those who are not yet players."[17] These kinds of reflective inquiries into the fundamentals of videogame design capture the very spirit of systemic dramaturgy.

But answering the question what a videogame is (or might be) isn't just a matter of being thorough and imaginative. Whether something is a videogame or not can be the subject of violent—sometimes literally violent—debate. Granted, characterizing as "debate" the kind of language one finds on troll-infested social media sites like Reddit, Twitter, and 4Chan is rather generous. The zealous defense of convention against those who would create new kinds of mechanics, rules, and game fictions reminds us that there are powerful ideological and social forces that shape the medium. But those pressures are just as evident, if more subtly, in the work of videogame historians. As Lana Polansky has noted, "If videogames can be said to possess an 'official history,' it is predicated primarily on the advancement of technology, the shifting of markets and the consolidation of multinational corporations."[18] Those histories tend to ignore popular genres that don't depend on powerful (and profitable) graphic processors or big-budget marketing campaigns: text-based videogames; experimental, art, and political games; and the diverse communities, both long-lived and emergent, profiled by Anna Anthropy in *Rise of the Videogame Zinesters*. And, no surprise, they tend to erase people who aren't straight and male.[19]

For these reasons and more, as systemic dramaturgs, we enthusiastically accept an invitation to think outside the box—in this case, the videogame console. (Dare we say, "Think outside the Xbox"?) But what exactly is that box? In his provocative essay "Defining the Videogame," Veli-Matti Karhulahti calls into question many of the assumptions we might have about what a videogame is—and opens up avenues for thinking about what a videogame might be. Karhulahti notes, to begin with, that scholars have yet to settle on a definition of *game*, let alone videogames. From there, Karhulahti ponders whether only those designed around "rule-bound gameplay" should count as videogames. After all, interactive fiction, visual novels, or walking simulators are built around playful interaction between a user and rule-bound gameplay, but in a way that lacks the typical kinetic feel and strategic thinking of most videogames. And what about the name of the medium? Why not "digital game," "electronic game," or "computer game?" And why the emphasis on seeing? Though videogames whose play centers on hearing or touching are rare, they do exist. Yes, it is perfectly acceptable to use a term as lingua franca, but the names we give things can keep us from recognizing other names, other ways of thinking and, ultimately, making. Let's continue: How does the visual bias of our thinking about these kinds of games keep designers and players from exploring other avenues of creative expression?

In *Metagaming*, Boluk and LeMieux explore forms of videogame play that involve "blind, low vision, and sighted players navigat[ing] videogame spaces without the use of video and invent[ing] new ways of playing according to alternate sensory economics." Doing so, they "hold a critical lens up to not only the games industry but the design, dissemination, and consumption of software in general."[20] And then there's the problem of distinguishing videogames in terms of whether they're software or hardware. We think of the former when we consider the kinds of games we play on the same devices on which we do other kinds of tasks—for example, writing a book, calling a friend, or responding to email. But we think of the latter when we consider the custom-built cabinets we find at arcades or the purpose-built games some of us played as children, such as *Merlin* or *Football Champ*.

The question of interactivity is equally fraught. Espen Aarseth's contention that videogames are unique as a medium because they require nontrivial interactive effort was obviously conceived by someone who was never involved in a tech rehearsal.[21] Drama seems like a medium that requires nontrivial effort only if we limit our analysis to the final product and the experience of the audience. The more useful comparison to make is between videogame players and actors and technicians. We might define videogames in terms of a particular kind of interactivity—exchanging information with a computer—but even that gets blurry when we think of other kinds of play that involve computational devices. In sum, it is difficult to pin down what exactly distinguishes videogames from other "playable media"—and it's not entirely clear that it's worth the effort to answer that question. But we do think it's our mission as systemic dramaturgs to keep asking.

The kinds of questions we ask about videogames can concern more than what and how we play—they're ultimately about who we are and how we see others. In "Queering Human-Game Relations," Naomi Clark and merritt k explore the ways videogames enforce heteronormative views of the world. They note that this question concerns much more than "narrative and representational content." No doubt, having more queer characters and storylines is important, but any discussion of heteronormativity in videogames needs to go deeper, they argue, needs to question, for example, the procedures and mechanics of games. Joli St. Patrick and Avery Alder advocate "consideration of the ways in which specific mechanics, like statistics or character ownership in role-playing games, can reinforce heteronormative dominant values."[22] merritt k cites Edmond Chang and Robert Yang, both of whom have interrogated code as an engendering language, the former asking "whether digital games can even meaningfully be queer when we consider the inherently binary structuring of all such works."[23] And what of the spaces in which we play games? Clark and merritt k ask us to consider how, for queer and trans people, family game nights and internet cafes can be spaces of unwelcome emotional and physical risk. Similar to the kinds of questions avant-garde and experimental theater artists have asked about the dramatic text, the stage, the audience, and so on, a dramaturgy of videogames must continually push against assumption and convention.

Not coincidentally, some of the most incisive, memorable, and fun thinking about videogames has come from artists who situate videogames within theatrical contexts. For *[giantJoystick]* (2006), Mary Flanagan created a six-foot-tall joystick that gallery visitors could use to play games projected on a nearby wall. On one hand, it is an obvious and quite hilarious pun on the phallic obsessions of the videogame industry and many of its players. On the other hand, it is an invitation to play in a different way. It's not easy to use a six-foot joystick! It requires patience and teamwork. Brian Schrank writes, "Figuring out how to collectively play the thing becomes the game, turning players into artistic performers."[24] In *Bad News: A Game of Death and Communication*, the UC Santa Cruz Expressive Intelligence Studio applies a similar strategy to the procedural generation of narrative space and character (figs. 4.2a and 4.2b). The player sits in a small booth with a window that allows them to interact with a live actor. The player is tasked with tracking down the next of kin of a body they have discovered in a small town. Meanwhile, a third person, out of sight and designated the "wizard," runs a computer program that generates the small town in which the body is found. The wizard responds to the player's queries and commands, procedurally generating information about whatever curious corner or denizen the player might encounter. They then pass that information to an actor (Ben Samuel), who improvises dialogue with the player in response.

The three channels of communication—player-actor, player-wizard, and actor-wizard—each require adept forms of play. Together they create a rich, dramatically compelling, and undeniably theatrical game experience—and, as Noah Wardrip-Fruin explains, they "leverag[e] the strengths of trained improvisers and computation systems both for narrative possibilities and for communication between the humans creating the performance."[25] Theatricalizing videogames can also foreground their geopolitical and ethical dimensions. In his 2007 work *Domestic Tension*, the Iraqi American artist Wafaa Bilal lived in a gallery space for a month during the U.S. occupation of Iraq while online participants shot (or attempted to stop others from shooting) a remote-controlled paintball gun at him. As he explains, the installation/performance/game "is designed to raise awareness about the life of the Iraqi people and the home confinement they face due to both the violent and the virtual war they face on a daily basis."[26] At the same time, it highlighted the callous cruelty enabled by anonymous online interactivity and the long history of representing non-Europeans in videogames as targets.

Ultimately, we affirm Michael Chemers's definition of dramaturgs as "the ones who question."[27] What is a videogame? is a question that is more productive to *ask* than to *answer*. But it's important that we ask that question the right way, considering with care the context, the diversity of platforms and players, and the assumptions we carry into every encounter with them.

Toward a Dramaturgy of Videogames

Figs. 4.2a and 4.2b. Images from *Bad News* showing the interplay of computational and digital technologies with live actors. *Photos courtesy of James Ryan, Benjamin M. Samuel, Adam J. Summerville, and Noah Wardrip-Fruin.*

WHAT DO WE DO WHEN WE PLAY A VIDEO GAME?

We shift now from what a videogame *is* to what we *do* with them. Typically, when we think of someone playing a game, the picture that comes to mind is someone sitting on a couch by themselves, controller in hand, fingers flicking, eyes intent on a glowing screen, nacho-flavored corn chips or cheese puffs optional but recommended.

This image of videogame play is a stereotype: simplistic, nostalgic, and far from the facts of the matter. More to the point, if we wish to be effective videogame dramaturgs, we need to consider the roles players play, the texts with which they interact, and the spaces in which they perform. Consider, for example, the game *Overwatch*. In many respects, *Overwatch* is a conventional videogame, a multiplayer first-person shooter in which one selects an avatar equipped with various kinds of weapons and abilities and competes with a small team against another small team in variations of king of the mountain, capture the flag, and so on. And yes, this mainly involves wiggling one's fingers over a controller of some sort while scanning the screen for visual cues and listening carefully for audio cues, an activity that works perfectly well on a couch. But this is only part of the player's performance. They may also participate in live in-game chat, trading tactical advice, trash talk, and casual conversation with their teammates, who may be complete strangers or good friends. There is no small amount of in-game time when they aren't shooting another avatar in the face. *Overwatch* provides the player with numerous "emotes"—dances, gestures, graffitilike stamps to apply on walls and floors—that allow them to interact in nonviolent ways with other players (indeed, there is a small but passionate BDSM community that has repurposed avatars and emotes so they "get their dom off" while playing a "healslut"[28]).

The dedicated *Overwatch* player can play the game in ways that don't involve a controller. They might, for example, spend time exploring *Overwatch*-focused websites, such as the official site of the game's producer, where they can keep up with changes in the game's mechanics and avatars, read digital comics and watch videos, get news about upcoming events, and get in touch with other *Overwatch* fans. They might visit fan-produced sites to discuss strategy and tactics or share stories they've written, pictures they've drawn, machinima they've produced, and costumes they've created. They might tune in to the latest match between the Guangzhou Charge and the Paris Eternal, two of the professional teams vying for the year's championship and the $1 million prize that comes with it. Or they might log on to their favorite Reddit forum to participate in the vibrant LGBTQ+ *Overwatch* community.

And they might be doing all this while they're shooting an opponent in their virtual face!

While not every videogame enjoys the support of a multinational corporation or the passionate international fandom surrounding characters like Tracer and D.Va, this kind of cross-platform, multimodal, performative, and utterly fun play is not at all unusual. Kiri Miller has written extensively about players of games like *Dance Central*, the videos they share of themselves dancing, and the community that has formed around them. She describes an intimate, honest, and supportive community that honors the "push and pull of trial and error" that comes with learning to dance.[29] And she shows the ways the dancers apply that ethos to overcoming shyness, achieving physical fitness, or coping with personal tragedy. Videogame dancers and cross-platform gamers epitomize the kinds of "social interaction and creative identity work" described by Michele Wilson, work that occurs not only in the game but across "the broader social network and the material conditions of access, including different devices . . . and different locations."[30]

That kind of cocreative activity is integral to one of the biggest trends in videogame entertainment: watching other players play. Platforms like Twitch.tv and eSports attract millions of viewers and generate billions of dollars in revenue. The 2014 *League of Legends* final in Seoul, Korea, was held in the same stadium that hosted FIFA World Cup games twelve years earlier; it boasted over forty-five thousand attendees and was broadcast to twenty-seven million online viewers in nineteen languages.[31] The performance of the professional gamers is fascinating in its own right, but even more so is that of the spectators. In an analysis of eSports consumers, Yuri Seo and Sang-Uk Jung demonstrate that eSports cultivate a "multifaceted social performance" in which spectators "adopt multiple roles" as players, viewers, and community members. Affirming the idea that videogame play is a complex, multifaceted, and mercurial activity, they show that eSports requires of its spectators a "nexus of understandings, tools, skills, and competencies" that blurs the line between the professionals who are the focus of attention and those whose attention is focused.[32]

The line between watching and playing is even more blurred in the world of livestreaming. Popular streamers like Ninja, Shroud, and TSM_Myth entertain millions by playing videogames in front of live online audiences and talking about it as they do so. Thousands of lesser-known, but no less beloved, others perform for much smaller, more intimate audiences. While the notion of playing a videogame and talking about it might sound fairly easy, when it happens on the streaming stage, it is decidedly not. Consider first the visual interface of Twitch.tv, one of the more popular platforms. Most of the screen is filled with a replica of the player-performer's own screen, which displays the game they are playing in real time. A small live image of the streamer typically appears in the bottom-left corner. One sees information about the stream (including code of conduct, subscription information, and so on) in another section and perhaps advertisements for companies that support the streamer. Finally, there is a column on the right side of the screen that displays a continually updating cascade of comments by spectators composed of text and emojis.

The variety of interfaces can be dizzying to the novice; however, as Rachel Linn notes, the total effect aims at the kind of intimate community that Kiri Miller observed among videogame dancers. "All of these features," Linn writes, "ease access between streamers and viewers, encouraging them to be in the moment with one another."[33] Which is not to say that those who stream (and those who watch) aren't doing something of breathtaking complexity and skill, especially when it comes not just to the creation of intimacy but to the presumption of intimacy among spectators. This is especially true of female streamers.

In a fascinating study of the professional streamers Kacey "Kaceytron" Kaviness and Tang "Eloise" Haiyun, Linn shows exactly how virtuosic a livestreaming performance can be, particularly for streamers who shoulder the additional burden of performing for a hostile, aggressive audience. Streaming involves multiple kinds of performance done simultaneously. The streamer plays the videogame, comments on the gameplay, monitors the live chat, and responds verbally to it. In other words, they play, talk, and read. For each of these activities, they construct a persona: within the game they play, as a person on view, and as a verbal respondent to written communications. The best streamers make all this look easy. Kaceytron and Eloise, both women, one of them Asian, not only play and comment for half a million followers with the same kind of skill as other top streamers but also have the additional burden of responding to the men who throw sexist and racist comments at them in the chat channel. But that's part of the "fun" of their performances. They "troll the trolls," as Linn puts it, with performances that "mockingly pla[y] up stereotypes often hurled at female streamers."[34]

Kaceytron, on one hand, parodies the hyper-sexualized "boob streamers," constructing a persona "that naively presumes sexual allure, pro-level skills, and all-around superiority to anyone she meets." Eloise, in contrast, plays the naive foreigner, asserting patently ridiculous opinions about U.S. culture, language, and history—for example, celebrating the June 4 victory of the United States over the alien horde under Will Smith's "tactful leadership." While all streamers construct personas, Kaceytron and Eloise construct "an imitation of themselves while a sea of viewers assault that imitation in an attempt to dismantle it." Linn admits that it's difficult, if not impossible, to come to terms with these performances—to decide whether they play into stereotypes or deconstruct them. Their mercurial, improvisatory nature confuses the line between insouciance and authenticity. Ultimately, she argues, the performances of live streamers reflect videogame culture's continuing "struggle with performance and the virtual body."[35]

Far less ironic but no less artful forms of play are staged by theater companies like EK Theater. Founded by Eddie Kim in 2007, the company's mission is "to keep the classics alive," which it does by staging theatrical entertainments in multiplayer videogame worlds such as *World of Warcraft, Minecraft, Grand Theft Auto, LittleBigPlanet 3*, and *Red Dead Redemption*. Stephanie Chan explains that Kim "views the videogame characters as marionettes or puppets, tools that can be used to perform a wide array of actions by getting creative within restraints." Beyond the challenge of manipulating avatars to express character, EK Theater must also address unique technical problems, including making sure that internet connections are consistent for all performers, microphones are functional, and timing is perfect.[36]

But technical excellence need not be the primary goal of videogame theater; indeed, in the same way that the trial and error of the theatrical production process can birth unexpected insights and innovations, the less-than-perfect performances that happen in the interface between enthusiastic players and videogames can produce remarkable, fun, even moving performances. Developed by Gina Bloom and the UC Davis ModLab, *Play the Knave* is best described as "Shakespeare karaoke."

Bloom describes the game as "an immersive, embodied experience of staging a scene from a Shakespeare play."[37] Up to four players stand in front of a large screen, in front of which is an inexpensive motion-capture device. Bloom describes the rest of the experience, which walks players through multiple production decisions:

> Users begin to craft their production of the scene by choosing set design (historical or fantastical), music, lighting, costumes/actors, and theater space (e.g., a proscenium or a thrust stage). Once these choices are selected, the screen shows a three-dimensional image of the theater stage the players have chosen, all done up to convey the selected setting, and each player's avatar (i.e., the costumed actor) appears on the stage ready to perform. Shakespeare's script lines scroll at the bottom of the screen, and in a kind of theater karaoke, the players perform, their gestures and voices mapped onto their avatars. The effect is that of seeing one's performance mirrored "live" on screen.[38]

As Bloom explains, *Play the Knave* "is inspired by an activity long popular among Shakespeare teachers: having groups of students perform scenes from a Shakespeare play in order to study its language, themes, plots, and characters." However, as anyone who has ever managed such an activity knows, it is difficult to get students both to comprehend simultaneously all the elements that go into a staged production and to take chances and experiment.[39]

Having witnessed students play on multiple occasions, we can affirm that this is never the case with *Play the Knave*. Indeed, we were struck by the enthusiastic fashion in which young people happily played avatars and characters that did not match their own identities. And we were excited by the fun the players had performing Shakespeare together. However, as systemic dramaturgs invested in crossing the boundaries between disciplines, we were most thrilled by the way *Play the Knave* "leverage[s] one discipline/practice against the other." As Bloom explains, "In the first case (theater), gaming is used to understand or produce theater: theater subsumes the game, and the resulting product or theory is considered as or in terms of theater. In the second case (gaming), theater provides models or tools for understanding how games work or for producing better games; in this case, gaming subsumes theater." In sum, "A session of *Play the Knave* is simultaneously both game play and theatrical work."[40]

WHO PLAYS THE VIDEO GAME?

Theater is a profoundly human endeavor, even if the performers are robots or light is cast by digital projectors controlled by offstage technicians. Thus one of the core responsibilities of a dramaturg is to assess the needs and expectations of the people involved in a production. Perhaps the most important group of people is the audience. Consideration of audience is one of the key factors in script selection. Does the company go with a classic, a dependable draw, hoping to court the regulars? Or does it take a risk with a new play or controversial production approach, aiming to challenge the tastes of the multiseason subscribers and attract newcomers? Consideration of audience is also a key factor in production decisions. What aspects of a script might be confusing, troubling, or offensive?

The dramaturg has the skills and knowledge to help a production team—whether those who focus on the stage or those who handle publicity and ticket sales—address these issues. The systemic dramaturg should also consider a broader set of questions that concern the people involved in a production: Who is directing? Designing? Casting? Performing? Who is lighting the stage? Managing the production? The ability to make a good choice about a script, a production, or a marketing strategy often depends on whether the right person is in the room to ask the right kinds of questions. In sum, the question, Who plays? implicates the theatrical gamut, from script selection to production process to audience reception. And it implicates the organizational context too: Who does the work? Who does the hiring? Who makes the decisions? Who determines what matters and to whom?

A dramaturgy of videogames should be no less concerned with the people who make and play and write and talk about them. Let's start with what kinds of people play videogames. There is a widely held stereotype of the videogame player: male, white, straight, middle-class, stuck in developmental limbo somewhere between high school and college. The truth is quite different. Since the first attempt to collect reliable data on gamers in 2008, scholars and market analysts have recognized that the community of videogame players is diverse in terms of race, ethnicity, gender, sexuality, age, and class and that gaming cultures vary widely within and across national boundaries, as do attitudes toward games, players, even the very labels *player* or *gamer* (an issue we'll return to in a moment).[41] A 2020 study by the Entertainment Software Association (ESA) identifies the average person who plays videogames in the United States as between thirty-five and forty-four years old, slightly less than half of them identifying as women.[42] But as relatively forward-looking as industry organizations like the ESA are in terms of paying attention to gender (at least in terms of data collection), they have not paid much attention to the way gaming is shaped by other identities or the histories and institutions that surround those identities. We simply don't have the same quality of data on nonwhite, nonstraight, nonbinary gamers. What data does exist suggests that, in respect to ethnicity, more Latinx and African Americans describe themselves as gamers than do whites and spend more time playing games.[43]

But data may not tell the whole story, particularly when it comes to telling the story of those who don't fit the straight, white, male, late-adolescent gamer stereotype. As Adrienne Shaw, Sarah Rudolph, and Jan Schnorrenberg note, "LGBTQIA* videogame players have not been fully recognized by the mainstream game industry," and while players "have always found ways to connect with one another and form communities that intersect their fandoms and LGBTQIA* perspectives," those communities and their archives have proven frustratingly ephemeral, and it has been difficult if not impossible to reconstruct their stories and their archives.[44] A dramaturgy of videogames should play a role in the preservation of the record and the telling of those stories.

Videogame cultures vary widely from region to region, so the question of Who plays? can't be answered without asking another question, Where do they play? And stereotypes tend to inform thinking about that too. When we think of the places where people play videogames, we tend to think of the United States, Western Europe, and Japan. The statistics tell a different story. Yes, the United States, Western Europe, and Japan are leaders in global revenues, but China is now the largest videogame market (48 percent of total global market revenue in 2020), and gamers from Asia Pacific constitute over a third of the total population of video game players. Australia, Canada, Russia, Mexico, and

Brazil each have large gaming communities, as do India, Indonesia, Saudi Arabia, and Turkey. The smartphone platform continues to grow the most rapidly, as the cost is far lower than for a dedicated console or personal computer, making it the most popular platform for gaming, with 48 percent of players regularly playing on phones or tablets (in the United States, that amounts to 209 million players).[45]

But to tell a more complete story about who plays videogames, it's not enough to simply add a basket of new players and places into the mix. Phillip Penix-Tadsen argues that any effort to understand a particular regional videogame culture must account for the particular relationship of citizenship to commodity culture, for the specific interrelationships of videogames with other commercial media in a given space, for the histories of hardware and software development, and for other economic and political factors that shape how videogame play happens and who makes it happen. As he puts it, "While the videogame industry is often described in global terms, it is important to pay attention to the ways cultural context affects videogame meaning, especially in areas outside the globally dominant markets." In the absence of government support and training programs, with endemic "digital poverty" that denies many access to digital media, Latin American designers have "historically produced their work in an atmosphere of relative isolation . . . working with small groups of friends, family, and associates and figuring out the process of putting games together from scratch."[46] Which is not to say that designers haven't made remarkable games or that national governments aren't now supporting the industry; rather, Who plays videogames? is not a question that can be answered in the abstract.

And it is often answered in ways that reflect endemic bias against certain kinds of players and certain kinds of games. Ask any group of people, "Who plays videogames?" and you will see a significant number raise their hands—in our experience, roughly a third to half of a given group. Remind them that games on phones—known as casual games—also count as videogames, then ask the question again. You'll see more hands. The often intensely insular, misogynist character of videogame culture can make identification as a "gamer" deeply fraught. The reluctance of "casual" players to identify themselves as gamers— and vice versa, to be recognized by those with the time and resources to play more often and with a higher degree of challenge—is not just an issue for the gaming community. As Shira Chess and Christopher A. Paul, as well as others, have shown, the bias against casual gaming in the videogame industry distorts the way academics study videogames, videogame players, and videogame culture.[47]

That bias is more than a question of marketing. For thousands of people around the world, playing videogames is more than a pastime; it's an identity. And that identity has been weaponized against others who are deemed unworthy of or alien to the gaming community. In 2013, months before the events that instigated Gamergate, Simon Parkin wrote a column for *New Statesman* magazine titled "If You Love Games, You Should Refuse to Be Called a Gamer." It begins with several anecdotes: a nationally broadcast American videogame awards show during which host Joel McHale makes a transphobic joke; a Microsoft representative sexually harassing a woman while they played a fighting game; a YouTuber making inappropriate comments and posting a series of "rape face" videos; the hostility expressed on internet forums toward Anita Sarkeesian and her *Tropes vs Women* videos.

Parkin sees nothing wrong with the desire to "form groups with like-minded people" and affirms the leveling power of the medium: "Games do not distinguish between privilege and under-privilege, between rich and poor, between gay and straight, between loved and abused: in their dimension, everybody is given an equal opportunity."[48] So while players, marketers, and commentators regularly speak of a "gaming community," all too often, that term names only one kind of player and one kind of community—that of the "hardcore gamer" who has the time and space to spend hundreds of hours on a game; the straight, white, Western, cis player who doesn't want "politics" involved in his gameplay; the angry isolate protecting the values of "true gaming" against "social justice warriors" and the "casuals." (This was discussed in more depth in chapter 3.)

As dramaturgs, we feel it is important to be conscious of the ways that the tastes and values of some communities can dominate and marginalize those of other communities. This isn't just a question of expanding our taste spectrums. Our understanding of the history of the medium can be distorted. Consider how this works in theater. In *Highbrow/Lowdown*, David Savran tells the story of how anxiety about "lowbrow" entertainment—dance music and unscripted, popular, and enthusiastically commercial entertainments—shaped the development of "legitimate theater." In *Playing Underground*, Stephen Bottoms upends the conventional wisdom that the 1960s was an era of performer-centered ensembles and director-driven productions, showing instead the robust and widespread presence of playwrights and script-based theater. Savran and Bottoms alert us not just to scholarly bias but also to artists that we may have forgotten or underappreciated because of that bias.

This kind of critical historiography is just as vital for the dramaturgy of videogames. In the United States, videogames are often equated with toys and juvenile forms of play. This distorts the facts of the matter (including the fact that this attitude is not prevalent in other countries), but more harmful still is the distortion that such stereotypes can inflict on our understanding of videogames, the uses to which they are being put, and who makes and play them. The gamer stereotype does not accommodate the older adults who are part of Semi Ryu's VoicingElder project. The gamer stereotype does not account for the way they use interactive virtual puppets and digitally mediated storytelling to cultivate sharing and storytelling with younger people. The VoicingElder project is not just a powerful therapeutic experience for those who play it; it is also a perfect example of the powerful creative potential that can be unlocked when we move beyond conventional answers to the question, Who plays videogames?[49]

The term *player* proves less than optimal when it comes to the line between those who play videogames and those who make them. Since their earliest days as an entertainment medium, videogames have provided tools so that players with a yen for making could build their own variants on the games they purchased. Games like *Super Mario Maker* and *Minecraft* are designed around the fun of doing your own thing. But the erasure of the line between player and maker is most evident in the "modding" community.

Game designer Will Wright considers the growth of modding culture as a sign that "game development is becoming a very collaborative process between the game developers and the players."[50] Modding culture emerged in the early 1990s among players of personal-computer-based first-person shooter games like *Castle Wolfenstein*, *Duke Nukem*, and *Doom*. Code-savvy players created new levels for favorite games, and companies like Id, the maker of *Doom*, released their games' source codes to the general public. But modding achieved something like a critical mass in 2002 when Valve Software released its online service Steam, whose offerings included a new level for its smash hit *Half-Life*, an add-on created entirely by fans. Industry attitudes toward modding vary. Some companies encourage it, viewing it as a way to sustain fan engagement and ensure rapid response within a highly competitive market, while others aggressively fight it, worried about damage to earnings and intellectual property claims.[51] As systemic dramaturgs (and videogame players!), we're excited by modding, which we feel democratizes the creative process and diversifies design perspectives. However, we're concerned about the way modding opens creators to exploitation. Julian Kücklich sees modding as part of a broader trend in creative industries he calls "playbour," a portmanteau of *play* and *labour*. He notes that modders "are rarely remunerated for taking the risks the industry itself shuns" and are just as rarely recognized or remunerated for the work they do, despite the value they generate for game companies.[52]

> Through modding, computer code that represents images and game play is stripped of context and redesigned by the player or group of players, passed through communities of fan developers who may create/appropriate and incorporate other bits of their cultural experience into the new game environments they create and eventually thrust it out into the internet where it may be downloaded by thousands who will then play the new code, layered onto the old.
>
> —Kyle Andrew Moody, "Modders," 30–31

Finally, limited understandings of videogame players may keep us from engaging critically and creatively with forms of "play" that have massive, material, mortal impact on real-life people and places. Jenna Altomonte has explored digital performances created in response to the use of telepresent technology, remotely guided weapon platforms, and electronically mediated representations in war. She shows how the creative work of artists like Wafaa Bilal, Adel Abidin, and Joseph Delappe deploys the technologies and tropes of videogame play to expose the insidious ways contemporary warfare depends on the specific skills and attitudes fostered by the mainstream videogame industry. And they reveal the insidious way those technologies and tropes have been used by corrupt authority to obfuscate the systemic trauma of the war on terror.[53]

Toward a Dramaturgy of Videogames

While a systemic dramaturgy of videogames should never lose sight of the actual people who make and play videogames, we would be remiss if we didn't attend to some of the more philosophically recondite aspects of the question, Who plays videogames? After all, videogames are one of the only other media besides theater in which a player commonly refers to an imaginary character as themselves. In the same way that an actor might say, "While I was terrified of Stanley at that moment, I also felt powerfully vindicated that my assumptions about him were correct," a videogame player might say, "When I discovered the magical gauntlet, I knew that I would be able to vanquish the troll." Videogames depend on the cybernetic interplay of human, machine, and text, an interplay that is mediated by the technological interface of a given videogame and the representational affordances that provide a sense of in-game embodiment. Gabriel Patrick Wei-Hao Chin has explored how kinesthetic empathy functions in videogames—in other words, the particular ways that physical embodiment in videogames produces affective identification. He builds on the work of Sarah Whatley and others who have shown that the peculiarly intense kinesthetic experience that occurs in virtual environments "complicate, entangle, and elide the division between self and other, watcher and performer, body and machine."[54] Why is this?

Chin argues that when we play a videogame, we experience two kinds of "blurring" between ourselves and the game. First, there is the blurring between body and machine (i.e., our hands and a controller). Second, there is the blurring between ourselves and the in-game avatar (i.e., our mind and the graphical representation of ourselves in the game, whether abstract or anthropomorphic). Together, the "body-object relation with the computer, console, keyboard, or controller" and the kinesthetic-empathetic relationship with the avatar blurs, if not erases entirely, the distinction between observer and performer.[55] We find this absolutely fascinating—but also not altogether unfamiliar. The thrill of participatory and immersive theater is generated by playing with the boundary between spectators and actors. And for actors, the idea that one might exist simultaneously within the reality of a character while at the same time observing that character is old hat. But that is the benefit of systemic dramaturgy's interdisciplinary, cross-media methodology: by expanding our understanding of dramaturgy from what it *is* to what it *might be*, we encourage a conversation between the familiar and the unprecedented and provide an opportunity for new kinds of conversations and new kinds of creativity.

THE SIX DRAMATURGIES OF VIDEOGAMES

Having considered these three questions—What is a videogame? What do we do when we play a videogame? Who plays videogames?—it is time to codify a dramaturgy of videogames. We have identified six ways that the knowledge and skills of the systemic dramaturg can be employed to cultivate creativity and critical consciousness in the interface between videogames and theater:

1. Ensure that the historical relationship between theater and videogames is properly represented in histories of theater and performance.
2. Assist directors, designers, and actors in the interpretation of plays and other performance texts in which videogames appear, whether incidentally or as a significant part of plot, character, or setting.
3. Facilitate collaboration among artists, technicians, and researchers in the designing of experiences in traditional theater spaces that use videogame technologies or other playable media.
4. Provide practical advice, critical perspectives, and innovative concepts to artists and companies wishing to create theatrical experiences that are interactive, environmental, gamified, or participatory, as well as to designers of videogames and other interactive digital experiences.
5 Educate audiences and promote productions through the use of videogames and other playful media.
6. Critique videogames and improve literacy about aspects of videogames, videogame play, and videogame culture that concern storytelling, the artistic use of space, character, interpersonal relationships, the modeling of affect, and other theatrical questions.

INTERVIEW 5

GENERATIONS

JENNIFER HALEY ON THE THEATER GAME

Jennifer Haley is a playwright whose work delves into ethics in virtual reality and the impact of technology on our human relationships, identity, and desire. She won the 2012 Susan Smith Blackburn Prize for her play *The Nether*, which premiered with Center Theatre Group in Los Angeles and has been produced off-Broadway, on London's West End, across the United States, and internationally. Other plays include *Neighborhood 3: Requisition of Doom*, a horror story about suburban videogame addiction, and *Froggy*, a noir thriller with interactive media. Haley has worked with the Royal Court Theatre, Headlong, MCC, Sonia Friedman Productions, Woolly Mammoth, the Humana Festival of New American Plays, the Banff Centre, Sundance Institute Theatre Lab, O'Neill National Playwrights Conference, the Lark, PlayPenn, and Page 73. For television, she has written on Netflix's *Hemlock Grove* and *Mindhunter*. She is a member of New Dramatists in New York City and lives in Los Angeles, where she founded the Playwrights Union.

MIKE SELL: What does theater as a medium afford you when it comes to exploring videogames, videogame players, and the culture of videogame play?

JENNIFER HALEY: Well, theater offers—and I learned this term from studying with Paula Vogel—a plastic space. You can use the plasticity of the space to your advantage. For instance, one way in which I use this with *Neighborhood 3* is by having my characters be types—son type, daughter type, father type, mother type—and having multiple roles played by a few actors. In some high schools and universities, the different parts are played by all different people just to accommodate the larger casting, which is cool, but for the most part it works organically the other way, because in a videogame you have one actor (the player) playing a variety of roles as avatars in a similar way. So, when you go into a game, you choose your avatar type. In *World of Warcraft*, I'm going to be a male or female and a troll or an elf or whatever. You have these prototypes. Using the actors as prototypes for the various characters gives the audience an entry point into the concept of how videogames work, how they overlap with the way that theater works.

In theater, you accept the plasticity of the space—you can totally accept that one actor can play a variety of characters, and you accept the reality of their character in the moment of that scene. So in some ways, there's already an overlap between virtual worlds and theatrical worlds. The world of theater creates a virtual space that involves the audience, and the actors are like avatars—you move them around to tell stories and focus the audience in certain directions.

I think that there is an interactive quality built into the theatrical space as well. As an audience member, you may not be driving the course of the story, although there are some cases where that happens, but this is similar to player interaction in videogames. In my plays, the audience is passively watching the story, but still there are [interactions] in the ways that I've described, and I can probably even go further into this in terms of what's real versus not real. In his book *Great Reckonings in Little Rooms*, Bert O. States, the phenomenologist, points out how something that is extraordinarily real onstage can take you out of the stage moment. So in many ways, because of that plasticity, theater is a perfect space for exploring digital culture, and it's just a question of learning to play with it, because the last thing I want is to see someone onstage typing into a computer.

SELL: This happens at the end of *The Nether*, when we see the in-real-life bodies of the characters Doyle and Sims enact the same script and gestures they did via their avatars earlier, avatars that were quite different than the ones we see now. That experience of watching those bodies, those aged and weathered bodies acting out this delicate, sensitive, loving moment, is just a knockout.

MICHAEL CHEMERS: Is this why you make theater and not videogames or some other kind of media? Is it that plasticity, that liveness, that presence? Is that what compels you to do theater, or is there is there something else about it?

HALEY: I think the easy answer is that I started out in theater and I was an actor for a long time. TV and film always seemed like a very distant and separate

Interview 5: *Generations*

thing until I came out of graduate school. So, now I live in LA and I'm actually having quite a good time translating into televisual media. I'm working on *The Nether* as a TV show, and I've been working on and off and on for a while to figure out it's an entirely different conversation how to translate these plays into television because the media is so different. We have to tell the story in a completely different way, a much less plastic way. But I am interested in making a living and retirement and exposure and having a wider conversation than with the few hundred people you can reach in a theater. But other media have their own pleasures and their own surprises. For example, the basic storyline of *The Nether* will make up the first season of the television show, but there are a lot of different stories I want to tell in that space. TV is going to be a great help in being able to focus in on the characters and follow their other arcs.

That being said, I don't intend to leave the theater because of the excitement of that live space. I don't think it's anything that I'll ever be able to give up. The challenges of that live space are so profound, and I love a great challenge. And actually, after writing those tech plays, I wanted to write a "living room play." I wrote one called *Sustainable Living*. I wanted to explore the tropes of the living room play: how do you set up those tropes and how do you knock them down?

SELL: That's something that I see across many of your works. You're fascinated with different kinds of narrative systems, with the way these stories work. You're *playing* with genre and you're playing with those tropes.

HALEY: I try to, I try to. Yes, yes. When I was at school, I was given a prompt by a teacher, which was "Write what you hate." I was responding to that prompt when I wrote *The Nether* because I was thinking about how much I hated police procedurals, how easy and pat they were, how the violence is very gratuitous and usually involves a young woman (fig. i5.1). And I realized that the power of that prompt is that if you can hate something, you feel kind of passionate about it. I was passionate about taking this idea of a police procedural, turning it on its head, making it completely surprising and different.

With *Neighborhood 3*, I morphed that idea into being about videogames. My script was originally focused on the idea of the supernatural occurrences in this neighborhood, but the underlying danger has to do with the relationships between the generations. It was like a potential exorcism going on. The different scenes were systematically related but didn't add up into that sculptural sort of traditional narrative that kind of builds and builds and builds. I came to a crossroads with that where I could have kept it more in this meditative experimental

Interview 5: *Generations*

Fig. i5.1. Two images from the Royal Court's 2012 production of *The Nether*. On the left, Morris (Amanda Hale) confronts Sims (Stanley Townsend) about his actions in virtual reality: "We can't control a person's body. Yours is free to walk out the door." On the right is the Victorian virtual reality in which Sims, in the form of his avatar, Papa, abuses and murders the simulated girl Iris. Design by Es Devlin. *Photos courtesy of Es Devlin.*

place or I could do that more traditional arc, but because I am a populist at heart, I wanted that arc, because I knew that a greater number of people would embrace that. That's the way we tell stories, and it gives you forward momentum and revelations. I felt like it was going to make the difference between the play being this experimental piece that a few people know about or a piece that a lot of people would do—and sure enough, that's what happened.

CHEMERS: Mike and I are interested in getting dramaturgs to think about the interactions between different media in a systemic way. Your work provokes deep thinking about systems of representation like genre, traditions of playwriting, theatricality, and staging. All of these are systems, and your characters rise or fall based on their facility with navigating these systems.

HALEY: Oh, interesting. To speak to that about *Neighborhood 3*, I've always thought that the suburban environment is like a very well-controlled virtual environment. A handful of probably male architects came up with this, you know, "We're on this grid and you've got four different homes and two different kinds of brick to choose from." It's real life, but it's like a videogame in that your choices are

188

Interview 5: *Generations*

delivered to you by a system. Like in a game, you lose your creativity and the ability to *wander.*

SELL: *Froggy* is a piece that is process oriented and very much about the different kinds of screens that one might use in the theater, whether narratively or in terms of design. You've got something that is, on one hand, completely live and depends on having real people there in the room watching and interacting, but it's also about mediated experience.

HALEY: Yeah. In *Neighborhood 3* and *The Nether,* I don't really specify how they should be done. Some directors have incorporated digital media; some have not. With *Froggy,* we have a production designer, set designer, sound designer, and we're going for a full-on experience like the actors are working in sync with all of the media. And it's all live, so the sound mixer is right there during the performance switching up the music based on the action. The actors are not waiting for some prerecorded thing. The entire thing has a soundtrack; it's very cinematic. We have screens to project on, but also the set designer is building a building. We're playing with vertical lines—when they're open, you can see through them, and then when they're closed, you can project on them. We have a TV that shows up a lot in that play; it's one of the few actual props. Our projection designer is able to project onto the TV as well. So, we have this huge playground and we were finally able to put a bunch of stuff together.

Just this past December, we did a workshop at La Jolla Playhouse. From that, we got a grant through the San Diego Foundation, with the director Matt Barros, the artistic director of Diversionary Theatre down in San Diego. For us, there was a kind of turning point of the whole play, a section that in some ways had been the vaguest and the most rewritten of the play. We put our heads together with our projection designer, Jared Mezzocchi, and we talked through how it could be done with media. Jared actually calls it "mediaturgy." It was a really fascinating moment. When we did it in workshop, I felt like for the first time that moment really worked.

SELL: You're describing a close interaction among a writer and a technician and a designer, and you're finding something that is dramatically meaningful, something that could only happen if you all were working in sync.

HALEY: In *Froggy,* some of the media is prerecorded, which is the woman remembering the videogame. You see scenes from the videogame, her memories, and stuff like that. But *Froggy* is also an examination of media itself *and* the entertainment business, so in the final section, the main character realizes that she is actually being filmed so that her actions can be used as content in future iterations of

189

Interview 5: *Generations*

this videogame. The way we talked through it with Jared that was so engaging was that the audience has just been fed this wall of media the whole time, and suddenly they're watching a piece of media that is actually being recorded live in the space. So they're seeing the stage replicated in the media with the character. It generates a great kind of telescoping effect and a breakdown of the world. Dramaturgically, it satisfies me that, after this wall of media, now suddenly you're shown a space that you recognize as the space that you are actually in.

SELL: Your other digital media plays, *Neighborhood 3* and *The Nether*, raise similar challenges, particularly for people who are ambivalent or lack knowledge about videogames and digital culture.

HALEY: Well, I've seen *Neighborhood* and *The Nether* staged with almost no media and then with full-on media. I think they're both successful. I actually still feel like the success of the piece comes down to how well the actors capture the humanity of the characters. With *Neighborhood 3*, I've seen productions where the walk-throughs are almost too explicit. One production literally had a first-person-point-of-view film of someone walking down the street, and to me that was too literal. You were taking away the audience's right to imagine that space.

CHEMERS: One of the pleasures of *Neighborhood 3* is that a great deal of it is written in the hacker slang leet [aka 1337] language, which is an entirely visual language. As a dramaturg, I would recommend some kind of visual representation of that language. Do you agree with that notion?

HALEY: It's never really been important to me that the audience understand that. I'm actually not even familiar enough with leet speak to know about those numbers or anything. I wrote in that format because I felt like it captured a sense of breakdown of communication, almost like text messaging. But especially in the early days, people who were producing it asked me how to present it, how heavily they should hit it. My response was always that slightly broken forms of communication were more naturalistic than those beautiful sentences that just pour out, where the actor speaks a whole block of text and then pauses. But the way we actually speak, we are constantly thinking and reforming, reformulating our thoughts. If I were directing my own play, I would have the actors hit these pauses ever so lightly, so that after a while, it actually just starts to feel like the way people really speak.

SELL: The language itself, as well as our attempt to decode it, takes on a kind of concrete reality on stage. That feels especially true of *Breadcrumbs*, where you have, on one hand, a woman suffering from dementia struggling to write an autobiography and her troubled caregiver, who has her own stakes in the telling of that story.

HALEY: With *Breadcrumbs*, I was definitely thinking about how, if we don't have language anymore, can we put our own identities together at all? How much is identity as we know it, or as we think we understand it? How much is it dependent upon us being able to string these words and thoughts together?

SELL: That sounds like a pretty good description of theater!

CHEMERS: Theater as a system.

HALEY: I'm so glad, really glad you said this, because I'm also very interested in systems. It's so interesting that you latched on to that exact same word. It goes back all the way to when I was about thirteen years old. I wanted to go to computer camp, so I learned BASIC. I've always been interested in technology, which for me is just a question of how things work. Computer languages are interesting to me. In fact, one of the ideas I want to explore in *The Nether* as a TV show is that the code for the Hideaway computer system is keyed to voice commands, so it's actually a spoken language, not a written one. That control over that code means verbal control over those languages. Figure out where the code comes from, and you can figure out that language. And if you can do that, you can break into the code.

In *The Nether*, I was interested in exploring the question of freedom of speech. Speech is expressed in code, which is now building technological systems, which is formulating our reality. There's a legal realm I explore here, based on an actual case where the government had gone after some hacker, but the hacker actually won that case arguing that his code was free speech. That's one of the ideas that I'm able to develop in a bigger story in the television medium. There's so much going on in the world today with free speech and what is allowed as free speech and what isn't. And there's overlap in there, somewhere, I want to tease out. I think it's easy to underestimate how much speech develops our sense of reality.

CHEMERS: *Neighborhood 3* and *The Nether* share a tension around the belief that the players of the game will start to act out in real life the violent fantasies that occur in the videogames. In 2004, there was the case in the UK of Warren Leblanc. Leblanc was believed to have been imitating the videogame *Manhunt* when he killed his friend with a claw hammer. Then in 2011, after your play was first produced, there was the case of a Philadelphian named Kendall Anderson who killed his mother with a claw hammer after she took his PlayStation away. This reminds me of the kids in *Neighborhood 3* who scream if you take away their consoles, and of course, there's the presence of a claw hammer as an important prop.

HALEY: It has to do with the feeling that is generated around digital culture. Obviously, if videogames were really affecting our behavior, then *Grand Theft Auto*

Interview 5: *Generations*

would be causing all kinds of chaos. Clearly, that's not the case. But to kill your parents because they won't let you get on a videogame—that's the danger of it. You can get addicted to those alternate realities, and if anyone gets in the way of that, then there's going to be trouble.

CHEMERS: This brings us to the question of empathy and the failure of empathy between the parents and the children in *Neighborhood 3*.

HALEY: I think it moves around one thing. One of the things I was interested in about *Neighborhood 3* was that younger viewers were zeroing in on those aspects of it that spoke to them, and older viewers were zeroing in on their fear that the younger generation might get lost in these games. Both generations were connecting to different aspects of the play. I'm also interested in that older generation who are not videogaming, introducing them to what it's like to get caught up in a game like that. On the other hand, one of the huge challenges I found with all of these pieces is, how do I educate people who don't play games or know about code? How do I convey how this whole virtual reality could work, not just in an ideal sense, but in a real technical sense, without heavy exposition and without explaining to gamers and coders and programmers who already know how that works? In terms of trying to work with technology onstage, how do I find that bit of language, that way of conveying an idea, that may educate one group without talking down to another group because we're coming at these concepts from different places?

CHEMERS: Well, every year I make about 350 students, mostly between the ages of eighteen and twenty-two, read your play, and they tend to side with the parents! They think the kids are assholes. It's surprising to me!

HALEY: That's great. I love that. That's funny. Thinking about empathy, in *Neighborhood 3*, the parents are more clueless than anything else, and their failure to really raise their children right in some ways indicates they're just big children themselves. They haven't figured out whatever formula it is in your life that gives you a real sense of meaning and a place to stand.

To come back full circle, it's down to tropes and archetypes. We always identify with the underdog. We like to identify with the underdog. We have a natural resistance to authority. So I think we'd be more on side of the kids if the parents were purposely trying to keep the kids down. But when we realize it's just sort of this cluelessness on the part of the parents, we also realize it's the kids that have the upper hand, so we empathize with the parents. In *The Nether*, Detective Morris is the authority, and it's Sims who's being repressed. They're trying to control him and his freedom of speech.

Interview 5: *Generations*

I wrote the first draft pretty quickly over the course of a month as a writing exercise with the playwrights' group that I'm with here in LA, and I didn't really do any research. I really started doing research *after* I had the draft. I just didn't want research to inform me too much. But then, once I wrote it, I thought, "Is any of this truth? Is any of this real?" And so, I started doing some googling around and I found that there's a Japanese videogame called *RapeLay*. When I found out there was an actual game with this kind of content, I was just furious. I was writing from the perspective of a liberal free-speech advocate, asking whether or not this sort of thing can even be policed, and then I find out there's an example of this in real life. Suddenly, my moral indignation kicked in, and I thought, "There's no way this kind of game should be out there for anyone to play, particularly for a young man to play a game where you can kidnap a mother and her children."

Once *The Nether* is on television, I'll be curious to see what happens. Right now, I am writing scenes that involve a real missing little girl who's been photographed, and Papa has used her likeness to create the Hideaway game avatar. The detective won't know if that's the real child or not, whether the real child has been hooked up to the Hideaway. Our protagonist starts out in the FBI in the Violent Crimes against Children unit, and I've been talking to people and reading stuff that these detectives really have to look at. They have to look at stuff all the time. How do I even write about this stuff when I don't even want to see it? But in the television media, where you have to show microscopically what the character is seeing and thinking, and we do need to see to a certain extent a piece of content with this little girl, I'm wondering, "How much can the audience take?" We're on a sliding scale. When it's on-screen, it's so blatant, because you don't have the protection like you do in the theater of seeing the actress and knowing that ultimately she's safe. It should be interesting to see.

SELL: The other risk there is that you've got characters in the play who earn and deserve our sympathy, and that sympathy feels to me a lot more precarious on television when you're being exposed in a much more mediated way to these images, despite the fact that in the play, you've got an actual girl who comes forward and invites the other character to brutally murder her. It feels like the sympathy that generates such dramatic friction in *The Nether* is going to be put at risk on the small screen.

HALEY: How do you hold that line? How do you create that sympathy or empathy? They'll be doing a lot of stuff off scene, of course, which I think spares us a lot. In the European productions of the play, the way that their rehearsal and

Interview 5: *Generations*

performance schedules sort out, they have a much harder time using children, so they often do use young women. I've seen productions where they get really explicit onstage. I indicate in the script that when possible, you should use younger actresses, because I didn't want it to be that explicit. It's too disturbing.

CHEMERS: That's interesting. You want the actor to generate empathy, but not by situating them within explicit sex and violence. The first time I read the play, I was concerned about the actress, if it was a little girl in the role of Iris. That was really disturbing. Of course, I was thrilled by that disturbance, even in the absence of explicit representation.

HALEY: I have a fun story about that. I workshopped the play at the O'Neill, and we had a college student playing Iris. And it was really creepy because they did more with her onstage. And then we went to the Lark, and I wanted to see what this feels like with an actual child. We found a twelve-year-old actress named Maya, and she came into rehearsal. The director and I were sweating bullets. We sat around the table to begin rehearsal, and the director said, "Does anyone have any questions about the piece before we read it?" Maya raised her hand and said, "So, that last scene, is that a memory or a dream?" And I was just like, we got this.

Maya came when it was done in New York. There was one show with a talkback afterwards. Maya, she was sixteen by this point, came to that talkback, and there were a couple of audience members who were very concerned about this actress and so on, and Maya stood up and she said, "I did this role four years ago, and I'm sixteen now, and I can tell you it was one of the best things I've ever done. And I wasn't scared of the material because the concepts were all out there. It wasn't a secret, and the adults were forthcoming about the content and what was going on, and I felt like at that age I already knew that was going on." To have it spoken, to have it all on the table in a safe space, was much better than, "Oh no, speak/see/hear no evil and then evil doesn't exist." It doesn't work like that. Across the board, the younger actresses in that role have all been crackerjacks. I have a dream of, you know, in another few years when all of these Irises are getting to be young adults, having like an Iris convention, and I get to ask them, "Hey, have I screwed any of you up?"

CHEMERS: Well, that's a play right there.

5

THE UNCANNY MOUNTAIN AND *NEIGHBORHOOD 3: REQUISITION OF DOOM*

the house you want is third from the left
as you face the cul de sac
all the houses look the same
be careful

. . . .

like all the other houses
this house will have a
flesh colored brick façade
and a welcome mat in front of the door

hint: if you kneel down and
take a closer look at this mat
you will see the word
'welcome' becomes
'help me'

—Jennifer Haley, *Neighborhood 3*

These are the spooky opening lines of Jennifer Haley's play *Neighborhood 3: Requisition of Doom (N3RD)*, which premiered at the Actors' Theatre of Louisville's Humana Festival in 2008. It is presented as a voiceover but intended as the theatrical version of a videogame "walk-through." The walk-through is a convention of game culture that describes the step-by-step process for completing an in-game task. Walk-throughs can be dry, utilitarian affairs, as is typical when presented in written form, or more performative, as tends to be the case with their video versions, which allow gamer geeks to show off their knowledge, skills, and personality. They can be quite entertaining.

The nine walk-throughs we hear in Haley's play are not just entertaining but also distinctly theatrical. First, while they are presented as walk-throughs of the fictional videogame featured in the play, their primary role is to provide hints and clues so the audience can piece together the thematic arc. Second, they are voiced from a body whose ontological status is as uncertain as anything else in the theater. We cannot see who is speaking, but we know they're here with us in the theater. Or are the walk-throughs recorded? And who exactly is saying these words? Are they a character in the play or an online semicelebrity providing fans of N3RD the guidance they need to win the game? Or are we to understand them as existing in our world, a fourth-wall-breaking presence like those we find in the works of Bertolt Brecht or in the direct-address moments of Shakespeare and Marlowe? This instability of voice and position is appropriate for a play about an innovative videogame technology that transposes a player's real-life neighborhood into the terrain of the game's zombie-hunting pleasures. As it happens, this kind of uncanny doubling and trebling, with all the uncertainty it produces, informs the play more generally, from the characters who exist simultaneously inside and outside the game to the technological and interpersonal forces that transform familiar loved ones into inhuman others deserving of violence. This makes this play an ideal case study for a dramaturg thinking systemically about digital technology specifically and representation more broadly.

A PLAY THAT PLAYS WITH VIDEOGAMES

Neighborhood 3: Requisition of Doom tells the story of a wealthy suburban American community suffering profound emotional and interpersonal crisis. The seeming source of that crisis is the neighborhood children's obsession with a videogame, an obsession that rewards antisocial behavior and leads to acts of brutal violence. But that crisis is not the only one suffered by the residents of this neighborhood. There are other problems riddling this affluent community: alcoholism, mental illness, adultery, mendaciousness, sexual abuse, and apathy. Further, it's suggested that one of the adults murdered his children and may have

The Uncanny Mountain

killed and mutilated a neighbor's pet. This doubling of concerns—one new (videogames), one old (suburban life)—is one of the reasons we find Haley's play both fascinating and relevant to the concerns of systemic dramaturgy. *N3RD* dramatically represents the technological and affective structures that shape contemporary life, showing that videogames are both cause and consequence of the problems plaguing the neighborhood. Thus it demands from those who produce it a systemic understanding of the play's content and the specific challenges that accompany the task of staging videogames, videogame players, and videogame culture.

To recall, our book is designed to enable dramaturgs to work and play effectively in the borderlands between theater practice and new media. In previous chapters, we've examined how new media like videogames both resemble and diverge from traditional theater, and therefore how dramaturgs who lack extensive experience with new technologies might nevertheless participate in the development of humane technocultural practices. In this chapter, we put these ideas into practice by describing the questions and challenges posed by Haley's play. Our analysis of this play drives home our twofold observation that, to properly understand technology, we need to stage that technology, and to properly stage that technology, we need to understand theater itself as a technology. We find *N3RD* particularly relevant to this project because it is a play not only about a new technology but of the effect of a new technology on the capacity to empathize. Haley's play targets the widespread (at least in the United States) concern about the ways videogames affect their players' ability to feel and express their feelings, particularly about and toward others. By staging the question of the relationship between videogames and violence, Haley challenges both the simplistic reasoning that would argue that videogames cause violence and the simplistic reasoning that would argue that they do not. Furthermore, a systemic analysis of *N3RD* reveals that staging the videogame teaches us much about theater itself.

So, to the task. What does a dramaturg do when first considering a script for staging? One thing we do is take a long, hard, loving look at the text as text. What's the story? Who are the characters? What are the themes? How might we read the play in the context of other plays like it? This is an essentially textual process. The other thing we do is identify aspects of the script that might be challenging to our creative team or intended audience. This might be a simple question of cast and casting: How many characters are there? Or of setting: How many scenes are there, and in how many different places do they take place? Or of problematic language or structure: Does the play include the use of a racist term or a plot that takes a twist toward misogyny? Or of audience accessibility: Are there uses of language or situations that are alien or easily misunderstood?

In the case of *N3RD*, these two traditional responsibilities benefit from the perspectives of a systemic approach to dramaturgy. This is a play about videogames. But let's consider two ways of articulating that statement. We might put the emphasis on the last word: This is a play about *videogames*. So we have to consider what videogames are and mean in the play and what they might mean in a possible production. Haley's script is easy to misunderstand. It flirts with naive and tendentious attitudes about and stereotypes of videogames, videogame players, and videogame culture. To avoid a production that is naive and tendentious, the creative team needs to understand the specific kind of game that the characters play: a cooperative, multiperson, mixed-reality, first-person shooter game. And it requires knowledge of the specific kinds of affect videogame players evince while playing that kind of game. Why is that important? Haley's play explores the causes and consequences of what might be called an empathy gap between adults and children. That gap is exacerbated by the videogame the characters play. But it's also a scapegoat, demonized because of the alien behavior exhibited by the children while they play.

Let's shift the emphasis to the fourth word: This is a *play* about videogames. That leads to a more practical set of questions: How do we communicate what videogames, videogame players, and videogame culture are to those who might be unfamiliar with them? How do we stage the characters playing the game? How should an actor perform those walk-through voiceovers? How do we clearly signal the difference between moments when characters are in and out of the game—and the moments when that difference is purposefully confused? Most importantly, how do we stage the play so the questions it raises don't lead to simplistic, stereotypical conclusions? Haley's play both dramatically and theatrically scuttles conclusive arguments about the relationship between videogames and violence. A production of it should do the same.

DIPPING INTO THE UNCANNY

Now let's rephrase the statement as a question: Why would someone want to stage a play about videogames? That's a question that leads us to a larger surmise about theater as a medium. This surmise concerns a well-known design problem affecting technologies intended to appeal to a sense of emotional identification: the problem of the uncanny. In a 1919 essay, Sigmund Freud uses this term to describe the psychological phenomenon of "doubling," a kind of cognitive dissonance that occurs whenever humans make cultural representations of themselves. Like statues, dolls, and the concept of the soul, these doubles function to alleviate anxiety about human mortality by representing a life beyond the ordinary confines of the body, satisfying an infantile but primal desire for eternal life. If the double confuses the viewer as to whether it is in fact alive or dead, it winds up threatening that primal desire and exacerbating anxiety to the point of horror.

It is this phenomenon to which computer scientist Masahiro Mori refers in a 1970 article describing a curious response to technology he calls "the uncanny valley." Mori was interested in the ways that robotic and digital simulations of the human can become unsettling, ridiculous, even nauseating because of something being slightly "off" about their simulated humanity (fig. 5.1). Mori notes that, as robots and digital simulations come to resemble humans more and more strongly, they provoke a more positive emotional response, until a critical point when they look *almost, but not quite* human. The more difficult it is to tell whether the object is alive or artificial, the greater the sense of revulsion, represented by a graph with a sudden, dramatic dip.[1]

One of the things that make N3RD fun and fascinating is the sci-fi gimmick at its heart, which produces a variety of uncanny doubles. The fictional videogame uses global positioning technology to simulate in-game the player's real-world neighborhood, producing a "mixed reality," though exactly how those realities are mixed is never quite certain. Apart from that twist, the videogame is otherwise familiar, even banal: a multiplayer zombie-hunting adventure that indulges extreme, often gratuitous, hand-to-hand violence. Something else is familiar about

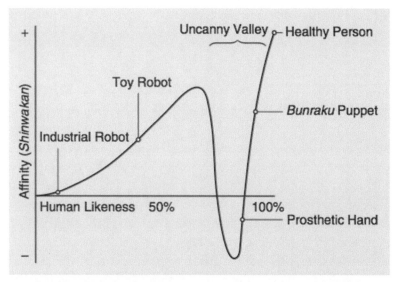

Fig. 5.1. Masahiro Mori's diagram charting the way the artificial representation of the human in robotic form affects our empathetic response to it. Mori suggests that a too-close resemblance that does not adequately disguise its mechanical qualities causes a failure in empathy. However, we see that Bunraku performers (and those who can perform perfectly as a "healthy person") do not cause this to occur. (We also note that prosthetics come in a variety of forms, and our responses to them may be more a question of experience than gut response.) Reprinted by permission from Mori, "Uncanny Valley," 99. © 2012 IEEE.

the play, though to a different sort of nerd community. Haley's script digs into one of the enduring topics of the modern dramatic canon: the deteriorating relationships between parents and children in a rapidly changing world. And it takes place in one of the tried-and-true settings of U.S. writers since at least the 1960s: the suburbs. N3RD recalls Edward Albee's *The American Dream*, Eric Bogosian's *SubUrbia*, Jackie Sibblies Drury's *Fairview*, and a host of other plays, movies, television shows, and songs, from Richard Kelly's *Donnie Darko* to Sonic Youth's *The Sprawl* to TV's *Roseanne*.

Finally, there are the zombies. While the walking dead are uncommon in theater, they are a time-tested trope in movies, as is their association with mindless conformity, dating at least as far back as George A. Romero's 1978 *Dawn of the Dead*, set in a suburban shopping mall just east of Pittsburgh. Haley, fluent in multiple pop culture dialects, knows that her audience is familiar with the hidden horrors of quiet suburbs, whether those horrors are designed to inspire thrills, high scores, or trenchant thoughts about the human condition.

Each of these tropes involves intense and confusing affect—the compulsive thrills of running and hiding and killing in a videogame, the seething but inexpressible anger and resentment between adult and child, the terror caused when a human is turned into a mindless machine of cannibalistic desire. Each involves the uncanny doubling of the human and the unsettling emotions that emerge as a result. The player of the videogame is doubled by their avatar, the child by their parent, the human by the zombie. Haley compounds and complicates the tropes. The game doubles the streets and denizens of the neighborhood, turning homes into places of thrilling terror and in-game achievement and mothers and fathers into zombies that must be destroyed. The Neighborhood Association enforces strict conformity of appearance—each house a perfect double of its neighbors. Parents insist their children become like them—successful, well adjusted, their pleasures properly calibrated and focused. But the children have come to understand that this only means joining a community of quiet desperation, hardly a community at all, so they choose a community of trash talk and make-believe violence.

The compounded doubling serves critical and dramatic ends. If staged well—that is, in a fashion that comprehends and communicates the entanglement of old social problems and new technologies—the audience for N3RD should come to understand that the videogame isn't the problem, at least not the only problem. Indeed, for the children, it's a kind of solution, providing them an escape, a community, and a cold, analytic view of the neighborhood in which they live.

Our immediate concern as systemic dramaturgs is the role of empathy in the play, especially the lack of empathy between neighbors, between parents and children, and between players and zombies. In the interest of financial and emotional security, the parents have traded their individuality for the superficial harmony enforced by the Neighborhood Association. This requires them to emotionally distance themselves from each other and their children. The walk-through notes that the houses all have a "flesh colored brick façade," a metaphor for the zombified parents who appear alive and are, in the game's ludic reality, nothing but lifeless shamblers that can (and must) be massacred. The adults have bought the subdivision's conformity package lock, stock, and barrel, and they live in abject terror lest the Neighborhood Association reprimand them for putting an unsanctioned garden gnome in the front yard. But they suffer from a litany of diseases of the affluent targeted by playwrights since Ibsen: hypocrisy, adultery, alcoholism, addiction, domestic abuse, neglect, and mental illness. Withdrawn, corrupt, and wracked with fear, the adults know they have lost contact with their children but can neither understand why nor muster up the necessary courage to rebuild their relationships.

We can't help but recall the final lines of Albee's *A Delicate Balance*, when Agnes says, "They say we sleep to let the demons out—to let the mind go raving mad, our dreams and nightmares all our logic gone awry, the dark side of our reason. And when the daylight comes again . . . comes order with it."[2] *N3RD*'s adults are as oppressed by their personal histories as Agnes is and will seek any means possible to erase them, however temporarily. But they carry the additional burden of living in a world haunted by an uncanny double whose denizens are familiar but whose rules are utterly alien: their children.

In contrast, the teenagers in *N3RD* see their parents' failures perfectly clearly, though they are none the wiser for it. Jared refuses to attend the intervention his mother has planned for his father, an alcoholic. Furious about all the hurt and embarrassment he's suffered, Jared wants to express his anger, but "you're not / supposed to be / angry." Indeed, he, like his sister and the other children, sees himself as a victim, orphaned by his parents' infelicities and feckless dedication to providing them "everything they need" (including the videogame their parents believe has caused this crisis).

Makaela, for instance, complains to her friend Trevor that her father bought her elder brother a Hummer (a very expensive, large, and resource-intensive car) and then, when the brother totaled it, almost killing someone, her father simply replaced it. "maybe / if I act like a giant jerk / who's totally circling the drain," Makaela muses in the play's first scene, "he'll buy me one to try to / save me." Her father's failure to hold his son accountable for his recklessness reinforces a moral system for Makaela that inverts the expected transactional logic: rather than behave in a responsible fashion in hopes of a reward, she is determined to engage in a performance of personal decay to get her father to shell out a car of equal value to what her brother has received. In similar fashion, Jared recognizes that his own behavior is simply an inverted version of his alcoholic father's:

> i think we play
> to get away from him
> like he's trying
> to get away from
> whatever he's trying
> to get away from

But he's no more capable of recognizing the "whatever" that he's fleeing.

This is the crux of the problem. Haley has written a world of two equally dysfunctional structures of affect, the children playing at their collision. The game is their primary site of social interaction and, more importantly, the only way they can experience intense feeling that connects with community and a sense of communal purpose. In contrast, their interactions with their parents lack narrative coherence and community feeling. Yes, they are irritatingly privileged, ungrateful, and emotionally stunted, delivering nothing but hostility and abuse to their worried, well-meaning, if hapless parents. And like the zombies they fight, they live only to mindlessly consume, and they are defined by what they consume. But it's not just the kids; the adult community is also defined by its consumption—of gasoline, drugs, booze, sex, grown-up toys, and the "American Dream" of bourgeois stability and conformity. For all intents and purposes zombified themselves, the adults move from one episode of dehumanizing, stultifying consumption to another. It is fitting, then, that the play's action really gets going when the mutilated body of a pet cat (ironically named Snickers) is discovered, and the gamers realize that even in real life, as Friar Lawrence says in Shakespeare's *Romeo & Juliet*, "these violent delights have violent ends."

The real promise of the game for the children is not just killing zombies with their friends, but something more classical and more affectively intense: revenge. This is realized by one of the adults in the play's sixth scene:

in the Final House
there's a wormhole
once you go in
you take your family with you
they appear to you as
Zombies
and finally you can
kill them
without
remorse

The kids are sucked into this world because it provides them a way of comprehending their world. It literally provides them a map. They play because it provides them both escape and narrative—a way to find a destination for their feelings and actions, however absurd and fantastic that destination might be. Most importantly, it is a place where they can play with their feelings, where they can murder zombies and dogs and cats and even their own family members, secure in the knowledge that the violence is merely computer rendered ("sometimes it's fun / to be sick," says teenager Trevor, "sometimes you need a place / to be sick"). But by the play's end, the boundary between the ludic world (with its obvious violence) and the real world (with its covert violence) has been inextricably compromised, and Tobias' prophecy comes true.

THE KIDS ARE NOT ALL RIGHT

What should a systemically minded dramaturg make of Haley's play? That's a question we ask in two directions: First, to what degree does it accurately and movingly describe our technocultural moment? Second, how do the answers we find to the first question help us think about how to stage it? One of the pitfalls of N3RD is the way it tarries with the clichés of videogame culture, both the culture of those who play and the culture of those who worry about those who play. It is a text that, if handled clumsily, can lead to tendentious interpretation.

There's no question that videogames can be a compulsive, even addictive pastime. The World Health Organization added "gaming disorder" alongside "gambling disorder" in its list of addictive behaviors. And there's little doubt that the children in the play suffer from "impairment in personal, family, social, . . . or other important areas of functioning."[3] But most people who play videogames suffer no such impairment. Regardless, videogames, like other digital pastimes, generate anxiety, particularly among parents—and particularly about violent videogames like the one in Haley's script. Though decades of research has provided conclusive evidence that violent media does not increase the risk of aggressive or violent behavior, videogames spur a unique kind of anxiety—and renewed attention among researchers and policy makers. Craig Anderson believes this is due to the "active role required by video games."[4] Notwithstanding the questions that remain unanswered about violent media and violent behavior more generally, the parents in Haley's play are convinced the videogame their children play is the cause of their children's withdrawal and aggression.

Which brings us to the zombie. In the horror genre, a zombie is generally understood as a creature incapable of empathy and deserving of none. Part of a hegemonizing swarm, a zombie exists only to consume and make others like itself—denuded of personality, communalized, and voraciously hungry. It is unquestionably to be eradicated without the least hesitation. But the real horror of the zombie is its relationship to the individual human it once was. Its gutted humanity clings to it in shreds, a ghostly, fragmented reminder of what it has lost. This is what makes the zombie uncanny in the Freudian sense: it generates uncertainty and anxiety about whether it is living or inanimate and, most importantly, why it desires the one it pursues. In just about every zombie film one might care to name, there is at least one scene where a zombie is mistaken for a living human, and that is the moment of the most acute peril in the story, for the zombie might take advantage of natural human empathy to sneak inside the defenses and destroy. To empathize with the zombie is to put the self and the community at risk.

This makes zombies an apt metaphor for the anxieties generated by fictive universes like those found in videogames. In fact, we might suggest that the fear of videogames is the fear of the zombified—of people turned into cybernetic dopamine addicts, locked into an unbreakable risk-reward cycle. Again, without dismissing the reality of addiction, we might posit that the anxiety at the heart of anti-videogame sentiment is that gamers will mistake fake feelings for real ones; that the supposedly instinctive human repugnance toward violence will be replaced by an equally instinctive urge to destroy. Paired with the often odd and alienating look and sound of a person playing a videogame—the intense blankness broken by sudden outbursts of anger and joy; the weird, often profane lingo; the spastic twitching of fingers—the interactive nature of videogame violence can frighten the uninitiated. Unfortunately, real-world tragedies bolster this anxiety. In 2004, British seventeen-year-old Warren LeBlanc was reported to have been imitating the extremely violent videogame *Manhunt* when he armed himself with a claw hammer and used it to murder his fourteen-year-old friend as a prelude to robbery. The link between the game and the murder was denied by the police investigators and was not proven conclusively, despite the victim's family's attorney making the case in court and their attempt to sue Rockstar, the company that produced *Manhunt*, for wrongful death. Nevertheless, the game was removed from retail stores in the UK.

In our interview with Haley, she told us that she was fascinated by the question of videogames and violence, but did not consider it a question that can be easily or finally answered. When we asked her about the anxiety parents and policy-makers feel about them, she answered: "It has to do with the feeling that is generated around digital culture. Obviously, if videogames were really affecting our behavior, then *Grand Theft Auto* would be causing all kinds of chaos. Clearly, that's not the case. But to kill your parents because they won't let you get on a videogame, that's the danger of it. You can get addicted to those alternate realities, and if anyone gets in the way of that, then there's going to be trouble." The power of addiction to generate fictive universes with a warped, asocial sense of morals in the minds of the addicted is widely accepted by psychologists. The capacity of violent media to increase aggression in viewers, however, is generally presumed on moral grounds rather than based on any qualitative scientific research. Theater historians are all too aware that moral panic about violence is far more likely than actual violence to erupt from exposure to media—through history, theater has been the subject of many inflammatory accusations of moral corruption (as have jazz, rock music, glam rock, and many other forms of popular performance).

This is why we feel it is vital for any production of *Neighborhood 3: Requisition of Doom* to clearly communicate to the audience that the kids are in fact getting the kind of emotional support, shared experience, intensity of feeling, and sense of community from videogames that they cannot get in real life, even though this puts their capacity to empathize at risk. Does this make their behavior any less alien, repulsive, or immoral? No. The game has revealed to them that their parents are soulless husks, incapable of empathy and perhaps deserving of none. The real reason the kids are overtly hostile to their parents is that they recognize their zombification, and they live in fear that if they are not careful to avoid the empathy trap of the zombie—the uncanny double of falling into the trap of suburban conformity—they will become just like them. The twist of N3RD is that the ludic world offers a more emotionally authentic life experience than the real world.

For those of us who spend significant time in playful, fictive story-worlds, the attack on videogames and the passions of those who play them is familiar. It is of a piece with attacks on theater launched by those who don't like it when people they wish to control decide to pretend to be whomever they please, create fictive universes that work differently than our own, or allow their passions to be expressed by and for that which is patently false. Even more than a vacuum, power abhors an alien and transformative passion—particularly if it is pursued in the spirit of play. This is threatening specifically to a certain type of mindset that understands dissent, alternative lifestyles, fantastic utopias, and unproductive pastimes as an attack on authority. It can be difficult to overcome the barrier that playful pastimes can erect. Which is why we find the exchange between Cody's mom, Barbara, and Blake, in the form of his videogame avatar ZOMBIEKLLR14. It is the only moment in N3RD when an adult and a child genuinely try to explain what they're feeling and the rules of expression. It is understandably awkward and difficult, as if they are each learning a new language.

Barbara finds herself in a kind of liminal space between the ludic world of the videogame and the real-world streets of the neighborhood. It is not clear what forces are at work that blur the boundaries between these worlds, but they are blurred enough that Blake, operating his avatar, can interact with her, though it's unclear how this is happening. What is immediately clear is that she doesn't have a clue about what she's doing or why. "i don't know how you got to the / Last Chapter / noob," he says, "but you better not give me away." But soon enough, Blake realizes that Barbara is not another player's avatar but his friend's

The Uncanny Mountain

mother, desperate to find her son. Sympathetic but not empathetic, Blake reveals his identity and tries to help Barbara. But Barbara's mission is entirely different from Blake's. Horrified, she begs him not to enter the Final House:

ZOMBIEKLLR14. that's the only way
out of the Neighborhood
BARBARA. that is not
the only way
get up
from your computer
get up
from your computer
and go talk
to your mom
ZOMBIEKLLR14. i don't talk
to my mom

By this point in the play, Haley has thoroughly intertwined the ludic and real-life worlds so they have become perversely coterminous. Blake's avatar opens the door of the game's representation of his own house (the Final House of the game, the finish line), and in real life, his mother, Joy, opens the front door, revealing Barbara with half her head smashed to pieces. Blake claims that he killed her in-game, but Joy has discovered her corpse and the bloody claw hammer on the stairs and brings it into the room. Blake demands that she give it to him, calling her Joy, which she despises. "I don't recognize you," she tells him." "I'm your son," he responds, and asks for the hammer. She begs him to speak to her: "You don't believe me. You don't even see me. You don't see anything outside of your game. You don't see me. You don't see anything outside of the game. You don't see anything that's real!" She realizes that he is cowering from her. She stops her attack, apologizes, and asks if it is too late for them to reconcile: "I just want to . . . I just want . . . the two of us . . . It's not too late, is it? It's not too late?" He shakes his head no.

This is the climax of the play, a moment of real connection, of genuine empathy between characters, perhaps the only such moment in the play. Joy exposes herself emotionally to her son, lets him know how desperately she wants them to be able to talk. And she apologizes for her own failures. Seizing the moment, she rushes toward Blake to embrace him, whereupon he seizes the hammer from her and beats her to death, raining down blows through her screams. The shock of the moment rings through the drop to darkness, and as the lights rise on Blake pushing himself away from his computer, looking around his now-empty room, and uttering a single question, that question that carries with it so much ambiguity: "Mom?" (fig. 5.2).

Why does Blake murder his mother? Has he simply transported the violent delights of the videogame into real life? Has he misrecognized his mother, mistaking a real person for an avatar as he did Barbara a few minutes before? Or are we asking the wrong question? Rather than failing to recognize his mother, he has recognized her all too clearly, recognized the pain and longing she feels. The terror of suddenly recognizing the emotional reality of his mother's life is a moment of radical uncanniness for Blake, causing him to enter a panic. And in that moment of panic, he relies on what the game has taught him—that closeness with the zombies of the Neighborhood Association results

Fig. 5.2. Joy (Kerry Ipema) begging Blake (Connor Johnston) to stop playing the game in the 2015 Flea Theater production of *Neighborhood 3: Requisition of Doom*, directed by Joel Schumacher. *Photo courtesy of Hunter Canning.*

The Uncanny Mountain

in the zombification of the player. In the end, whether he has actually committed murder is unclear. According to the script, Joy's body is not present in the final scene when Blake calls for her. But the barrier between the ludic world and the suburban world is now so porous that it is impossible to say with certainty what has happened. This is why the question that Blake asks is perhaps the most dramaturgically difficult decision a production of N3RD must make. What does "Mom?" mean? The decisions a team makes will affect how the audience understands the play as a critique of videogames, videogame players, and videogame culture. That decision will be driven by two questions: First, where is Joy's body? Second, what is Blake feeling?

The solution to these questions lies in whether or to what extent we consider N3RD to be a "videogame play." In fact, Haley's script is barely about videogames at all, though videogames are critical to its import. It is rather about what happens to a community when people cannot speak about their trauma and have to express it elsewhere and otherwise: the alcoholic father, the psychotic Tobias, and the disaffected Leslie are as trapped in their own fantasies of consumption, addiction, and fear as are Cody, Chelsea, and Blake. But unlike their children, the adults are isolated from one another too. In contrast, the children have a vibrant (if misogynistic, exploitative, and abusive) virtual community to sustain them. Ultimately, this is a play about generational conflict. Each has found its own level of tolerance for hypocrisy, addiction, and loneliness and can't understand why the other generation has chosen a different way of living with its shortcomings.

Staging the videogame is Haley's way of articulating this generational conflict in a way that resonates with a modern audience. In our interview with Haley, she spoke about her choice to have only four actors play all the roles in the play: a mother type, a father type, a daughter type, and a son type. While doubling is a well-worn strategy in the theater, serving both thematic and financial ends equally, in a play about videogames, this overlap with the way theater works enables audiences to better understand the concept of the videogame avatar. Ironically, audiences tend to empathize along generational lines. Haley noted that younger and older viewers each "connect[ed] to different aspects of the play. But in fact, the generational conflict in the audience is more likely about the degree of knowledge concerning videogames, videogame players, and videogame culture. In our own experience teaching *N3RD*, we have noted that young people tend to side with the adults.

Thus the question of whether and to what extent an audience empathizes with Blake depends on how a production communicates the gaming experience to its audience. Haley recognizes this, explaining that she wants to show those who are not involved in videogaming "what it's like to get caught up in a game" while seeking to "educate one group without talking down to another group." These dramaturgical questions lead Haley into territory hitherto unexplored by theater, one that communicates effectively with and educates both gamers and nongamers about the opportunities and terrors of a highly mediatized existence. In particular, she plays with the theater's ability to present ethical and emotional dilemmas in a way that is obviously a representation but also carries the impact of actual experience.

This is why the decisions a team makes about the final scene of the play—particularly the disposition of Joy's body and the tone of Blake's question—are so vital. What the moment requires is a sense of uncanniness. Dan Solomon, critic for the Austin *Chronicle*, responded to this quality in a 2012 production:

> What price gamers pay for doing horrible things in a virtual world is one question that the gaming media has struggled to ask seriously, as developers thrill to their ability to raise ethical dilemmas that they're ill-prepared to properly address. In the theatre, though, where the uncanny valley is far away and the comfy confines of the couch are abandoned for real people doing real things in front of you, those questions are visceral and hard to ignore. Smashing a zombie's face with a hammer is a good time on a PS3, but watching it enacted a dozen feet from you onstage is less comfortable. Credit [this production] for utilizing the strengths of an "irrelevant" medium to better explore the weaknesses of our most popular.[5]

Solomon's tongue may be firmly in his cheek when he refers to theater as "irrelevant," but he recognizes that one of the great joys of playing videogames comes from the *simulation* of immediacy enabled by the medium's particular structures of affect. And he recognizes equally that the same thrill can be had in the theater, though it requires a different kind of suspension of disbelief, a different negotiation of technological systems and the particular structures of affect that produce emotional experience. The murder of Joy struck Solomon as "real," but the reality of that moment was enabled by everything that preceded it. The viscerality of that moment was prepared by the compounded uncanniness of the previous scenes: Ryan attempting to express his sadness about the murder and mutilation of his pet, Chloe defending herself with a golf club against her father's advances as the lights fade, the intensifying coincidence between the events described in verbally in the walk-throughs and the onstage sights and sounds. The murder of Joy by Blake is no less "unreal" than anything else on the stage, but its unreality is forgotten because the violence that we've experienced to that point was presented in a fashion that divorced the verbal from the physical. Though only four actors played all the roles, attenuating the specific actor's physicality from any particular character's, the violence feels (or should feel) utterly specific.

THE UNCANNY MOUNTAIN

Solomon's experience of that moment—presumably one shared by other audience members—is due not to the reality of the experience, but rather to its very unreality. Thus while Solomon describes the theater as "far from the uncanny valley," we, as systemic dramaturgs, would describe it as precisely the opposite. If the original problem of theater is technology, then the enduring challenge of theater is the uncanny. The theater is a place where artifice and reality can become indistinguishable, where it can be impossible to tell the difference between real emotions and those conjured by dramatic fantasy and technical virtuosity. But it's also a place where we find thrills in the exposure of that artificiality, where we marvel at a special effect and share that marvel in passionate whispers to our companion, where we admire the technique of the stars. That tension between the artificial and the real—and the feelings it catalyzes in audiences—has driven much of theater history in both its practice and theory.

Some would seek to occlude that artificiality, to create an illusion so convincing that we all but forget that we're in the theater. This might be accomplished for naturalistic ends—for example, recall August

The Uncanny Mountain

Strindberg's diatribe against footlights (discussed in the introduction) and flats—or to simply convince us that a combination of sleight of hand and verbal distraction is magic. However, some would seek to foreground artificiality, to remind us that we are in the theater and nowhere else. We think here of Bertolt Brecht or Karen Finley. But whatever the attitude toward its artificiality, we expect a theatrical experience to feel emotionally authentic, regardless of the kind and quality desired. When it isn't, when it has either failed to abjure the frisson of unreality or failed to delve convincingly into it, we feel something quite similar to the feelings Masahiro Mori identified in robotic and digital simulations that aimed for the human but fell . . . somewhere else. In the same way we feel discomfited by a digital simulation that falls a little too closely to success, we can feel discomfited by theater. But we can also marvel at such representations. If you take a second look at the graph, you'll see that Mori includes Bunraku on his scale of uncanny experiences, viewing it as something that closely resembles the human but whose artificiality provides a sense of pleasant uncanniness. We'll return to this idea later.

For those of us who enjoy both theater and videogames, the experience of a representation that fails to properly calibrate the artificial and the human feels remarkably similar to the experience of watching an actor almost but not quite plumb the emotional truth of a character or observing a set try to achieve something that it almost can but does not accomplish. Indeed, it is far more likely that a theatrical production will have these uncanny moments, as so much of the technology of theater is material and embodied, and so much of that material, embodied stuff is being asked to be something just as material and embodied, but otherwise. This is the brilliance of Haley's play. *N3RD* juxtaposes the uncanniness of videogames and those who play them with the uncanniness of suburban privilege and those who dwell within it. In so doing, she refines our understanding of the way structures of affect shape the relationships of neighbors and families. Earlier, we asked the question, Why stage a videogame? A systemic approach to that question unveils the shared territory between stage and game, a territory of affective distortion and hampered empathy. In the end, we find Haley's play offering little in terms of our understanding of videogames as a media, but much when it comes to understanding how two media might work

The Uncanny Mountain

in concert to alert us to the ways our emotional and material lives might be reoriented toward honesty.

In previous chapters, we explored the ways that theater can capitalize on digital media to generate thrilling imagery, exciting new territories for exploration, and a renewed engagement with empathy. We explored the ways that digital games can capitalize on theatricality and expanded notions of presence to enhance the thrill of the experience for the audience, augment the capacities of designers and players, and amplify and protect the material and emotional lives of those who design and play them. We've described a densely intertwined relationship among theater, play, and technology—a relationship that led us to conclude that many of the questions being asked by today's theater artists about digital and computational technologies might be answered in part by looking to the past. We conclude here by suggesting once again that a systemic conception of theater can reveal to us the essential character of theater.

We think here of the uncanny. We find something limiting about Mori's conception of the uncanny, precisely because it presumes an attitude and response that is entirely alien to people committed to theater in all its forms, today and in the past, here and elsewhere. Anyone who loves theater has had an experience when the proximity of the real to the fake has proven disturbing, in a way that leaves us shaken, disturbed, shocked, upset, but has done so in a way that feels utterly authentic on an emotional and existential level. That experience of uncanniness is, if not ubiquitous to theater, certainly common and often sought by creators and audiences alike. So, perhaps it is time for us to revise our geographical coordinates. If there is an uncanny valley, a shadowy vale of artistic death, then there is also its opposite, a place where recognition of the brute and inescapable materiality and fictionality of the human experience is placed in the riskiest, most precarious proximity to that which most resists objectification.

We would call this uncanny other of the uncanny valley the uncanny mountain, and we would advocate that it be thoughtfully, carefully, knowledgeably, and courageously climbed rather than fastidiously avoided. No doubt, it is an artistic challenge, a human challenge, to enter a state of empathy with others while sustaining the full and constant consciousness that everything around you is constructed, that you are always already a congeries of things and processes. To enter that state of empathy, you must expose and explore that which would seem most resistant to emotional authenticity and identification. Is there anything more uncanny than watching a contraption made of wood, cloth, and paint become irresistibly human? It is not the elision of artificiality that fuels the theatrical moments that move audiences. It is not technology that threatens theater. Rather, it is the failure, as Zeami noted when he discussed the phenomenon of sokyokuchi, to properly ascertain the conception of, relationship to, and manifestation of technology in the construction of empathic structures. It is at the peak of the uncanny mountain that we find those treasured opportunities for deep examination.

By staging a videogame (that is to say, staging one uncanny representation within another), Haley inverts the uncanny valley to underline the challenges faced by middle-class children and their parents to find common, empathic ground—and to find that ground at moments when they seem most alien to each other. She signals a broader challenge to theater makers in a digital age. As we noted earlier, many of the problems of new media and performance actually have solutions in long-standing dramaturgical traditions. By staging a videogame and staging the failure of empathy, Haley maps the terrain of the uncanny and marks the routes to rock bottom and peak. It's not videogames that are the problem—or, more precisely, the problems of videogames aren't new problems. The problem, as always, is how technologies are used to promote empathy, and whether empathy is directed toward positive, progressive social change or the invidious, the pernicious, and the violent.

SYSTEMIC DRAMATURGY ROUNDTABLE

On January 14, 2019, a group of critics, educators, artists, and makers assembled at the Digital Arts Research Center of the University of California–Santa Cruz to explore the concept and future of systemic dramaturgy. In addition to micha càrdenas, Elizabeth Swensen, Noah Wardrip-Fruin, and Marianne Weems, we were joined by Nick Junius and Allucquére Rosanne "Sandy" Stone.

Nick Junius is an interactive narrative researcher, game developer, and playwright at UC Santa Cruz currently working on an interactive drama visual novel as part of their masters of fine arts in the Digital Art and New Media program. They have published papers at the Foundations of Digital Games conference and Digital Games Research Association conference discussing methods of building computational systems inspired by theatrical practice and the ways games can use their mechanics to reinforce narrative beats.

Allucquére Rosanne "Sandy" Stone is an American academic theorist, media theorist, author, and performance artist. She is an associate professor emerita and founding director of the Advanced Communication Technologies Laboratory (ACTLab) at the University of Texas–Austin. Concurrently, she is the Wolfgang Kohler Professor of Media and Performance at the European Graduate School, senior artist at the Banff Centre for Arts and Creativity, and University of California Humanities Research Institute fellow. Stone has worked in and written about film, music, experimental neurology, writing, engineering, and computer programming. Stone is transgender and is considered a founder of the academic discipline of transgender studies. She has been profiled in *Artforum, Wired, Mondo 2000,* and other publications and interviewed for documentaries such as Traceroute. She is a recipient of a State of California Lifetime Achievement Award.

MICHAEL CHEMERS: Mike and I are honored to bring together such a unique group of pioneers, people who are established leaders in their various fields, and people who are up-and-coming. Despite the fact that we all come from different backgrounds and have different creative and scholarly interests, we are all interested in using new technologies in new spaces to create art.

MIKE SELL: We want to explore the questions that you ask when considering whether you want to use a specific platform, digital medium, or other technological affordance to tell a story and reach an audience.

CHEMERS: We think about these questions in terms of a continuum. We are interested, on one side, in Marianne Weems's work integrating computational digital elements into live performance in a way that both enhances and challenges what we think about when we think about live performance. On the other side, we are interested in digital games, social media, interactive media, artificial intelligence, and how a systemic dramaturgical approach can inform how you make and use those technologies. We contend that dramaturgs have a unique understanding of how the multiple systems of theater operate, not just the systems of production and collaboration but also the hermeneutic, heuristic, research, political, social, and collaborative systems that surround and support the theatrical enterprise. It seems to us that the incorporation of new technologies into what might broadly be termed "dramatic media" requires a comprehensive understanding of these systems as well as the ability to harness the collaborative energy of people who are experts in different types of systems.

SELL: We believe there's a way of thinking dramaturgically that is different—and differently valuable—from how we typically think about technology and performance. As we engage as thinkers, creators, players, and performers with digital and computational technologies, we think about old technologies as well. We want to think broadly about technology and techne. In other words, we want to talk about technology but also how we think about technology.

CHEMERS: Let's start by talking about empathy.

SELL: One of the enduring concerns of theorists and makers of theater is how we are helping people to feel. The term we use for that concern is *empathy*. But *empathy* is not a monolithic term. In fact, it's wonderfully problematic. Empathy means different things to psychologists, political scientists, and artists. The concept Michael and I have been exploring frames *empathy* as a value-neutral term that designates in broad fashion any of the effects used by artists for emotional connection and the opportunities that audiences have to experience different kinds of affect in a performance context. What does empathy mean to you? What are the problems that you find with empathy, either as a concept or as a component of your creative work?

NOAH WARDRIP-FRUIN: Well, a few years ago, I took some potshots at the game *Uncharted 2* when it came out, but I hadn't ever finished playing it. So I thought, "Okay, I really have to sit down and play this game if I'm going to criticize it." And as I got into it, I thought it was a pretty linear story. I did not have a lot of sense that I could make decisions in the game that would cause the story to unfold differently, which is often one of the things that makes me more emotionally invested in a game.

But then I was doing this escort mission where there's a wounded cameraman that you have to limp your way through the battle zone with, and because you're holding the cameraman, you can only use one hand, so a number of your weapons are taken away. You can't jump, you can't run, and so on. Turns out I was really bad at this. I just died over and over again, trying to get through this without my normal abilities. But eventually, we limped into the safe zone. Then the cartoonish, horrible bad guy comes in and shoots him in the head, of course. This is not some well-drawn fictional character. And I was genuinely angry. I was pissed off, which I certainly would not have been if I'd been *watching* this action like a film. I would have thought, "Oh, this is so trite." But because I had worked so hard to get to this point, I was furious. I see I'm not the only one who had this experience.

ELIZABETH SWENSEN: I have not played that game, but just listening to you describe the emotional arc as a player is visceral. I would be so angry.

WARDRIP-FRUIN: I think there is a kind of empathy that comes even from the most basic things that require the audience to enact something, which we can do with digital technology and in lots of other ways. I think for me, it really is different than the empathy I would feel watching or reading the same story.

CHEMERS: Matthew Causey approaches this through the Lacanian concept of split subjectivity—as in when a baby looks at a mirror and recognizes that it's not an empty image but, in some nontrivial way, itself.[1] Noah, you said, "I was stripped of my weapons. I could not jump." There's a transference of the self into the media.

Marianne, if I can throw this over to you, in your most recent show, *Strange Window*, at one point, a character played by Moe Angelos was subjected to a microstudy of her own face when she was reacting to some bad news. Her face was projected onto giant screens and time-dilated so we could see the tiny movements in her face that revealed her inner turmoil (fig. 6.1). Some critics say that digital

Fig. 6.1. The actor's face projected onto large screens in *Strange Windows*, enabling the spectators to examine the smallest subtleties of expression, something that would normally be available only in movie theaters. *Photo courtesy of Krannert Center for the Performing Arts/University of Illinois at Urbana-Champaign.*

technology built into the theater decreases the ability to empathize, but I had the exact opposite experience watching that show.

MARIANNE WEEMS: We were doing a takeoff on a 1970s pop-psych concept of microexpressions. The idea is that if you zoom way in on someone's face and slow the motions down, the subject will betray their true emotions with little tells. For instance, a person might roll their eyes in a way you'd never notice normally, but if you magnified and slowed the face, you'd see the sardonic reaction. I grew excited about this idea and how it reveals layers of truth and information, representation, masking, and staging.

The horrible thing about proscenium-based theater is that it is so passive, so minimally interactive, that it's hard to expect a high level of investment. The traditional theatrical technique of creating empathy is to set up a protagonist's struggle so that the audience member identifies with them. Postdramatic theater, on the other hand, is allergic to empathy. I really *don't* want people to worry about how the characters feel. It's much more about creating a framework where the audience is asked to analyze their own relationship to what's happening onstage, as well as between the characters. People may say this results in a more clinical experience, less straight-up empathic, but there's no reason to expect a twenty-first-century audience member to identify with and feel anything.

SELL: But your work is not clinical in the least. It fosters a different kind of empathy. You are still looking for an emotional core and an emotional experience, but it's happening somewhere else or in a way that might feel strange to somebody who's expecting it to be coming from that actor, right?

WEEMS: Well, I would really like people to have the experience of wondering about or questioning presence itself. I'm sitting in the theater. I'm sitting next to other people. We're watching something onstage. We're also watching it in some digital representation. What I hope is happening is that you, as the audience member, seeing the real actor and the mediated one, are enmeshed in this moment of thinking about digital presence.

CHEMERS: You also put onstage the technology itself. We see the engineers working on the systems that are digitizing the action in front of our eyes. That becomes another one of the relationships for interrogation. One of those presences that you're targeting is our relationship with technology. In your 2005 *Super Vision*, for instance, which is a play about data-veillance, one of the things that struck me the most was when you had the house manager come onstage and reveal to the audience personal information about themselves. The audience thinks they are out for a splendid evening at the theater and suddenly they realize, oh my god, this is a threat that I personally am under right now.

WEEMS: We used data to deconstruct the house. People in the upper balconies are usually people with lower income, while the orchestra has the blue-chip subscribers. We also analyzed people's zip codes, and then we held a mirror up to the spatial distribution of economic standing in the house.

SELL: So we have two ideas in play right now. The first concerns how to engage in conscious fashion with systems that might otherwise be invisible to us or function in a purely utilitarian fashion. Then we have the idea of systems that are generally visible to us that we expect a specific experience from—say, a videogame or a movie—positioned in a way that produces an unexpected feeling.

CHEMERS: Sandy, you're someone who has a strong background in traditional theater, but then started moving into what is called making. You developed a much more expansive definition of what performance is. We see you as someone who's always moving across these spectra.

SANDY STONE: When I was writing about this stuff in the 1980s, I broke it down like this: here's the audience member, whatever form that takes; here's the performer, whatever that means; in between, you have the interface. If you call it technology, then you get involved with Douglas Adams's definition of technology as anything that wasn't around when you were born.[2] But whatever is in that thin, invisible line that contains all the machinery is what we're talking about, and that's the thing that involves changes over time. When we were doing whatever the hell we were doing before, the machinery was how the actors prepared themselves and thought about what they were doing in relation to the audience. When we do it now, the machinery is some kind of electronic device which is a concretization of a whole bunch of social relationships that you have to go and unpack in order to figure out what the hell "newer technology" means.

When I get to that point in talking about digital dramaturgy, I'm just laying out the pseudo-code by which we can kind of dig into it. That's all I can do. Because how you implement that, how you take the interface and unpack it in relationship with those social interactions and identify where the "quasi-guys" lie—that's what I call the entities that are made up of combinations of humans and some kind of machinery, device, or technology. That is how you wind up understanding what the hell you're doing, even though I noticed that most people who do this stuff, including me, have no real understanding of how the hell we're doing it.

SWENSEN: When I think about empathy, I'm always in dialogue with practice. To put yourself in a position of imagining emotional response or imagining some kind of experiential or embodied feeling in an audience is certainly a part of game design practice. I imagine there's a connection between theater practice and game practice in that, in addition to the more clinical testing of early audiences and previews, a game designer has to imagine and create some personal distance from their own experience with what they're working on in order to imagine how someone else would see it for the first time. If one cannot do that, there are other sorts of methods to perfect one's work involving relying solely on testing and putting things in front of other people. But you could speed up your own development process if you could cultivate, if not an empathy, a theory of mind—that is, how someone who is not me will see this—as a way to test one's own experiential goals for a project.

CHEMERS: This gets to one of the core problems in working with a term like *empathy*. In primatology, the operational definition of *empathy* is the ability to consider matters from a point of view that's not your own, the ability to imagine how the person across the table from you is feeling. That's why it should be considered value-neutral, since that ability to empathize can be used to help or harm. In fact, primatologists link it to a type of cognitive ability they call Machiavellian intelligence.

SWENSEN: But it's not just an awareness of how someone's feeling in a moment, during a performance or during a testing session or play.

It's anticipating and designing and intending experience that grows from your previous literacy in that same space or medium.

SELL: When we're talking about the creation of these kinds of operational systems that we hope will induce some kind of embodied emotional experience, would you hold to the idea that there are particular techniques that will have a similar or limited range of effects on the player? In other words, is there a kind of technological essentialism here?

SWENSEN: It's a complicated question, because the environment is very rich. There are many different elements that in different combinations will create different feelings, and different people coming up to experience your work will come in with their own literacies and experiences. One thing that I try to stress as an educator when discussing systems-driven work is that, whether a designer intends it or not, systems express a designer's values. The designer should know that those values can then be mediated or enhanced with other elements of production.

WARDRIP-FRUIN: And there you have a conversation with vocabulary in other media, like a "shot/reverse shot" or a "swelling music cue" or something like that. There are elements in game systems that tend to have reliable effects. Stéphane Bura has an article where he lays out a number of these, such as if you put a player in a situation where the tools at their disposal don't work and then you remove one of the barriers—that almost inevitably will create a moment of hope and optimism, which you can then undercut, or you can go on with, or whatever.[3] But I don't think these are different from other forms of media, except maybe in that there hasn't been as much work to understand the vocabulary.

CHEMERS: We perceive a certain resistance among gamers and designers to this kind of critical engagement that you're talking about, an unwillingness, as it were, to consider what the impact will be on a target audience, but also on someone who might not be the target audience. Another way to put this is, What's wrong with being able to punch a suffragette in *Red Dead Redemption 2*? I have to think that somebody spent many long hours programming many millions of lines of code to enable the player to punch a suffragette. Was there no self-awareness of that task? We observe that our own students in theater are generally energized about engaging theater as a tool for advancing social discourse toward justice, whereas in games and digital culture in general, there seems to be a hesitancy or even a backlash against progressive critique.

NICK JUNIUS: I think some of this has to do with this perception that computers aren't inadvertently importing the designer's worldview into that system. That's not something we talk that much about, especially in engineering education, where we talk mainly about how to do a particular task, and we might talk about the person who first made the thing, but we don't care that much about where it came from. Mostly, it's a linked list: this is what it's good for, this is what it's not good for. We don't talk about why this exists in any more meaningful way.

SELL: So you've identified a problem, and I heard a kind of a solution there, which concerns the context in which a person is learning to do something creative, but also the related problem of becoming uncomfortable with creativity, so that we stop and ask, Wait, who am I? And why am I taking pleasure in this? Why am I not taking pleasure in this particular moment? So to my questions: Can we be more consistent with creating that contextual consciousness? Where's that education happening? How is education about a given system built into or baked into a particular use or experience of that system?

We seem to agree that we need to have lots of conversations about these systems, conversations about practical techniques as well as ethics. But there needs to be another conversation that considers how the systems that are the immediate concern of the artist or audience are connected with other systems. As an example, how might artists and educators raise consciousness of the interconnection of videogame culture, videogame design, and the social and digital strategies of the radical right?

STONE: I want to talk about that for a second, because we had that challenge in the ACTLab.[4] Our principles in that group were to make something, make anything, take risks, be awesome, and the way to get in was to knock Sandy's socks off. We didn't want to treat the classroom as a machine for encouraging those principles. We had to develop practical means to get the students to do it without exhorting them. Over a period of quarters, we built up a cadre of students who took the class every quarter, and they would ask questions about the social meaning of what we were doing: What's the social meaning of this art? How can we make this relevant? How can we use it to change minds or lives? Things like that. This cadre formed twenty percent of the class and were a long-standing cohort who knew where we were going, and the rest of the class would come along. That worked pretty well.

SELL: Let's follow up on that. How can we raise consciousness and create critical community like the one Sandy describes, but within virtual spaces, whether gaming spaces or social media spaces?

micha cárdenas: Something that is coming up for me is Tara McPherson's essay "Why Are the Digital Humanities So White?"[5] She looks at how oftentimes people want to separate technologies from their social, ethical, and political contexts. She's basically arguing that we can't do that. She discusses how Unix was first designed in the 1960s within a few years of desegregation laws being passed, and how the kinds of racism that were going on in the U.S. are, of course, encoded in decisions that people were making when designing the system. So thinking about people in online communities trying to have positive interactions, we can't separate the hateful people from the system. The systems are designed for that particular kind of communication, and that's what they've produced. It's like the internet: designed by the military, it's not a surprise that it's a great surveillance tool. Maybe what we need is to think about how to move on.

SELL: What are the kinds of things that you do to intervene in that conjunction of persona and system?

cárdenas: One thing I've tried to do is to think about how we could build more autonomous networks. I did a project called Local Autonomy Networks, where I made mesh networked clothing for people to build safety networks.[6] But sometimes I just want to be more practical and timely and put things where people's eyes are. So I did a project about digital security called *Hold Your Boundaries*, which I did right after the election of President Trump, who lost the election, but still took office.[7] I saw a lot of people getting involved in activism, newly, freshly, and doing things online that were really dangerous, like planning illegal protests in public and releasing Google documents with their first and last names attached, which is just a ticket to jail. I made this project with security tips for people targeted by the administration, like trans people, immigrants, and Muslim people. I made short little poems out of those security tips and then put them in cute little Instagrammable squares, and then put them on Instagram and social media so that people would see them and share them. In this case, I am using extant social networks, but in a way that subverts them with tips about like how Siri and Alexa are always listening, and there have already been numerous court cases in which people have been put in jail based on recordings and conversations recorded by Alexa and Siri. That's how "Hey, Siri!" works. So if you're planning civil disobedience, your phone should be far away, preferably with the battery out of it. Some of those squares get saved, some of them get deleted.

WARDRIP-FRUIN: I'm kind of sad that none of our phones just responded when you said, "Hey, Siri!"

cárdenas: I've also been thinking about empathy. I've been thinking a lot about this game that I really love and used to teach called *Lim* by merritt k.

SELL: It's hard to find these days.

cárdenas: It is. I think she took it down. A lot of my favorite games are by trans women, who are now saying, "I don't want you to see that or talk about that early content." That's something to think about. Anyway, *Lim* is this wonderful, very simple game. Basically, you're a square, maybe you're brown, and then you're changing colors. Then there are some simple wall shapes that you're navigating around. And then you encounter some other squares that are blue. And if you walk too close to the squares, they attack you and the screen shakes a little bit, and there's just this sound that's like, "Kchh Kchh Kchh," over and over again. The only controls are move up or down, left and right, or you press the Z button to mimic the color of whoever's attacking you. This makes me think about, you know, empathy and representation. My experience of it was like, wow, this is really violent, even though it's just squares and basic sound. When I would show it to students, I got the same response over and over again: they were cringing and saying "Stop, please stop." Whereas, you know, I could show them like, super-high-resolution video of *Quake* or *Gears of War* and they wouldn't have that reaction. And I often don't have that reaction either.

Frankly, I love watching *Critical Role*, a *D&D* livestream, so much more than playing a video game, and I think it's partly just because I can look at the actors in the face. They are feeling and expressing emotions, even though they are just talking about what they are doing in the game. I've cried a bunch of times, watching *Critical Role*. But as a game studies person, I do like buying new games all the time, playing whatever the new high-resolution thing is, and usually my emotional response is just to roll my eyes and stop playing after like an hour. The voice acting is compelling, but maybe it's the glitches, maybe it's the uncanny valley. *Horizon Zero Dawn* is trying hard to be realistic, but when I watch it, my emotional response is like, hmm, meh, I don't know, there's something missing.

SELL: It's the emotional and affective dimensions, rather than the idea of looking at the digital face and thinking it feels a *little* human, but it's just inhuman enough that it's creating that sense of alienation, if not nausea. You're talking about something that's working on an affective level.

cárdenas: Yeah.

WARDRIP-FRUIN: Plus, the teeth are always wrong.

SELL: The eyes are better than they used to be.

SWENSEN: They've got that glint sometimes. But on the subject of thinking about solutions to negative discourse online, of thinking about the relationship between hateful discourse and an understanding of the systems that they're in, I think game designers are at a point now that we are thinking about how we draw an audience and about our audience's awareness of those systems. We are not taught systems-based literacy. I mean, we are surrounded by systems and we learn from systems, but we aren't given a critical language to talk about them.

There are a number of game designers that take real-world systems, put them in front of you in an abstracted way through play, and tell you to learn the strategies. If it's a real-world system, you begin to think about who designed this, what the ideal strategy to navigate it is, whether it is a behavior I want to engage in. It's something I run into often in educational work, and a lot of the games I make are to teach something or to make someone think about some kind of learning material.

Some of the earliest games I made when I was still in graduate school, as a part of the Game Innovation Lab at the University of Southern California, were designed to increase college-going in underserved communities. To do that, many of our games presented, "This is the system; these are all the rules that are in place in that system that will never be taught to you in school and also are not on any application checklist." Like how to "game" extracurriculars so you will look like an attractive applicant. This project was very focused as an intervention to teach folks how to apply to college successfully. But one could imagine taking that system one step further: "Okay, now you've played the system. Now, let's think critically about the system. Who benefits from the system? Who made this system? Who is the system for? How can we rebrand, retake, or change the system?" That's the step those games don't quite take. But I think games could become a way to teach us about the other systems that are informing the discourse about the media we love.

CHEMERS: There was a game that I played some years ago called *High Tea*, released by Preloaded. The game is set in the period of the Opium Wars, and the idea is that you are an importer of tea from China to Britain. In order to facilitate your ability to move tea, you need to smuggle opium from India into China, where you sell it and then take the profits to buy tea to send to England. It starts being a game about resource management, but sooner or later you start to realize that in order to make the profits that you need to match the accelerating demand for tea, you need to start undermining the civil structure of China. You need to bribe government officials and police, you need to get people looking the other way, and you need to maintain pockets of opium addiction all over the country, which accelerates crime and ruins the social infrastructure, and if you're going to play the game well, you really need to be absolutely ruthless about that sort of thing. What you are doing it for ultimately is to feed the tea addiction of the British, and so you begin to realize that you are the central figure in a global drug deal scam, and by the end of it, you are suckered into learning a lot about this real history and reflecting on your own lack of ethics in what you did to win.

I think my own sense of ethics interferes with my ability to be a good videogame player. In *Skyrim*, getting married is this elaborate quest, but divorce is by the sword. Now, my wife in *Skyrim* was glitchy, but I was never able to kill her and replace her. I just couldn't look her in the eye and kill her, even though I *knew* she wasn't a person, she was just a pile of pixels, that there were no real-world consequences to anyone, except maybe to me and my own sense of myself.

SWENSEN: As a dramaturg and an actor, Michael, if your character has to murder another character, what is the interaction with your own sense of yourself?

CHEMERS: It's troubling. Actors talk about this a lot: if they have to behave in evil ways onstage, then sometimes they fear it does psychological damage to them. It's part of the reason why actors tend to go crazy, because they're constantly having to split their subjectivity with characters that are horrifying to themselves. Marianne, you don't think so?

WEEMS: My actors are very distanced.

CHEMERS: In this last work of yours that I saw, your actors were doing exceedingly cruel things to one another, but on the whole, they were pretty flippant about it, right?

WEEMS: They did it with gusto!

CHEMERS: With gusto, yeah! And then the action stops, and another character comes out and addresses the audience: "Now we're going to see what happens when we put someone in an ethically compromised situation that they cannot possibly get out of. Hmm. Look, look at the brow lines descending, showing the cracking of the inner personality." At the same time, these time-dilated magnifications of the actor's face are being projected on big screens. Is that a reflection of your observation that we've become a callous society?

WEEMS: I don't know. What do you guys think?

cárdenas: I think about Molleindustria's game *Phone Story*. I love this game. I teach it to my students all the time. It's a really simple game about how smartphones are made. Apple banned it from the App Store, so you can't get it on your iPhone anymore, but you can get it on your Google phone. It's a really simple pixelly game. Level one is, you are a guard with a machine gun in a coal mine. The miners are children, and you have to prod them when they stop working.

That's level one. If you just stand there and try to act ethically, then the game ends and you are given a message: "Don't pretend you're not complicit. You're using this game on this device. You know what to do. Let's try it again." So then you think, "Oh god, I really want to see level two. I'd better, you know, jab these child workers in the mines." You do that and you get to level two, which is about the suicides in the Foxconn factories in China, when people making iPhones were jumping out of windows. Now you are a rescue crew with a trampoline, and your job is to try to move back and forth and catch the jumping workers that are trying to kill themselves.

I love this game. I think it's really good, really putting things in people's faces and not trying to be realistic. Very silly, very simple game. I don't think there's an answer for if we're becoming a more callous society. It's too broad a question. But some of my students said, "This is horrifying, I had no idea." Some of my students were like, "Oh, it was a really easy game." A lot of students were like, "I thought level one is too long. And then level two was too easy, blah, blah, blah, blah." But you could not have missed the larger point.

SELL: It seems like one of the things we're privileging, in this conversation and in general, is that we want to "break" play, we want to break systems, and we want to stage the breaking of those systems. Are we all just closet modernists baring the device and smashing the device? Is that the only way forward to teach people how to feel and how to be ethical? And how to understand how systems work? It feels like there's a bias or assumption in our conversation that feels a little old-fashioned to me.

WARDRIP-FRUIN: Maybe this is true of many disciplines, but I think students often recapitulate the history of the field as their way of learning it. That is, students often come in with a very naive idea of what it means for a game to be *about* something. A *Simpsons* chessboard, for instance, is about *The Simpsons*. "Look, I'm moving Marge, she is the queen." Then you have a conversation with them: "Okay, what if I just replaced all these pieces with bottle caps? Or with glass pebbles? Would this still be the same game? And in what ways would it be, and in what ways wouldn't it be?" They usually say, "Oh yeah, it would be exactly the same game." I say, "Great, then why don't you go ahead and market *Mr. Bean Tomb Raider*? Why do you laugh when I say that? Okay, well, maybe it isn't right." There is this set of canards that when students work through it, they begin to get a nuanced sense of what it might mean for a system to be *about* something, what it might mean to learn something from a system, what it might mean to challenge something through a system. And part of it, I think, inevitably, is a recognition of the need to expose the mechanism. But I don't think that's the end point. I think that's part of the transition.

SWENSEN: Yeah, because sometimes to teach about systems, we have to make them clear, but later on, we can appreciate a nuance or a subtlety. We appreciate systems as people making them. There can be a discovery process through design that you stumble across—systems that work without ever having been critically analyzed. In the same way that a typical enjoyer of your book of poetry is probably not explicating to everyone in a formal way, a way that they might learn to do in a classroom, but it's important to know how to do that to understand poetry, especially if you ever hope to write a poem. Even if your own discovery process feels more natural, feels more punk, ultimately, understanding the mechanisms is really important.

There's a step that is often skipped, and I think it doesn't come from malice or even straight up ignorance—I think that would be a simplification—but it comes from a position of the consumer, someone who only plays games. We want to jump to the point where we can play it. So they will skip many of these important critical steps because they're used to the product as players. They think if they get to the play faster, as long as it barely works, or as long as it's about the thing even if the system doesn't support it, that the game is done and that's what making a game is. It's coming from just being a consumer.

CHEMERS: So certainly, this kind of uncritical practice is not limited to games.

SWENSEN: No.

CHEMERS: We want to jump straight to the consumable, straight to the movable, straight to the product, and not worry so much about the processes of creation. Perhaps that is why we get otherwise well-meaning people doing terribly racist, terribly sexist, extremely homophobic, transphobic things with their art. I'm actually not even convinced that in theater we have a broadly better practice than this—I think we do it a lot. We also see a backlash against progressive aesthetics in the theater, although I think it is the minority voice in the U.S.

cárdenas: A big part of this conversation is about audience. The audience sizes for those kinds of media are very different. My question about empathy is usually, "Empathy for whom, and from whom?" My games are made for other trans people or people of color, mostly. Other audiences are secondary. Also, my games are probably really "bad," because they are "art games." So, you know, I'm not trying to make my games entertaining and I haven't spent a lot of time thinking about emotional arcs, although maybe I might in the future.

But I'm more interested in those games like *Redshift and Portal-metal* that ask interesting hard questions about the intersections of decolonial politics, immigration, and climate change (figs. 6.2a and 6.2b). The audience I am trying to reach is people that are already neck deep in thinking about and working on social justice, and I'm introducing to them some nuance like, "Even though trans women of color are a main target of violence, they can also be complicit in other kinds of violence, like colonization."

So I'm not trying to target my games at a mass multimillion-dollar audience. I'm just making art that's interesting to me. I have made games thinking that they would reach a different audience but only to a small extent, because usually my games are shown in an art or academic context.

CHEMERS: One of the virtues of dramaturgy is that, even in an era where a good scholar understands cultural relativism and eschews things like "Truth" with a capital *T*, we have these ontological positions that we know are empty or, more appropriately to this conversation, centered around one particular type of experience: Truth, Justice, whatever. The dramaturg is always searching for what is "best on stage," and *best* is a term that has been defined by thousands of years of dramaturgical writing on the subject as being "that which generates the most compassionate person in the audience." We find this in Aristotle, Bharatamuni, Zeami. The purpose of theater is to make us more compassionate. So we don't need to talk about the most *popular* when we talk about the most *successful* from that point of view.

Figs. 6.2a and 6.2b. Screen captures from *Redshift and Portalmetal*, by micha cárdenas. *Images courtesy of micha cárdenas.*

Mike and I feel it is right for us to direct our readers to consider their notions of what is *best*, and I think that there's an agreement around this table that, even though there's not one particular way to pursue these questions around games and pieces of theater, we can still say it is part of our best practices to strive for those things that make us more compassionate and more empathic.

cárdenas: Maybe. But my favorite dramaturg, Augusto Boal, would say something different: that the best outcome for an audience member is not that they be more compassionate, but for them to be more engaged so that they actually do something to improve their community.

WEEMS: That's more the Brechtian tradition. More active activism.

CHEMERS: Yes, that's interesting. I guess I think of those things as complementary.

SELL: Aren't we just putting forward a traditional kind of humanism here? Let's also keep in mind those really effective forms of dramaturgy that inspired vast numbers of people to assemble to hate Jews, in the case of the Nuremberg rallies. It took some truly talented dramaturgs to figure out how to bring people together to enthusiastically feel together how much they wanted to kill Jews. There are different forms of dramaturgy and ways of thinking about performance, affect, and dramatic arcs that can serve different kinds of ethical and moral purposes.

STONE: I agree. I see similarities between this and what several others have said in the course of this dialogue, which is that the machinery itself is neutral, and you put your interpretation of what you would like that machinery to be and do onto it. So saying the goal of the machinery of theater is to produce compassion is a valid goal, but it's also not the only goal.

SELL: Kimberly Jannarone has done work on the avant-garde that discusses how techniques that were developed for progressive reasons were borrowed, appropriated, and détourned for very different purposes.[8] The fascists were particularly inventive about that kind of borrowing.

STONE: On this campus, there was a quite violent discussion (which still, fortunately, remained only a discussion) about whether the internet was in fact neutral. There was a large faction here that maintained quite angrily that the internet was in fact not only neutral but tended to the good, and that left to its own devices, it produced positive changes in society. Others were going around saying, "You're out of your gourd." But the fact that it got so angry and violent, I think, is an indication of how much contention there is around the idea of what the role of performance culture is, to change the subject rather quickly. How can we be aware of the fact that theater itself doesn't help you one way or the other, and you have to make it into what you want to be? That's a conscious act of violence in its own way.

SELL: It's interesting how often the conversation, the techniques, the advice get down to the point where we say, "Okay, so you're in this place with these people, these resources, these constraints, these opportunities, this potential audience, this definite audience, this possible audience. What are you going to do with that stuff?" In the ethical dimension, that's where the rubber hits the road, because it's no longer an abstract concept. You say, "Okay, so what are we going to do at this place in this time? What can we achieve here?" As a literary scholar who loves drama best, and who loves to play video games and tabletop roleplaying games as well, I often think about these things that exist free from context.

When I think about the many productions of plays I've seen that were important to me, I realize they were important because of one moment that made all the difference. As we think about operational systems like games and theater, I think it is important to sustain the situational dimensions of their operation in mind. And so I wonder if we might speak a little bit about the value of performance, not as an abstract, not as in the performative, but in terms of actual performance, in this space at this time.

WEEMS: Well, theaters are a kind of ancient technology of mass social cohesion, because the participants are committing to being in the same room at the same time as these other people to witness this live event, which is a specific and kind of niche moment. Just making that commitment to connect is very specific to theater. I mean, where else do you do that? If you go to a movie house, it's not really the same, because you don't have the live component onstage. So there's something that's quite antiquated but I think still intact about that social cohesion.

SELL: Here's an interesting twist on that notion: right now, around the world, there are thousands, hundreds of thousands, of people who are watching other people play videogames. They might be watching on their phones and computers or gathered in massive sports arenas. In these situations, live performance is essentially televisual, mediated by screens, multiple screens, and yet that feeling of being there comes through. Do you feel that a kind of mediated televisual presence is different in kind from being in a theater together?

WEEMS: I think that the experience of connection and cohesion is what I see when I see people watching other people play. It's virtuosic; it's operatic. You want to see the performance. But is that different from athletics? Can't that happen in any medium? It is intensely seductive and engaging to see somebody be really good at something.

CHEMERS: Mike and I are by no means Luddites or technophobic, but our interest in the idea and practice of systemic dramaturgy is due to the advent and proliferation of digital technology that has inarguably changed the way we experience *presence*. Yes, digital presence is a type of presence, and yet one of the things that I keep coming back to is why I think it's different for me to be teaching my class in a room full of students than it is for me to put it online. I realize that online courses increase access and accommodate different learning styles, but I still think that there's something important about liveness. But I'm not arguing that the digital is the enemy of the live. I don't believe that these things are opposite or even in opposition. As an example, we watched *Bandersnatch* the other night.

SWENSEN: My favorite quip that I heard about whether *Bandersnatch* is a movie or a game is "It's a movie, because everyone who made it is in a union."

CHEMERS: Love it! *Bandersnatch* is an episode of the *Black Mirror* series on Netflix. But it has an interactive component, which is that the viewer is asked to make a decision, and that decision creates a branch in the narrative. It requires several kinds of engagement, and the engagement itself—whether you choose to eat one cereal or another, whether you choose to work for a company or not—becomes a piece of content that is consciously acknowledged and even analyzed by the characters in the story. It starts to get really weird to the point where you, the viewer-participant, are implicated in the bad things that are happening to the characters. I watched/played that in a room with four people, all of whom were yelling at each other, "Don't make that choice! Pick that choice!" and that made it much more pleasurable and much more exciting to me than if I played it all by myself. I'm not sure what that was. Was it a TV show with a game component? Was it interactive TV? I've never seen anything like it. But I do know that there was a liveness component of it that I found valuable.

Similarly, I want to play *Dungeons & Dragons* with my friends who are in the room. But I don't know how to talk about that desire and that experience without feeling like I'm illegitimately privileging liveness—a naive understanding of liveness. I know I'd rather go to the theater than go to a movie. I'd rather play videogames than go to the theater. Oh my god, did I just say that out loud? And I would rather play *Dungeons & Dragons* with a group of people than play a videogame about *Dungeons & Dragons*.

WEEMS: I think that part of the pleasure is that it is a gray area where you and your friends get to exist in this little continuum between this mediated space rather than just sitting on the couch with nothing to do. It's the combination of those two things that make it so pleasurable, don't you think?

SELL: There's a term related to *liveness* that I feel just as suspicious about but is a common part of our conversation about interactive entertainment: *immersiveness*. When I was first learning film theory, I was always told to think about how we identify with characters. I've never been particularly good at identifying with characters. Maybe I lack a basic ability or willingness to empathize. But I've always been conscious of a kind of oscillation or strobing that happens as I watch or play. I'm identifying and not identifying when I'm playing a game. I'm in that game, I'm with my avatar, and I'm also thinking more systemically and strategically, "What's happening here? What am I supposed to do?" And that's been my experience in theater. I'm never not aware that I'm sitting in a seat with a program tucked under my leg. I'm never feeling comfortable about where my pleasure in my activity is landing. But I'm definitely experiencing pleasure. There's something to that particular way of being in a live audience, aware of the stage and being in the world staged on that stage at the same time, that feels to me both very old and very much of our technocultural moment.

CHEMERS: I think this goes back to the invisible screen that was there before we ever had a concept of digital culture or anything, right?

We called it the fourth wall or, from the audience's side of things, the willing suspension of disbelief. Is that relevant to our discussion anymore?

STONE: When you go into the movie theater and sit in the dark, that invokes dream logic, which is to say a particular kind of neurological efficiency. It feels to you as if you're putting yourself in the hands of storytelling. I abandon myself. I give myself up to the experience of having something happen to me narratively. I participate. I put my caboose on that particular train. And for a while, I don't have to do any work. It's all done for me and it brings me out, and then I get out on the other end of it and I've been wrung out, and it feels good without my having had to do any particular work on my own. But in live theater, this is totally different. You have to work, but everyone comes out, hopefully, feeling like they've been struck by lightning, and everybody is happy.

I'm really interested in the problem that you've laid out by describing that there are things that we take great pleasure in, and it feels like we have a kind of agency in that pleasure. It has to do with maintaining a kind of analytic and emotional control and agency over what we're doing. Maybe what's happening there is actually something that is either hardwired, because it's somehow essential to our neurological wiring, or it's something that has been built into my system. And as somebody who's been playing a fair amount of the game *Tetris* recently, I'm very conscious of that so-called Tetris effect. Once you finish playing, you see, you organize the shapes around you the same way.

I was playing another game called *Into the Breach*, which is a grid-based game, and you're constantly thinking of lines. I played that for a while, and I was walking around my house and mentally rearranging furniture to make sure I wouldn't get blown up by giant insects. There's something very important about that kind of cognitive training or rewiring that happens. It's why I read certain kinds of books or why I love certain movies. Teresa de Lauretis characterizes film as a technology of gender, pointing out that there's only so much we can do with the machine.[9]

This goes back to the point that micha raised—that there's only so much you can do with the machine that was specifically designed toward certain attitudes, toward military efficiency, toward preserving think tanks after the nukes dropped and destroyed everybody else, and so on. There's only so much you can do with the machine that was designed to represent whiteness, to represent masculinity, to represent a certain kind of agency. For Teresa de Lauretis and others, one of the solutions was "Well, let's show movies in different kinds of social spaces. Let's think about how we lay out the seats and how we frame the frame," those kinds of things.

I think the problem you've laid out is really important. It's a dramaturgical question: How do you work if you have a problematic text? How do you frame it? How do you produce it? What are the different ways that you put it onstage so that we can get the pleasures that we find in the text, but also to make us conscious of those pleasures and what we seek from them?

CHEMERS: That is the way we think about dramaturgy. The British horror and comic book author Mike Carey spoke to me once about his concept of "fractal protagonist," which I think is an outgrowth of what Noah Wardrip-Fruin and Pat Harrington in 2009 called "vast narratives."[10] These are incredibly complex, convoluted stories that we find in comic books, for example, but also in different stories in different media colliding with each other: movies and TV shows and websites and figurines and cosplay and fan fiction, and then the comic book stories themselves overlapping and going back and retconning and changing themselves as they incorporate fan feedback and change again.

Look at something like *Game of Thrones*, a television show initially based on a novel, but the television show overtook the novel in terms of the release of episodes versus the release of new books, and the television show started changing what used to be considered the original source material, but now the books haven't come out yet, and so now what's the original source material and what's the adaptation? Nobody knows and maybe the only person who cares is a literary critic. Plus, there are all these other factors that would not go into the making of a novel that go into the making of a TV show, like actor salaries, shooting locations, craft services, gas and vehicles that are now going into the creation of the Ur-story. The next novel is actually going to be an adaptation of the TV show. Phew! How do we do dramaturgy in a situation like that?

SWENSEN: It's a common story that animes often overtake the manga, and I am not a scholar in that field at all. But oftentimes anime series are rebooted once the source material is finally done. It's as if they said, "Well, this is the first version of *this* anime, this is our interpretation of where we think the story was going, but now there is a new base text, so let's just start over." Speaking about when process leaks into the production of something and tells an additional narrative, a process narrative, that happens a lot in games. It happens in theater.

My personal experience of playing a game, my performance of the game, is a different story than the scripted narrative of the game. My personal story would not even be possible in a procedural narrative. How do you talk about the game script as an anchor text, if you will, as a part of dramaturgy? The fact that you know someone can play *World of Warcraft* trying to get to the top level without murdering anything, experiencing a completely pacifist playthrough—that is a very different story than most other players' stories. Some of it comes from attention and some from randomness. That's the nature of a procedural system.

AFTERWORD: SYSTEMIC DRAMATURGY THEN, NOW, AND TOMORROW

> If we take this process of technological extension seriously enough—not just on the level of theoretical argument but also through our experiential being with technologies and media such as cell phones almost permanently attached to our ears, pacemakers, virtual reality goggles, human growth hormones, or Botox—we are obliged to recognize that we human users of technology are not entirely distinct from our tools. They are not a means to our ends; instead, they have become part of us, to an extent that the us/them distinction is no longer tenable.
>
> —Sarah Kember and Joanna Zylinska, *Life after New Media*

A few more words about systemic dramaturgy. As we've discussed, a systemic approach to dramaturgy does not diverge from the work that dramaturgs have been doing for millennia. Like those who came before us and, if all goes reasonably well, those who follow, we believe in the power of dramatic performance, of play that entertains, moves, unsettles, and enlightens. There is something undeniably special about people gathering together to play and present what they've created to others in playful fashion. It feels undeniably *human* to do such a thing. Indeed, our very understanding of what it means to be human has been shaped by those who have played—played beautifully and well or played badly and with cruel intent. A systemic approach to dramaturgy enables us to do more effectively the traditional tasks of the

Afterword

dramaturg—comprehending the dramatic text in all its complexity, providing critical perspectives and practical advice to our team members, helping audiences experience fully and thoughtfully. But it also provides vital perspectives on other forms of dramatic, playful, meaning-making performance, particularly in the digital era. The bridge between the traditional and the new, the conventional and the unconsidered is built on this conception of dramaturgy that we call *systemic.*

Our approach is systemic because we use our skills and knowledge to comprehend the *entirety* of the performance production as an interrelated system of systems encompassing the people, places, things, processes, principles, concepts, and everything else that guides the conception, creation, and reception of play. It is systemic in the sense that we approach each aspect of production as a technical challenge, as a problem that can be solved by thinking and making carefully and consistently in terms of the relationship between ends and means, between the tool and the mind that directs the tool, between solutions that clearly articulate with the larger social, political, and economic context in which conception, creation, and reception occur and solutions that do not. It is systemic insofar as it recognizes that the boundary between *us* and *our tools* is at best quite murky.

Our systemic approach is grounded in three conceptual frameworks. The first is an expanded understanding of the history of theater and technology. While we recognize the unprecedented nature of digital, robotic, and computational technologies, we don't see the problem qua problem of technology as new to theater or live performance. In fact, quite the opposite. The problem of technology is the original problem of theater. Including the technologies of language, gesture, and light, there is no theater without technology, and every technology poses unique problems to those who would play with it, whether that be a simple technical problem (e.g., where a light source should be placed) or something more troubling, something that cuts to the crux of the art form or the community that loves it. We see theater history as, in part, the history of approaches and solutions to the problem of theater and technology. Among those we find particularly compelling is the sokyokuchi aesthetic of Zeami Motokiyo, which advocates a practice of dynamic interrelationship, of "mutuality in balance," between a human performer and the techniques and tools of performance.

An investigation of an older and non–Euro-American approach to the problem offers not only a different conception of technology (what the philosophers call techne) but a different history of that conception, as Zeami's theory can be traced through three major figures in the modern Euro-American theatrical tradition: Vsevelod Meyerhold, Jerzy Grotowski, and Richard Schechner. The persistence of the sokyokuchi approach in their work, when recognized by historians and practitioners, can help us avoid simple dichotomies between pro- and antitechnology. Did Grotowski and Schechner advocate the elimination of many theater technologies from their work? Undoubtedly, yes. But that doesn't mean they were antitechnological. In fact, such an assertion is logically impossible, as the very moment a space is transformed into a stage or a body into a motile, magnetic source of significance is a technological moment, a moment when something that exists in itself is turned into something that exists for the purposes of communication, beauty, and mutual presence. In our conversations with Marianne Weems and Noah Wardrip-Fruin, we find exactly that kind of pragmatism. Though both enthusiastically embrace new technologies, they never lose sight of the well-worn tools that remain useful or beloved. They do this for reasons that are practical (e.g., a soda bottle with the top cut off does a fine job of creating an echo effect) or speculative (e.g., as Wardrip-Fruin suggested in his interview for this book, "Why don't we do it with real people? Then we'll get all these ideas we would never have had if we just sat down and went with the assumptions that were built into the tools.").

The second conceptual framework in which we ground systemic dramaturgy concerns the idea of play. Play is the essence of theater, encompassing script (a text designed to be played with), process (playing with options and ideas), and final product (playing for the audience). But it's also the essence of so much more, as has been established by historians and theorists of play like Johan Huizinga and Bonnie Ruberg and historians and theorists of performance, like Richard Schechner and Diana Taylor. A systemic approach to play that recognizes its full historical, conceptual, aesthetic, and practical dimensions enables a dramaturg to be more alert to dimensions of the theater and performance that might otherwise escape their attention. It enables them to identify other forms of expression, interaction, and community to which their skills can be smartly applied, like videogames. In our conversations with

Weems, Wardrip-Fruin, Elizabeth Swensen, micha cárdenas, Jennifer Haley, Nick Junius, and Sandy Stone, we see a wide range of playful dramaturgies. While none of them describe what they do as dramaturgy, we do. Textual analysis, thoughtful process, and attentiveness to audience needs structured around play—that's what connects the traditional dramaturg to the broader ecosystem of playful media.

Our third conceptual framework is empathy. Empathy informs all aspects of play. An actor must be able to imagine themselves as their character, feel what that character feels, experience the character's experiences with the same level of embodied heart, pleasure, and pain as they do their own lives. A player of a tabletop roleplaying game must imagine themselves through the statistics on their character sheets, the rules in the rulebook, and the roll of the dice to express whom they want their character to be. A videogame designer must imagine how their game will be experienced by all possible players, not just those like them. A parent must be able imagine themselves into their child's mind and heart when they see the child impassioned by play, project their own experiences and feelings to recognize moments of sympathy or empathy and moments that require a more constructive and interventionist approach. And children, too, must learn how to translate their own playful experiences, the languages of their playful texts and player communities, in terms that are meaningful to their parents, as we see go tragically wrong in Jennifer Haley's *Neighborhood 3: Requisition of Doom*.

In light of our systemic approach, we argue that empathy is best understood as an effect of technology and technique—what we call a "structure of affect." We treat empathy as a tool that can be turned to many tasks. As cárdenas reminds us in her interview, "Empathy is not monolithic." There are innumerable examples of works designed to generate empathy for some and against others or works that were intended to generate empathy for others but failed, instead generating feelings of disgust and antipathy. And sometimes empathy should not be asked of artists and their works, whether because that is not their intent or because they refuse to be obligated to reach out to those who have victimized them.

These three conceptual frameworks—the theater-technology relationship, an expanded conception of play, and a technological approach to empathy—enable dramaturgs to do the traditional labors of dramaturgy better and to apply dramaturgical practice in other and emergent fields of performance, including games of all kinds. But there's another benefit of a systemic approach to dramaturgy, perhaps the most important one. If, as Michael argued in *Ghost Light*, everybody involved in a theater production is a dramaturg, even if they aren't officially designated as such, then wouldn't we want everyone who's involved in any kind of dramatic play to know how to do the work of dramaturgy—or to recognize what they're doing as essentially dramaturgical? We think here of the Dungeon Master managing a game of *Dungeons & Dragons* for a group of friends and family. Like the traditional dramaturg, they must understand the "script" (in this case, a published adventure outlining the twists and turns of an adventure); they must understand the technical requirements of production (arranging the table, knowing the rules, performing the various nonplayer roles); and they must understand the needs of their audience (the players, who are also the performers). Wouldn't it be wonderful if our skills could help all kinds of players play better, more thoughtfully, and with a sense of critical consciousness, even an eye for social justice?

A systemic approach to dramaturgy provides a compelling argument for the inclusion of dramaturgy in the core curricula of high schools and colleges. If we are living in a "ludic century," as Eric Zimmerman argues, then the dramaturgy of play should be as widely taught as basic math and writing. Dramaturgy, from this perspective, is a critical life skill and a core cultural competency of contemporary life.

The very nature of work that includes discourses of technology is that it is always changing—perhaps never more so than now. That's what makes systemic dramaturgy effective and fun. As dramaturgs, we welcome problems because we know that, in the end, we'll have been part of something fun, memorable, beautiful, important. Or something that didn't come off quite as well but can be chalked up to a learning experience. Who knows what new tech is on the horizon that will instigate new changes in the experience of being human? How will it change the way we understand who we are, what we are, when we are, and most importantly, how we can shape these experiences to share with others? Systemic dramaturgs don't predict the future, but we do prepare for it by transforming our practice as dramaturgs into the most flexible, most engaged, and most wide-ranging practice possible.

Afterword

The book you are reading is at best an interim report from the field, a critical engagement with what we perceive to be going on right now informed by what's been going on for millennia and what's going on all around us. We invite you to surpass us by generating your own interventions in these important discourses. We invite you to a further exploration of the uncanny and its particular powers in representation. We invite you to identify other systems and pursue a deeper analysis of the systems we describe—and those we failed to describe—that involve drama, performance, and play. We urge you to apply what we have learned to new areas of dramatic play: videogames, tabletop roleplaying games, live-action roleplaying games, cosplay, and anything else that moves some people to build something that moves others. The future of systemic dramaturgy—and its past—is for you, dear reader, to design.

NOTES

BIBLIOGRAPHY

INDEX

NOTES

Introduction

1. Proehl, *Toward a Dramaturgical Sensibility*.
2. Zeydel, *Ludwig Tieck*, 261.
3. Some engineers call this "downward compatibility," but we feel the derogatory connotations of backwardness are already sufficient.
4. Carlson, *Haunted Stage*, 2, 3, 165.
5. Schechner, *Environmental Theater*, 32, 33.
6. Taylor, *Archive and the Repertoire*, 20.
7. Zola, "Naturalism on the Stage,"5.
8. An incomplete list of the most important of these works follows: Auslander, *Liveness*; Bay-Cheng, Parker-Starbuck, and Saltz, *Performance and Media*; Bay-Cheng et al., *Mapping Intermediality in Performance*; Bloom, *Gaming the Stage*; Causey, *Theatre and Performance in Digital Culture*; Dixon, *Digital Performance*; Eckersall, Grehan, and Scheer, *New Media Dramaturgy*; McKenzie, *Perform or Else*; Parker-Starbuck, *Cyborg Theatre*; Salter, *Entangled*.
9. Eckersall, Grehan, and Scheer, *New Media Dramaturgy*, 6.
10. Eckersall, Grehan, and Scheer, *New Media Dramaturgy*, 7.
11. Eckersall, Grehan, and Scheer, *New Media Dramaturgy*, 13.
12. Eckersall, Grehan, and Scheer, *New Media Dramaturgy*, 3.
13. Salter, *Entangled*, xxii.
14. van Kerkhoven, "Theatre is in the City."
15. Salter, *Entangled*, xxxv.
16. Deleuze and Guattari, *A Thousand Plateaus*.
17. McKenzie, *Perform or Else*.
18. Zimmerman, "Manifesto for a Ludic Century."
19. Eckersall, Grehan, and Scheer, *New Media Dramaturgy*, 2.

1. Sokyokuchi

1. Motokiyo, *Art of the Nō Drama*, 97–98. For Zeami's work, we rely on the excellent translations and analysis of J. Thomas Rimer and Yamazaki Masakazu in this source.
2. Schechner, *Environmental Theatre*, xli, xl.
3. Proehl, *Toward a Dramaturgical Sensibility*, 28.
4. See Salter, *Entangled*, 1–47.
5. See Salter, *Entangled*, 5.
6. Grotowski, *Towards a Poor Theatre*, 19.
7. Rozik, "Ritual Origin of Theatre," 138–39.

Notes to Pages 50–86

8. Meyerhold, "Stylized Theatre."

9. See Tian, "Meyerhold Meets Mei Lanfang."

10. Regarding Meyerhold's desire to draw attention to the black-clad assistants, see Fischer-Lichte, "Reception of Japanese Theatre," 36. The comprehensive work of Tian, "Authenticity and Usability," calls into question how minutely Meyerhold actually understood classical Asian dramaturgy and how authentic the productions he witnessed actually were.

11. Fischer-Lichte, "Reception of Japanese Theatre," 30.

12. Meyerhold, *Meyerhold on Theatre*, 197.

13. Meyerhold, *Meyerhold on Theatre*, 128.

14. Meyerhold, *Meyerhold on Theatre*, 128–29.

15. Quoted in Braun, Meyerhold, 176.

16. Meyerhold, *Meyerhold on Theatre*, 197.

17. Phelan, *Unmarked*, 147.

18. Auslander, *Liveness*, 3.

19. For more on *Super Vision*, see Jackson and Weems, *Builders Association*, 243–90. For more on the Builders Association, see Dixon, *Digital Performance*, 344–51 and 518–20; Salter, *Entangled*, 141–63.

20. Salter, *Entangled*, 222.

21. Causey, *Theatre and Performance in Digital Culture*, 61.

22. Causey, "Postdigital Performance," 436.

23. Salter, *Entangled*, 303.

24. Salter, *Entangled*, 351.

25. Eckersall, Grehan, and Scheer, *New Media Dramaturgy*, 7.

2. Playing with Play

1. Bloom, *Gaming the Stage*.

2. Shakespeare, *Henry V, I*, ii, lines 261–3, 940.

3. Zimmerman, "Manifesto for a Ludic Century."

4. Schechner, *Future of Ritual* 43.

5. Barish, *Antitheatrical Prejudice*, 161.

6. Huizinga, *Homo Ludens*, 13.

7. Milton, *Paradise Lost*, 376, lines 1027–32.

8. Gray, *Friday*.

9. Schechner, *Performance Studies*, 106–7.

10. Sample, "Play."

11. Bloom, *Gaming the Stage*, 1.

12. Zimmerman, "Manifesto for a Ludic Century."

13. Bloom, *Gaming the Stage*, 2.

14. Kramer, "What Is a Game?"

15. Carlson, *Haunted Stage*.

16. Roach, *Cities of the Dead*, 11.

Notes to Pages 86–131

17. Taylor, *Archive and the Repertoire*, xviii.
18. Bloom, *Gaming the Stage*, 58, 14.
19. Bloom, *Gaming the Stage*, 59.
20. Harrigan and Wardrip-Fruin, *Second Person*, xiii.
21. Hart, "Getting into the Game."
22. Hart, "Getting into the Game."
23. van Kerkhoven, *Listen to the Bloody Machine*.
24. Eckersall, Grehan, and Scheer, *New Media Dramaturgy*, 2.
25. Eckersall, Grehan, and Scheer, *New Media Dramaturgy*, 1, 13.
26. Parker-Starbuck, *Cyborg Theatre*, xiv, 8.
27. Huizinga, *Homo Ludens*, 1.
28. Suits, *Grasshopper*, 34.
29. Rothenberg, "Mixing Old and New."
30. Eckersall, Grehan, and Scheer, *New Media Dramaturgy*, 14.
31. Thomas, "Digital Dramaturgy," 30, 511.
32. Thomas, "Digital Dramaturgy," 506–11.
33. Dixon, *Digital Performance*, x, xii.
34. Bay-Cheng, Parker-Starbuck, and Saltz, *Performance and Media*, 1.
35. Eckersall, Grehan, and Scheer, *New Media Dramaturgy*, 3.
36. Eckersall, Grehan, and Scheer, *New Media Dramaturgy*, 7.
37. McKenzie, *Perform or Else*, 139.
38. Huizinga, *Homo Ludens*, 10.
39. Consalvo, "There Is No Magic Circle," 415.
40. Consalvo, "There Is No Magic Circle," 416.
41. Kelley, *Freedom Dreams*.
42. Kelley, *Freedom Dreams*, 2–3.
43. Costantino, "Politics and Culture," 194.
44. Bloom, *Gaming the Stage*, 1.
45. Zimmerman, "Manifesto for a Ludic Century."
46. Miller, *Playable Bodies*, 1.
47. Blast Theory, *Can You See Me Now?*
48. Salter, *Entangled*, xxii.

3. The Empathy Machine
1. Bharatamuni, *Natyasastra*, 4.
2. For a critical summary, see Chemers, *Ghost Light*, 12–65.
3. Belman and Flanagan, "Designing Games to Foster Empathy," 7.
4. Belman and Flanagan, "Designing Games to Foster Empathy," 8.
5. Belman and Flanagan, "Designing Games to Foster Empathy," 8.
6. Sell, "Avant-Garde Theory."
7. Donovan, "First They Came for the Black Feminists."
8. Suellentrop, "In the Footsteps." See also Carpenter, "Tropes vs. Women."

253

Notes to Pages 131–57

9. Most of the corporations that dominate the internet are governed by U.S. law, which at the time of the report held that corporate agencies that provided internet services were not liable for the actions of their users.

10. Boluk and LeMieux, *Metagaming*, chap. 6.

11. Boluk and LeMieux, *Metagaming*, chap. 6.

12. Geek lost both its Germanic/Old English meaning of "fool" and its nineteenth-century associations with carnival performers whose acts were notably disgusting in some way, and in the twentieth century, the word evolved into an (initially) derogatory descriptor for a person whose enthusiasm for (or obsession with) outré behavior has resulted in their marginalization from mainstream society.

13. Massanari, "#Gamergate and the Fappening," 332.

14. Shaw, "On Not Becoming Gamers."

15. Massanari, "#Gamergate and the Fappening," 332.

16. Fan, "Not All Nerds."

17. Massanari, "#Gamergate and the Fappening," 332.

18. It is worth noting how similar this evidence is to observations made by Roach in *Cities of the Dead* when discussing "surrogation" and the role that theater plays in this process (1–7).

19. Sarkeesian, address delivered at the 2014 XOXO Festival. The entire talk can be found at https://www.youtube.com/watch?time_continue=3&v=ah8mhDW6Shs.

20. This may go some way toward explaining the belief that *Depression Quest*, a play-for-free game that donated part of its proceeds to suicide prevention charities, could be understood by gamers as a threat to AAA franchises like *Call of Duty*, which in December 2015 had reported earnings in excess of $11 billion.

21. Robin Hunicke, interview by the authors, July 12, 2017.

22. ESA, "2020 Essential Facts."

23. Handrahan, "PewDiePie Dropped."

24. Bezio, "Ctrl-Alt-Del."

25. Donovan, "First They Came for the Black Feminists."

26. Dorothy Kim, interview by the authors, March 27, 2019.

27. Phelan, *Unmarked*, 163.

28. Phelan, *Unmarked*, 163–64.

29. Phelan, *Unmarked*, 164.

30. Phelan, *Unmarked*, 175.

31. Phelan, *Unmarked*, 164.

4. Toward a Dramaturgy of Videogames

1. Taekema and van Klink, "On the Border," 7.

2. Chemers, *Ghost Light*, 8–9.

3. Schechner, *Performance Studies*.

4. Takahashi, "SuperData."

5. ESA, "2020 Essential Facts."

6. Zimmerman, "Manifesto for a Ludic Century."

7. Laurel, *Computers as Theatre*, xi, 79–82, 199. See also 145–48.

8. Murray, *Hamlet on the Holodeck*, 29.

9. Dixon, *Digital Performance*, 609–16.

10. Gough, "Top-Selling Console Games Worldwide in 2018."

11. Wijman, "Newzoo's 2018 Report."

12. "Global Digital Gaming Market 2018–2023"; Gough, "Leading Mobile Game Titles Worldwide in 2017."

13. Morris, "4 of 2018's Best-Selling PC Games."

14. Boluk and LeMieux, *Metagaming*, intro.

15. For more on Semi Ryu's work, see her Ted Talk, "Virtual Reality for Han," at https://youtu.be/BLPARGjvwfc.

16. Sicart, "Queering the Controller."

17. Marcotte, "Queering Control(lers)."

18. Polansky, "Towards an Art History."

19. Anthropy, *Rise of the Videogame Zinesters*.

20. Boluk and LeMieux, *Metagaming*, chap. 3.

21. Aarseth, *Cybertext*, 1.

22. St. Patrick and Alder, "Beyond Representation."

23. Clark and merritt k, "Queering Human-Game Relations."

24. Schrank, *Avant-Garde Videogames*, 92.

25. Noah Wardrip-Fruin, email to authors, August 23, 2019.

26. Bilal, "Domestic Tension."

27. Chemers, *Ghost Light*, 8–9.

28. Winkie, "Overwatch."

29. Miller, *Playable Bodies*, 177.

30. Wilson, "Social Games as Partial Platforms."

31. "Biggest Live Esports Events."

32. Seo, and Jung, "Beyond Solitary Play," 639.

33. Linn, "We Third-Rate Monsters."

34. Linn, "We Third-Rate Monsters."

35. Linn, "We Third-Rate Monsters."

36. Chan, "EK Theater."

37. Bloom, "Videogame Shakespeare," 119.

38. Bloom, "Videogame Shakespeare," 119–20.

39. Bloom, "Videogame Shakespeare," 121–22.

40. Bloom, "Videogame Shakespeare," 123.

41. Williams, Yee, and Caplan, "Who Plays, How Much?; Shaw, "What Is Video Game Culture?"; Penix-Tadsen, *Cultural Code*; Anderson, "Views on Gaming Differ"; Shaw, "Do You Identify as a Gamer?"

42. ESA, "2020 Essential Facts."

43. Anderson, "Views on Gaming Differ"; "Children and Video Games."

Notes to Pages 177–240

44. Shaw, Rudolph, and Schnorrenberg, *Rainbow Arcade*, 92.
45. "Video Game Industry Statistics."
46. Penix-Tadsen, *Cultural Code*, 6, 21, 97.
47. Chess and Paul, "End of Casual."
48. Parkin, "If You Love Games."
49. Semi Ryu, "VoicingElder."
50. Au, "Triumph of the Mod."
51. Au, "Triumph of the Mod."
52. Kücklich, "Precarious Playbour."
53. Altomonte, "Witnessing Violence, (Re)Living Trauma."
54. Chin, "Observed Bodies and Tool Selves," 206.
55. Chin, "Observed Bodies and Tool Selves," 208.

5. The Uncanny Mountain and *Neighborhood 3: Requisition of Doom*

1. Mori, "The Uncanny Valley."
2. Albee, *Delicate Balance*, 174–75.
3. WHO, "Addictive Behaviors: Gaming Disorder."
4. Anderson, "Violent Video Games."
5. Solomon, "Theatre Proves a Most Relevant Medium."

6. Systemic Dramaturgy Roundtable

1. Causey, "Postdigital Performance."
2. Adams, "How to Stop Worrying."
3. Bura, "Emotion Engineering in Videogames."
4. ACTLab was the informal name of the New Media program at the University of Texas–Austin, which Professor Stone founded in 1993. The program formally ended in 2010 when Professor Stone retired from UT, but its principles are replicated in the educational training programs of the European Graduate School in Saas-Fee, Switzerland, the Entertainment Technology Center at Carnegie Mellon University, and the New Media Innovation Laboratory at Arizona State University.
5. McPherson, "Why Are the Digital Humanities So White?"
6. Dr. cárdenas can be viewed discussing the work of her Local Autonomy Networks as part of the "Feminist & Queer Approaches to Technoscience" colloquium held at the University of Toronto, March 27, 2014, at http://sfonline.barnard.edu/traversing-technologies/micha-cardenas-local-autonomy-networks-post-digital-networks-post-corporate-communications/.
7. The *Hold Your Boundaries* project can be found at https://www.instagram.com/holdyourboundaries/.
8. Jannarone, *Vanguard Performance.*
9. De Lauretis, *Technologies of Gender.*
10. Mike Carey, interview by the authors, July 31, 2017; Harrigan and Wardrip-Fruin, Third Person.

BIBLIOGRAPHY

Aarseth, Espen J. *Cybertext: Perspectives on Ergodic Literature*. Baltimore: Johns Hopkins University Press, 1997.

Adams, Douglas. "How to Stop Worrying and Love the Internet." *Sunday Times*, August 29, 1999.

Albee, Edward. *A Delicate Balance*. New York: Samuel French, 1967.

Altomonte, Jenna A. "Witnessing Violence, (Re)Living Trauma: Online Performance Interventions in the Digital Age." PhD diss., Ohio University, 2017.

Anderson, Craig A. "Violent Video Games: Myths, Facts, and Unanswered Questions." *Psychological Science Agenda*. American Psychological Association. October 2003. https://www.apa.org/science/about/psa/2003/10/anderson.

Anderson, Monica. "Views on Gaming Differ by Race, Ethnicity." December 17, 2015. Pew Research Center. https://www.pewresearch.org/fact-tank/2015/12/17/views-on-gaming-differ-by-race-ethnicity/.

Anthropy, Anna. *Rise of the Videogame Zinesters*. New York: Seven Stories, 2012.

Aristotle. *The Poetics of Aristotle*. Translated by Preston H. Epps. Chapel Hill: University of North Carolina Press, 1984.

Attridge, Derek. "Jacques Derrida: The Problems of Presence." *Times Literary Supplement*. November 2018. https://www.the-tls.co.uk/articles/jacques-derrida-problems-presence/.

Au, Wagner James. "Triumph of the Mod." *Salon*. April 16, 2002. https://www.salon.com/2002/04/16/modding/.

Auslander, Philip. *Liveness: Performance in a Mediatized Culture*. 2nd ed. Oxford: Routledge, 2008.

Barish, Jonas. *The Antitheatrical Prejudice*. Berkeley: University of California Press, 1981.

Bay-Cheng, Sarah, Chiel Kattenbelt, Andy Lavender, and Robin Nelson, eds. *Mapping Intermediality in Performance*. Amsterdam: Amsterdam University Press, 2010.

Bay-Cheng, Sarah, Jennifer Parker-Starbuck, and David Z. Saltz. *Performance and Media: Taxonomies for a Changing Field*. Ann Arbor: University of Michigan Press, 2015.

Belman, Jonathan, and Mary Flanagan. "Designing Games to Foster Empathy." *Cognitive Technology* 14, no. 2 (2010): 5–15.

Bezio, Kristin MS. "Ctrl-Alt-Del: Gamergate as a Precursor to the Rise of the Alt-Right." *Leadership* 14, no. 5 (2018): 556–66. https://doi.org/10.1177/1742715018793744.

Bharatamuni. *The Natyasastra: English Translation with Critical Notes*. Translated and edited by Adya Rangacharya. New Delhi: Munshiram Manoharlal, 1996.

Bibliography

"The Biggest Live Esports Events on the Planet." Bet O'Clock. July 8, 2020. https://betoclock.com/biggest-esports-live-events/.

Bilal, Wafaa. *Domestic Tension*. Accessed June 11, 2019. http://wafaabilal.com/domestic-tension.

Blast Theory. *Can You See Me Now?* Accessed March 21, 2021. https://www.blasttheory.co.uk/projects/can-you-see-me-now/.

Bloom, Gina. *Gaming the Stage: Playable Media and the Rise of English Commercial Theatre*. Ann Arbor: University of Michigan Press, 2018.

———. "Videogame Shakespeare: Enskilling Audiences through Theater-Making Games." *Shakespeare Studies* 43 (2015): 114–27.

Boluk, Stephanie, and Patrick LeMieux. *Metagaming: Playing, Competing, Spectating, Cheating, Trading, Making, and Breaking Videogames*. Minneapolis: University of Minnesota Press, 2017. https://manifold.umn.edu/projects/metagaming.

Borges, Jorge Luis. *Collected Fictions*. Translated by Andrew Hurley. New York: Penguin, 1998.

Bottoms, Stephen J. *Playing Underground: A Critical History of the 1960s Off-Off-Broadway Movement*. Ann Arbor: University of Michigan Press, 2006.

Braun, Edward. *Meyerhold: A Revolution in Theatre*. Des Moines: University of Iowa Press, 1995.

Bura, Stéphane. "Emotion Engineering in Videogames: Toward a Scientific Approach to Understanding the Appeal of Videogames." Updated April 23, 2008. http://www.stephanebura.com/emotion/.

cárdenas, micha, Zach Blas, and Wolfgang Schirmacher, eds. *The Transreal: Political Aesthetics of Crossing Realities*. New York: Atropos, 2012.

Carlson, Marvin. *The Haunted Stage: The Theatre as Memory Machine*. Ann Arbor: University of Michigan Press, 2003.

Carroll, Lewis. *The Complete Illustrated Works*. New York: Gramercy, 1982.

Carpenter, Nate. "Tropes vs. Women in Video Games." *Women & Language* 36, no. 1 (2013): 97–99.

Causey, Matthew. "Postdigital Performance." *Theatre Journal* 68, no. 3 (2016): 427–41.

———. *Theatre and Performance in Digital Culture: From Simulation to Embeddedness*. London: Routledge, 2006.

Chan, Stephanie. "EK Theater Is What Happens When You Mix Video Games and Shakespeare." *VentureBeat*. September 8, 2017. https://venturebeat.com/2017/09/08/ek-theater-is-what-happens-when-you-mix-video-games-and-shakespeare/.

Chemers, Michael M. *Ghost Light: An Introductory Handbook for Dramaturgy*. Carbondale: Southern Illinois University Press, 2010.

Chess, Shira, and Christopher A. Paul. "The End of Casual: Long Live Casual." *Games and Culture* 14, no. 2 (2019): 107–18.

"Children and Video Games." Accessed January 18, 2017. https://www.kff.org/other/fact-sheet/children-and-video-games/.

Chin, Gabriel Patrick Wei-Hao. "Observed Bodies and Tool Selves: Kinaesthetic Empathy and the Videogame Avatar." *Digital Creativity* 28, no. 3 (2017): 206.

Clark, Naomi, and merritt k. "Queering Human-Game Relations: Exploring Queer Mechanics & Play." *First Person Scholar.* February 18 2015. http://www.firstperson scholar.com/queering-human-game-relations/.

Consalvo, Mia. "There Is No Magic Circle." *Games and Culture* 4, no. 4 (2009): 408–17.

Costantino, Roselyn. "Politics and Culture in a Diva's Diversion: The Body of Astrid Hadad in Performance." In *Holy Terrors: Latin American Women Perform*, edited by Diana Taylor and Roselyn Costantino, 187–207. Durham, NC: Duke University Press, 2003.

de Lauretis, Teresa. *Technologies of Gender: Essays on Theory, Film, and Fiction.* Bloomington, IN: Indiana University Press, 1987.

Deleuze, Gilles, and Félix Guattari. *A Thousand Plateaus: Capitalism and Schizophrenia.* Translated by Brian Massumi. Minneapolis: University of Minnesota Press, 1987.

Dibbell, Julian. "A Rape in Cyberspace; or, How an Evil Clown, a Haitian Trickster Spirit, Two Wizards, and a Cast of Dozens Turned a Database into a Society." *Village Voice*, December 21, 1993. http://www.juliandibbell.com/articles/a-rape -in-cyberspace/.

Dixon, Steve. *Digital Performance: A History of New Media in Theatre, Dance, Performance Art, and Installation.* Cambridge, MA: MIT Press, 2007.

Donovan, Joan. "First They Came for the Black Feminists." *New York Times*, August 15, 2019.

Eckersall, Peter, Helena Grehan, and Edward Scheer. *New Media Dramaturgy: Performance, Media, and New-Materialism.* New York: Palgrave MacMillan, 2017.

ESA (Entertainment Software Association). "2020 Essential Facts about the Video Game Industry." Accessed October 8, 2021. https://www.theesa.com/esa-research /2020-essential-facts-about-the-video-game-industry/.

Fan, Christopher. "Not All Nerds." *New Inquiry.* November 6, 2014. https://thenew inquiry.com/not-all-nerds/.

Fischer-Lichte, Erika. "The Reception of Japanese Theatre by the European Avant-Garde (1900–1930)." In *Japanese Theatre and the International Stage*, edited by Stanca Scholz-Cionca and Samuel L. Leiter, 27–42. Leiden, Netherlands: Brill, 2001.

"Global Digital Gaming Market 2018–2023: Key Growth Factors & Threats andKey Players." Press release. July 24, 2018. https://www.apnews.com /07331e2fdb674e59817041989a3ef436.

Goffman, Erving. *The Presentation of Self in Everyday Life.* New York: Doubleday, 1956.

Gough, Christina. "Leading Mobile Game Titles Worldwide in 2017, by Revenue (in Million U.S. Dollars)." Statista. Accessed February 19, 2018. https://www.statista .com/statistics/505625/leading-mobile-games-by-global-revenue/.

Bibliography

——. "Top-Selling Console Games Worldwide in 2018, by Unit Sales (in Millions)." Accessed August 9, 2019. https://www.statista.com/statistics/273335/sales-of-the-worlds-most-popular-console-games-in-2011/.

Gray, F. Gary, dir. *Friday*. Featuring Ice Cube and Chris Tucker. Burbank, CA: New Line Cinema, 1995.

Grotowski, Jerzy. *Towards a Poor Theatre*. New York: Grove, 1968.

Haley, Jennifer. *Neighborhood 3: Requisition of Doom*. New York: Samuel French, 2008.

Handrahan, Matthew. "PewDiePie Dropped by Maker & YouTube Ad Platform over Antisemitic Content." *GamesIndustry.biz*. February 17, 2017. https://www.gamesindustry.biz/articles/2017-02-14-pewdiepie-dropped-by-maker-studios-over-antisemitic-content.

Harrigan, Pat, and Noah Wardrip-Fruin, eds. *Second Person: Role-Playing and Story in Games and Playable Media*. Cambridge, MA: MIT Press, 2007.

——, eds. *Third Person: Authoring and Exploring Vast Narratives*. Cambridge, MA: MIT Press, 2009.

Hart, Casey. "Getting into the Game: An Examination of Player Personality Projection in Videogame Avatars." *Game Studies* 17, no. 2 (December 2017). http://gamestudies.org/1702/articles/hart.

Higgins, Jeanmarie, ed. *Teaching Critical Performance Theory: In Today's Theatre Classroom, Studio, and Communities*. London: Routledge, 2020.

Huizinga, Johan. *Homo Ludens: A Study of the Play-Element in Culture*. London: Routledge, 1949.

Hunicke, Robin, Marc LeBlanc, and Robert Zubek. "MDA: A Formal Approach to Game Design and Game Research." In *Proceedings of the AAAI Workshop on Challenges in Game AI*. San Jose, CA: AAAI Press, 2004.

Jackson, Shannon, and Marianne Weems. *The Builders Association: Performance and Media in Contemporary Theatre*. Cambridge, MA: MIT Press, 2015.

Jackson-Schebetta, Lisa, ed. *Theatre History Studies*, vol. 39. Tuscaloosa: University of Alabama Press, 2020.

Jannarone, Kimberly, ed. *Vanguard Performance beyond Left and Right*. Ann Arbor: University of Michigan Press, 2015.

Karhulahti, Veli-Matti. "Defining the Videogame." *Game Studies* 15, no. 2 (December 2015). http://gamestudies.org/1502/articles/karhulahti.

Kelley, Robin D. G. *Freedom Dreams: The Black Radical Imagination*. Boston: Beacon Press, 2003.

Kember, Sarah, and Joanna Zylinska. *Life after New Media: Mediation as a Vital Process*. Cambridge, MA: MIT Press, 2012.

Kramer, Wolfgang. "What Is a Game?" Translated by Jay Tummelson. *Games Journal*. December 2000. http://www.thegamesjournal.com/articles/WhatIsaGame.shtml.

Kücklich, Julian. "Precarious Playbour: Modders and the Digital Games Industry." *Fibreculture Journal* 5 (2005). http://five.fibreculturejournal.org/fcj-025-precarious-playbour-modders-and-the-digital-games-industry/.

Laurel, Brenda. *Computers as Theatre*. 2nd ed. Upper Saddle River, NJ: Addison-Wesley, 2014.

Linn, Rachel. "We Third-Rate Monsters: Twitch Streaming Trolls." Presentation at American Society for Theatre Research/Theatre Library Association Conference, Atlanta, November 18, 2017. https://cdn.ymaws.com/www.astr.org/resource/resmgr /2017_conference/ASTR-Program-2017.pdf.

Marcotte, Jess. "Queering Control(lers) through Reflective Game Design Practices." *Game Studies* 18, no. 3 (December 2018). http://gamestudies.org/1803/articles /marcotte.

Massanari, Adrienne. "#Gamergate and the Fappening: How Reddit's Algorithm, Governance, and Culture Support Toxic Technocultures." *New Media & Society* 19, no. 3 (2015): 329–46. https://doi.org/10.1177/1461444815608807.

McKenzie, Jon. *Perform or Else: From Discipline to Performance*. London: Routledge, 2001.

McPherson, Tara. "Why Are the Digital Humanities So White? or Thinking the Histories of Race and Computation." In *Debates in the Digital Humanities*, edited by Matthew Gold, 139–60. Oxford: Oxford University Press, 2012.

Meyerhold, Vsevelod. *Meyerhold on Theatre*. 4th ed. Edited and translated by Edward Braun. New York: Bloomsbury Methuen, 2016.

Miller, Kiri. *Playable Bodies: Dance Games and Intimate Media*. New York: Oxford University Press, 2017.

Milton, John. *Paradise Lost: The Poetical Works of John Milton*. London: Henry Frowde, 1904.

Mokalsky, Stefan Stefanovich [Mokul'skii]. "The Japanese Theatre and the Soviet Theatrical Managers." *Weekly News Bulletin* (USSR Society for Cultural Relations with Foreign Countries) 4, no. 34–35 (September 1928): 7–8.

———. "Pereotsenka traditsii" [Re-evaluation of traditions]. In *Teatral'nyi Oktiabr': Shornik I* [The theatrical October: Collection I], 9–29. Moscow: Leningrad -Moskva, 1926.

Moody, Kyle Andrew. "Modders: Changing the Game through User-Generated Content and Online Communities." PhD diss., University of Iowa, 2014.

Mori, Masahiro. "The Uncanny Valley." Translated by Karl F. MacDorman and Norri Kageki. From the Field. *IEEE Robotics & Automation Magazine* 19, no. 2 (June 2012): 98–100. https://doi.org/10.1109/MRA.2012.2192811.

Morris, Chris. "4 of 2018's Best-Selling PC Games Are at Least 5 Years Old." *Fortune*. July 5, 2018. http://fortune.com/2018/07/05/2018-best-selling-pc-games -so-far/.

Motokiyo, Zeami. *On the Art of the Nō Drama: The Major Treatises of Zeami*. Translated by J. Thomas Rimer and Yamazaki Masakazu. Princeton, NJ: Princeton University Press, 1984.

Murray, Janet H. *Hamlet on the Holodeck: The Future of Narrative in Cyberspace*. 2nd ed. New York: Free Press, 2017.

Bibliography

Parker-Starbuck, Jennifer. *Cyborg Theatre: Corporeal/Technological Intersections in Multimedia Performance.* New York: Palgrave MacMillan, 2011.

Parkin, Simon. "If You Love Games, You Should Refuse to Be Called a Gamer." *New Statesman.* December 9, 2013. https://www.newstatesman.com/if-you-love-games-you-are-not-a-gamer.

———. "Zoe Quinn's Depression Quest." *New Yorker,* September 9, 2014.

Penix-Tadsen, Philip. *Cultural Code: Video Games and Latin America.* Cambridge, MA: MIT Press, 2016.

Phelan, Peggy. *Unmarked: The Politics of Performance.* Oxford: Routledge, 1993.

Piaget, Jean. *Plays, Dreams, and Imitation in Childhood.* London: Routledge, 1999.

Polansky, Lana. "Towards an Art History of Videogames." *Rhizome.* August 3, 2016. https://rhizome.org/editorial/2016/aug/03/an-art-history-for-videogames/.

Proehl, Geoffrey S. *Toward a Dramaturgical Sensibility: Landscape and Journey.* Madison, NJ: Fairleigh Dickinson University Press, 2011.

Roach, Joseph R. *Cities of the Dead: Circum-Atlantic Performance.* New York: Columbia University Press, 1996.

Rothenberg, Ben. "Mixing Old and New, Williams Began Surge with Racket Change." *New York Times,* June 30, 2013. https://www.nytimes.com/2013/07/01/sports/tennis/mixing-old-and-new-serena-williams-began-surge-with-racket-change.html.

Rozik, Eli. "The Ritual Origin of Theatre: A Scientific Theory or Theatrical Ideology?" *Journal of Religion and Theatre* 2, no. 1 (Fall 2003): 105–40.

Ryu, Semi. "VoicingElder." Accessed October 19, 2021. http://semiryu.voicingelder.com/post-16.

Salter, Chris. *Entangled: Technology and the Transformation of Performance.* Cambridge, MA: MIT Press, 2010.

Sample, Mark. "Play." Digital Pedagogy in the Humanities. Accessed June 28, 2019. https://digitalpedagogy.mla.hcommons.org/keywords/play.

Sarkeesian, Anita. "Damsel in Distress (Part 1): Tropes vs Women." March 7, 2013. *Feminist Frequency.* https://feministfrequency.com/video/damsel-in-distress-part-1/.

Savran, David. *Highbrow/Lowdown: Theater, Jazz, and the Making of the New Middle Class.* Ann Arbor: University of Michigan Press, 2011.

Schechner, Richard. *Environmental Theatre.* New York: Applause, 1994.

———. *The Future of Ritual.* New York: Routledge, 1993.

———. *Performance Studies: An Introduction.* New York: Routledge, 2002.

Schrank, Brian. *Avant-Garde Videogames: Playing with Technoculture.* Cambridge, MA: MIT Press, 2014.

Sell, Mike. "Avant-Garde Theory and Right-Wing Ideology." In *Vanguard Performance Beyond Left and Right,* edited by Kimberly Jannarone, 283–306. Ann Arbor: University of Michigan Press, 2015.

Seo, Yuri, and Sang-Uk Jung. "Beyond Solitary Play in Computer Games: The Social Practices of eSports." *Journal of Consumer Culture* 16, no. 3 (October 2016): 635–55.

Shakespeare, William. *Henry V.* In *The Riverside Shakespeare.* 2nd ed. Edited by G. Blakemore Evans and Joseph Jay Tobin. Boston: Houghton-Mifflin, 1997.

Shaw, Adrienne. "Do You Identify as a Gamer? Gender, Race, Sexuality, and Gamer Identity." *New Media & Society* 14, no. 1 (2011): 28–44.

———. "On Not Becoming Gamers: Moving beyond the Constructed Audience." *Ada: A Journal of Gender, New Media, and Technology* 2 (2013). https://doi.org/10.7264/N33N21B3.

———. "What Is Video Game Culture? Cultural Studies and Game Studies." *Games and Culture* 5, no. 4 (2010), 403–24.

Shaw, Adrienne, Sarah Rudolph, and Jan Schnorrenberg. *Rainbow Arcade: Over 30 Years of Queer Video Game History.* Berlin: Schwules Museum, 2019.

Shaw, Debra Benita. *Technoculture: The Key Concepts.* New York: Berg, 2008.

Sicart, Miguel. "Queering the Controller." *Analog Game Studies* 8, no. 2 (July 2017). https://analoggamestudies.org/2017/07/queering-the-controller/.

Solomon, Dan. "Theatre Proves a Most Relevant Medium for Addressing Issues about Video Game Culture." Review of *Neighborhood 3: Requisition of Doom*, Blue Theatre, Austin. *Austin Chronicle*, July 20, 2012. https://www.austinchronicle.com/arts/2012-07-20/neighborhood-3-requisition-of-doom/.

St. Patrick, Joli, and Avery Alder. "Beyond Representation: Queer Mechanics in Tabletop Games." Accessed July 13, 2021. http://buriedwithoutceremony.com/beyond-representation/.

Strindberg, August. Preface to *Miss Julie*. 1893. In Strindberg, *The Plays*, vol. 1, translated by Michael Meyer, 111–12. London: Secker & Warburg, 1964.

Suellentrop, Chris. "In the Footsteps of Lara Croft." *New York Times*, December 15, 2013.

Suits, Bernard. *The Grasshopper: Games, Life, and Utopia.* Toronto: University of Toronto Press, 1978.

Sutton-Smith, Brian. *The Ambiguity of Play.* Cambridge, MA: Harvard University Press, 1997.

Taekema, Sanne, and Bart van Klink. "On the Border: Limits and Possibilities of Interdisciplinary Research." In *Law and Method: Interdisciplinary Research into Law*, edited by Bart van Klink and Sanne Taekema, 7–32. Tübingen, Germany: Mohr Siebeck, 2011.

Takahashi, Dean. "SuperData: Games Grew 12% to $139.9 Billion in 2020 amid Pandemic." *VentureBeat.* January 6, 2021. https://venturebeat.com/2021/01/06/superdata-games-grew-12-to-139-9-billion-in-2020-amid-pandemic/.

Taylor, Diana. *The Archive and the Repertoire: Performing Cultural Memory in the Americas.* Durham, NC: Duke University Press, 2003.

Thomas, LaRonika. "Digital Dramaturgy and Digital Dramaturgs." *The Routledge Companion to Dramaturgy*, edited by Magda Romanska, 506–11. London: Routledge, 2015.

Bibliography

Tian, Min. "Authenticity and Usability, or 'Welding the Unweldable': Meyerhold's Refraction of Japanese Theatre." *Asian Theatre Journal* 33, no. 2 (Fall 2016): 310–46.

———. "Meyerhold Meets Mei Lanfang: Staging the Grotesque and the Beautiful." *Comparative Drama* 33, no. 2 (Summer 1999): 234–69.

van Kerkhoven, Marianne. *Listen to the Bloody Machine: Creating Kris Verdonck's End.* Utrecht, Netherlands: Utrecht School of the Arts, 2012.

———. "Looking without Pencil in the Hand." *Theatreschrift* 5–6 (1994).

———. "The Theatre Is in the City and the City Is in the World and Its Walls Are of Skin." *Etcetera*, October 1994. Translated by Gregory Ball. http://sarma.be/docs/3229.

"Video Game Industry Statistics, Trends, and Data in 2021." WePC. 2021. Accessed October 9, 2021. https://www.wepc.com/news/video-game-statistics/.

Wardrip-Fruin, Noah. "Playable Media and Textual Instruments." *Dichtung Digital* 34 (2005). http://www.dichtung-digital.de/2005/1/Wardrip-Fruin/index.htm.

WHO (World Health Organization). "Addictive Behaviors: Gaming Disorder." September 14, 2018. https://www.who.int/news-room/q-a-detail/addictive-behaviours-gaming-disorder.

Wijman, Tom. "Newzoo's 2018 Report: Insights into the $137.9 Billion Global Games Market." June 20, 2018. https://newzoo.com/insights/articles/newzoos-2018-report-insights-into-the-137-9-billion-global-games-market/.

Williams, Dmitri, Nick Yee, and Scott E. Caplan. "Who Plays, How Much, and Why? Debunking the Stereotypical Gamer Profile." *Journal of Computer-Mediated Communication* 13, no. 4 (July 2008): 993–1018.

Wilson, Michele. "Social Games as Partial Platforms for Identity Co-Creation." *Media International Australia* 154 (February 2015): 15–24.

Winkie, Luke. "Overwatch: 'Healsluts' Turn Playing Support into an Erotic Experience." *Kotaku.* September 12, 2016. https://kotaku.com/overwatch-healsluts-turn-playing-support-into-an-erotic-1786553002.

Working Group on Broadband and Gender. *Cyber Violence against Women and Girls: A World-Wide Wake-Up Call.* UN Broadband Commission for Digital Development. September 2015. https://en.unesco.org/sites/default/files/genderreport2015final.pdf.

Zeydel, Edwin. *Ludwig Tieck, the German Romanticist: A Critical Study.* Princeton, NJ: Princeton University Press, 1935.

Zimmerman, Eric. "Manifesto for a Ludic Century." *Kokatu.* September 9, 2013. https://kotaku.com/manifesto-the-21st-century-will-be-defined-by-games-1275355204.

Zola, Emile. "Naturalism on the Stage." In *Playwrights on Playwriting: From Ibsen to Ionesco*, edited by Toby Cole, 5–14. New York: Cooper Square Press, 2001.

INDEX

actors, 2, 4, 9, 11, 12, 38, 41, 42, 46, 47, 49, 52, 55, 56, 64, 75, 86, 89, 90, 93, 140–41, 182, 186, 189, 193, 198, 230
Adams, Douglas, 222
addiction, 185, 192, 202, 204–06, 210, 229
adults, 79, 82, 104–6, 109–10, 137, 201, 203, 207
Aeschylus, 7, 11, 32, 36, 48
aesthetics, 5, 10, 12, 16, 19, 20, 25, 27, 37, 40, 41, 46, 48, 49, 51, 53, 61, 71, 111, 157
affect, 20, 122–24, 126, 131, 138–43, 183, 198, 201, 203, 211–13, 219, 235, 246
Albee, Edward, 200, 202
algorithms, 26, 91
Alladeen, 65
alt-right, the 23, 77, 132, 139, 146, 225
analysis, x, 1- 4, 13, 15, 19, 27, 29, 30, 31, 42, 56, 71, 76–77, 87, 96, 98, 119, 122, 130, 145, 147, 159, 167, 172, 197, 201, 221, 239, 246, 248
Anthropy, Anna, 141, 166
Appia, Adolphe, 8, 45, 48
archives, 7
Aristotle, 12, 37, 40, 41, 117, 123, 143, 158, 233
Artaud, Antonin, 48
artificial intelligence, ix, 61, 67
Assassin's Creed, 15
assemblage, 6, 13
Attridge, Derek, 47
audience, 3, 8, 9, 10, 11, 13, 16, 38, 39, 42, 44–45, 46, 49, 52–53, 56, 57, 59, 65, 83, 85, 94, 140, 141, 147, 176, 186, 222, 233, 235, 236, 238

augmented reality, 16, 55, 59, 68, 146, 153
authenticity, 42–44, 46, 49, 54–55, 81, 108, 134, 174, 215
Auslander, Philip, 10, 55, 59
avatars, 42, 68, 87, 165, 171, 174, 175, 182, 186, 188, 193, 201, 207–10, 238

Bad News, 23, 169–70
Bandersnatch, 237
Behn, Aphra, 85, 157
Belasco, David, 8
Belman, Jonathan, 151
Bey-Cheng, Sarah, 97
Bezio, Kristin, 138
Bharatamuni, 9, 12, 37, 117, 233
biases, x, 167, 178–80, 231
Bilal, Wafaa, 169, 181
biology, 11, 12
biomechanics, 50, 52
Black Arts Movement, 36
Blast Theory, 16, 56, 101–2
Bloom, Gina, 76, 84, 86–87, 100, 174–76
Blume, Kathryn, 13
bodies, 16, 24, 25, 42, 50, 53, 55, 58, 60, 64, 78, 82, 88, 89, 93, 98, 99, 122, 141, 152, 169, 174, 182, 186, 188, 196, 199, 203, 210, 211, 245
Boal, Augusto, 235
Boluk, Stephanie, 163, 167
Box, 88
Brecht, Bertolt, 89, 118, 196, 213, 235
Brice, Mattie, 152
Brook, Peter, 48
Builders Association, ix, x, 1, 10, 16, 53, 58, 63, 64–70, 88
Bunraku, 36, 38–39, 43, 50, 157, 200, 213

265

Index

Bura, Stephanie, 224
Burke, Edmund, 9
Butler, Judith, 75

Candy Land, 110
Can You See Me Now?, 101–2
cardenás, micha, x, 23, 121, 141, 145–53, 217–41, 246
Carey, Mike, 240
Carlson, Marvin, 6, 86
Causey, Matthew, 58–59, 220
CAVE (Cave Automatic Virtual Environment), 24
Centipede, 22
Chemers, Michael, ix, x, 21–33, 63–73, 103–15, 144, 145–53, 156, 169, 185–94, 218–41, 247
Chicano theater, 36
Chin, Gabriel Patrick Wei-Hao, 182
China, 50, 177, 229, 231
cinema, 45–48, 57, 83. *See also* film
Clark, Naomi, 168
collaboration, 3, 7, 9, 10, 41, 57, 60, 72, 113, 156
colonization, 7, 10
commercial theatre, ix, 49, 71
compassion, 8, 19, 38. *see also* empathy
computers, 10, 14, 16, 19, 21, 23–29, 32, 33, 44, 57, 67, 91–94, 101, 133, 158, 160–63, 167–69, 178, 180–82, 186, 191, 199, 204, 208–9, 217–18, 236
Consalvo, Mia, 99
Continuous City, 65
Craig, Edward Gordon, 48
critics, 1, 4, 29, 30, 32, 45, 98, 100, 108, 136, 139
cybernetics, 9, 10, 61, 182, 205
cyborgs, 37, 40, 53, 88, 145

dance, 7, 72, 76, 80, 82–84, 86, 94, 96, 100, 172, 179
DeLappe, Sarah, 93–94

de Lauretis, Teresa, 239–40
Deleuze, Gilles, 13
Depression Quest, 127–28, 149
Derrida, Jacques, 47, 142
designers, 2, 4, 10, 13, 18, 31, 39, 47, 55, 57, 75, 100, 109, 111, 113, 136, 157, 175, 178, 183, 189, 224
Dibbell, Julian, 146–47
digital games. *See* videogames
digital media, ix, 10, 21, 57, 59, 61, 95, 133, 140, 178, 189, 190, 214. *See also* new media
directors, 1, 2, 4, 9, 13, 40, 47, 51, 55, 57, 94, 175, 183
diversity, 16, 19, 37, 89, 96, 118, 119, 126, 135–37, 139, 150, 153, 164, 166, 169, 177
Dixon, Steve, 96, 159
doubling, 199–202, 207, 210
Dungeons & Dragons, 15, 25, 32, 87, 90, 107, 112–13, 228, 238
drama, 8, 10, 16, 19, 41, 43, 57, 76, 93, 167, 248
dramaturgs, 9, 13, 15–19, 28, 36, 37, 39, 40, 41, 43–44, 52, 57–61, 70–72, 77, 81, 89, 94–96, 99, 118–23, 143, 144, 156, 157, 162, 176, 179, 190, 197, 218, 235, 244, 247
dramaturgy, and adaptation, 241; border-crossing, 157; business of theatre and, 4; digital, 95, 223; minor, 12–13, new media and, 9–11, 19, 58, 76, 88, 93, 97, 190; Nuremberg and, 235; of Gamer-gate, 137–40; of geek triumphalism, 132–35; of problematic texts, 240; of videogames, 135–36, 143, 155–60, 176–77, 183, 211; postdigital, 59; systems and, x, 2, 4–5, 10–13, 19, 35, 41, 53, 57–61, 70, 72–73, 77, 79, 89, 91, 92, 94, 96, 97, 99, 100, 102, 126, 134, 140, 142, 144, 156, 160, 164, 166, 182, 196, 204, 217, 218, 243–44, 246, 247;

Index

technology and, ix, 2–3,10–13, 15–17, 35, 36, 53, 54, 64, 76–77, 97, 118, 196, 243; traditional ix, 12, 28, 35, 36, 61, 65–66, 71–72, 233, 243
dumb type, 10, 41, 56, 88, 93

Eckersall, Peter, 10, 60, 88, 97
ecosystems, 12, 129, 137, 246
Eisenstein, Sergei, 52
Elements of Oz, 16, 64, 68–69
empathy, 3, 19, 20, 46, 117–26, 131–44, 145, 150–52, 192–94, 198, 200, 205, 207, 208, 210, 211, 213, 214, 215, 218–22, 227, 233, 235, 238, 246
engineers, 8, 13, 27, 30, 32, 221
eSports, 172
entanglement, 8, 13, 44–45, 78, 102
ethics, 3, 5, 38, 47, 53, 56, 81, 120–21, 129, 143, 152–53, 225, 229–31, 236
Euripides, 8
experimental theatre, 1, 9

film, 15, 17, 33, 45–48, 55, 68, 108, 121, 125, 186, 190, 205, 217, 219, 238, 239
Flanagan, Mary, 141, 151, 160, 168
4chan, 23, 134, 166
Freud, Sigmund, 9
Friday, 81
Froggy, 189

Gamergate, 16, 23, 59, 126–30, 135, 137–41, 145–46, 149, 150, 179
Game of Thrones, 107, 240
games, x, 1, 14, 22–23, 25, 27, 30–33, 54, 59, 76–102, 103–10, 118–19, 126–32, 136–38, 141–43, 149, 163, 164, 175, 177, 189, 233. *See also* videogames
gamification, 99–102, 157, 164
geeks, 96, 107, 132–37
George Gordon, Lord Byron, 117
Ghost Light (Chemers), 3, 143, 247
Glaspell, Susan, 123–24

Glengarry Glen Ross, 93
Goffman, Erving, 26–27, 75
Gone Home, 23
Grand Theft Auto, 31, 191–92, 206
Greeks, the, 6, 7, 8, 12, 48, 123, 139
Grehan, Helena, 10, 60, 88, 97
Grotowski, Jerzy, 18, 36, 47, 48, 53, 54, 139, 245
Guattari, Felix, 13

Hadad, Astrid, 99–100
Haiyun, Tang 173–74
Haley, Jennifer, 16, 19, 160, 185–94, 195–97, 201, 203, 204, 205, 208, 210, 211, 213, 215, 246
Hamlet, 6, 41, 75, 81, 82, 88, 89, 91, 159
Hansberry, Lorraine, 162
Harrington, Pat, 87, 240
Harry Potter and the Cursed Child, 39
Hart, Casey, 87–88
Heidegger, Martin, 13
hellmouths, 8
High Tea, 229
historiography, 35, 60, 61, 85, 180
history, 2, 4, 8, 10–11, 15, 19–20, 28–29, 31, 35, 37, 40, 44–45, 47–48, 53, 55, 58–61, 76, 83, 85–86, 96, 97, 99, 109, 124, 142, 147, 157, 163, 183, 212, 229, 244
homophobia, 16, 20, 23, 59, 131, 134, 137, 143, 149, 232
Hrosvitha of Gandersheim, 11, 36
Huizinga, Johan, 80, 89, 98, 245
humanism, 27, 28, 29, 30, 33, 77, 89, 90, 118, 139, 143, 235
Hunicke, Robin, 111, 137

ideology, 10, 22, 59, 61, 89, 98, 122, 147, 163, 16
immersive theatre, 24, 59, 159, 175, 182
innovation, 8, 11, 13, 19, 52, 58, 61, 72, 77, 157, 196

267

Index

Inspector General, the, 1
intermediality, 10
interactivity, ix, 13, 23, 57, 60, 71, 72, 82, 87, 95, 96, 103, 108, 109, 127, 159, 167, 180, 183, 185, 186, 206, 217, 218, 221, 237–38. *See also* new media
internet, the, 13, 58, 59, 102, 105, 131, 133–34, 146, 159, 161, 163, 168, 174, 179, 181, 226, 235

Jacquet-Droz, Pierre, 92–93
Jannarone, Kimberly, 235
Japan, ix, 35, 37, 38, 43, 49, 50, 177
Johnston, Brian, 32
Junius, Nick, 217, 225, 246

k, merritt, 168, 227
Kabuki, 35–36, 43, 50, 139
Kakyo, 38, 42, 51
Kalidasa, 11, 36, 85
Kaviness, Kacey, 173–74
Kelley, Robin D.G., 99, 100
Kember, Sarah, 243
Kim, Dorothy, 139
Kim, Eddie, 174
Kiyotsugu, Kan'ami, 37
Kramer, Wolfgang, 85
Kutiyattam, 164
Kyoden, Santo, 35

Lanfang, Mei, 50
Laurel, Brenda, 158–59
Legend of Zelda, the, 94, 115, 161
LeMieux, Patrick, 131, 132, 135, 163, 167
Lessing, Gotthold Ephraim, 41, 118, 125
Lim, 227
Linn, Rachel, 173–74
liveness, ix, 9–11, 25, 36, 40, 46, 53–56, 58, 68, 72, 86, 108, 140, 186, 236–38
Living Theatre, the, 53
Lysistrata Project, the, 13

Macbeth, 95, 160
machine learning, 64
magic circle, the, 98–99, 109
Manhunt, 206
Mario, 113–15, 161
Massanari, Adrienne, 133, 135
mass media, 13
Master Builder, the, 1, 72
McKenzie, Jon, 14, 97–98
mechanics-dynamics-aesthetics framework, the, 110–11
Medea, 8
mediation, 8, 10, 48, 55, 56, 57, 59, 63, 67–69, 83, 97, 101, 146, 160, 180, 181, 182, 189, 193, 211, 221, 224, 237, 238
mediaturgy, 189
memory, 6, 7, 72, 81, 86, 160, 164, 194
metagames, 163–64, 167
Méténier, Oscar, 8
Meyerhold, Vsevelod, 18, 36–37, 49–53, 54, 58, 245
Miku, Hatsune, 8
Miller, Kiri, 100–101, 172, 173
misogyny, 16, 20, 131, 134, 136–39, 141–43, 146, 149, 157, 173–74, 198, 232
Mnouchkine, Ariane, 8, 41, 48
mobile phones, 16–17, 18, 56, 59, 68, 69, 70, 94, 107, 110, 159, 161, 162, 163, 178, 227, 230, 236, 243
modding, 180–81
Monzaemon, Chikamatsu, 43
Moody, Kyle, 181
Motokiyo, Zeami. *See* Zeami
Mori, Mashiro, 199–200, 213, 214
multimedia, 1, 17, 49, 69, 88, 159
muntu, 36
Myst, 31

Natyasastra, the, 9, 12, 37, 117–8
Neighborhood 3, Requisition of Doom, 16, 19, 185, 187, 189, 191–92, 195–97, 201–02, 206–12, 246

nepantlerismo, 36
Nether, the, 186–94
new media, 9–10, 13, 15, 16, 40, 46, 52, 53, 55, 57, 58, 61, 88, 140, 145, 188–90
Noh theater, 37, 38

Oresteia, 32
Othello, 124–25, 137
outreach, 3
Overwatch, 171

Paine, Thomas, 9
Pantages, Alexander, 45–46
Parker-Starbuck, Jennifer, 88, 97
Parkin, Simon, 179
performance; actors and, 32, 42, 50–52; behavior as, 156, 203; digital, ix, 53, 55, 60–61, 67, 76, 96, 145, 244; dramaturgy of, 3, 15, 28, 41, 43, 71, 122, 222, 235, 243, 245, 247; empathy and, 119–21, 123, 140–42, 219; future of, ix; history of, 20, 37–38, 83, 117, 183, 206; identity and, 77; interactive, 72; live, 3, 9, 28, 36, 43, 45, 46, 55, 108, 114, 140, 175, 189, 218, 244; liveness and, 54, 55, 86, 140; mediated, 67, 237; multimedia, 17, 101 146; new media and, 10, 40, 55, 88, 102, 215; online, 77; psychology and, 26; reality and, 58; ritual and, 48; role-playing and, 112, systems and, x, 6, 18, 19, 25, 29, 58, 60–61, 78, 100, 126, 142, 248; teaching as, 71; technology and, x, 2, 7, 8, 10–13, 16, 17, 39, 44–45, 53, 54, 60–61, 97–98, 102, 108, 158, 159, 160, 169, 171, 172, 173, 174, 215, 241; text and, 3, 124, 183; value of, 236
Performance Group, the, 7
performance studies, 27, 30, 98, 156
performance theory, 2, 4, 9, 15, 20, 39, 61, 75, 98, 126, 175, 212, 245
performativity, 82, 112, 123
Phelan, Peggy, 53–54, 59, 140–43

Phone Story, 230–31
phones. *See* mobile phones
Piaget, Jean, 79
Piscator, Erwin, 36, 49, 124
play, adults and, 107–9, 180; as doing, 79, 80–83, 160, 186; as human activity, 22, 77, 78, 79, 100, 104, 105, 137, 153; as thing, 79, 83–89, 160; critical, 78, 98, 104, 147–48; definitions of, 22; design and, 111; digital, 96–97, 105; dramaturgy and, 20, 94, 95, 96, 99, 102, 142, 158, 176, 177, 197, 210, 245, 247; empathy and, 3, 19, 143, 150–51, 246; identity and, 79, 148; instruments and, 91–93; games and, 21, 22, 30, 31, 32, 54, 67, 91, 93, 99, 101, 102, 103, 108–14, 126, 127, 157, 158, 163–73, 177, 181, 182, 183, 185, 192, 193, 198, 203, 205, 213, 214, 219, 223, 229, 232, 236, 238, 241; learning and, 22; performance and, x, 15, 19, 75–76, 172, 174, 176, 243, 244, 247, 248; power and, 22, 75, 77, 90, 98, 207; psychology of, 104; self and, 22; systems and, x, 12, 14, 19, 77, 94, 119, 144, 158, 228, 231, 245, 246; technology and, 14, 214, 244; toxic, 136, 149, 157
Play the Knave, 174–76
playable media, 21, 87, 103, 119, 145, 168, 183
plays, x, 11, 13, 37, 83, 84, 108–9, 112, 185–92
playwrights, 9, 13, 29, 41, 47, 111, 112, 114, 185, 188
pleasure, 18, 55, 67, 68, 70–71, 108, 117, 225, 238, 239, 246
politics, 5, 9, 12, 13, 23, 14, 37, 40, 51, 54, 56, 57, 59, 79, 80, 81–82, 89, 97, 98, 99, 100, 101, 102, 107, 118, 120, 125, 132, 135, 139, 140, 145, 146, 148, 150, 153, 155, 156, 163, 164, 166, 169, 178, 179, 218, 219, 226, 233, 244

Index

postdramatic theatre, 221
presence, ix, 6, 13, 24, 46, 47, 54, 55, 68,
   81, 105, 108, 124, 128, 130, 134, 138,
   139, 140, 141, 180, 186, 191, 196, 214,
   221, 237, 245
Proehl, Geoff, 3–4, 41
projections, 17, 24, 39, 46, 47, 55, 56, 189
Prometheus Bound, 7
Prom Week, 27
psychology, 9, 11, 50, 78, 120
puppets, 18, 35, 38–41, 43–44, 51, 55, 57,
   71

Quinn, Zoë, 127–29, 131, 132, 141,
   145–46
Quintillian, 9

racism, 23, 107, 122, 124–25, 131, 134,
   136–39, 143, 152, 157, 162, 173–74, 198,
   232
rasaesthetics, 36
Raisin in the Sun, A, 162
Red Dead Redemption, 174, 224
Redshift and Portalmetal, 233–34
Reinhardt, Max, 48
remediation, 27
Renaissance, the, 2, 7, 90
ritual, 48
Roach, Joseph, 86
robots, 9, 10, 16, 55, 57, 61, 67, 93, 199,
   200, 213, 244
roleplaying, 15, 24, 87, 111–13, 236, 248
Rove, Karl, 146
Rozik, Eli, 48
Ruberg, Bo, 245
Ryu, Semi, 164–65, 180

Salter, Chris, 8, 12, 13, 44, 57, 59, 60, 102
Saltz, David, 97
Sample, Mark, 82–83
Sarkeesian, Anita, 130–32, 135–37, 141,
   143, 148, 179

Schechner, Richard, 7, 18, 36, 40–41, 48,
   53, 58, 78, 82, 156, 245
Scheer, Edward, 10, 60, 88, 97
Schopenhauer, Arthur, 9
science, 9, 11, 26, 27, 29, 120, 122, 159,
Sell, Mike, ix, x, 21–33, 63–73, 103–15,
   124, 145–53, 185–94, 218–41
Shakespeare, William, 41, 75–81, 84, 89,
   160, 174–75, 196, 203
Shaw, Adrienne, 134, 177
Shaw, Debra Benita, 14
Sim City, 28, 31
Simpsons, the, 231
Skyrim, 230
social media, ix, 2, 10, 13, 14, 16, 37, 44,
   54, 59, 76, 78, 94, 100, 101, 218, 226,
   227
software, 12, 14, 18, 27, 30–31
sokyokuchi, 18, 19, 35, 37, 42, 43, 49, 52,
   55, 56, 58, 60, 77–78, 97, 215, 244
Solomon, Dan, 211–12
Sophocles, 48
Soyinka, Wole, 156
Stanislavski, Konstantin, 42, 50
States, Bert, 186
Stone, Sandy, x, 217–41, 246
storytelling, 21, 23, 24, 29, 32, 67, 108,
   125, 160, 164, 165, 180, 183, 187, 218,
   239
Strange Window, 65, 220
Strindberg, August, 11, 212–13
Super Vision, 56, 65, 222
surveillance, 14, 56, 65, 67, 70, 97, 101,
   222, 226
Sutton-Smith, Brian, 22
Swensen, Elizabeth, 103–15, 217–41,
   246
systems, ix-x, 2, 4–5, 9, 13–15, 18–19, 27,
   29, 30, 36, 38, 52–53, 57–60, 77, 80, 89,
   94, 107–8, 122, 132, 142, 156, 160, 181,
   182, 187, 191, 213, 218, 222, 224, 232,
   236

Taymor, Julie, 8, 71

Taylor, Diana, 7, 245

techne, 7–8, 36, 52, 53, 61, 78, 102, 135, 218

technoculture, 10, 14, 15, 53, 54, 56, 77, 238

technology, aesthetics and, 12, 18, 20, 199; as problem, 45, 55, 212, 224; backwards compatible, 5–7; culture and, 14, 98, 138, 197, 218; digital, 14, 15, 17, 59, 76, 77, 95, 102, 112, 164, 170, 196, 218, 237, 244; dramaturgy and, 2–5, 9, 11, 12, 15, 17, 35, 36, 40, 44, 53, 58–61, 65, 67, 70, 88, 89, 91, 93, 95, 96, 97, 102, 139, 140, 156, 247; empathy and, 126, 215, 220, 221, 246; entanglement and, 201; exclusion and, 20, 59, 135, 145; film and, 239; games and, 181–83, 196, 197; interactive, 13, 158, 223; limits of, 105, 140, 141, 142, 224; liveness and, ix, 10–11; politics and, 51, 226; performance and, ix, x, 2, 7–11, 13, 16, 35–37, 39, 44–48, 52, 53, 55–58, 64, 83, 89, 97, 98, 101, 102, 124, 139, 159, 164, 191, 192, 197, 213, 214, 215, 221, 222, 236, 244, 245; puppets and, 38; social media and, 54, 133; surveillance and, 97, 222; systems and, 5, 30, 77, 115, 132, 166, 191, 212, 243

text, 5

That Dragon Cancer, 108

theater, antitechnology and, 18, 40, 44; business of, 119; changing definition of, ix, x, 41, 47, 49, 59, 72, 95, 155; dramaturgy and, 4, 15, 36, 58, 65, 79, 95–96, 102, 119, 121, 158, 183, 212, 247; commercial, ix, 4, 49, 84; culture and, 80, 104, 155–56, 225, 232–33; empathy and, 118, 123–25, 140, 142, 219, 221, 233, 235; experimental, 1, 71, 82, 168, 197; experience of, 6, 46, 55, 98–99, 213, 238, 239, 241; games and, 19, 84–86,

108–9, 111, 112, 141, 143, 157, 160, 174, 175, 176, 182, 185–86, 197, 210, 211, 234, 236; history of, 1, 2, 7, 8, 20, 28, 29, 37, 40, 47, 50, 55, 85–86, 89, 183, 206, 223, 238, 244; immersive, 182; mediated, 59; multimedia, 88; pedagogy and, 1, 32; plague and, 90; play and, 75, 77, 104, 245; postdramatic, 221; presence and, 46, 67, 68, 187, 237; psychology and, 26; ritual and, 48; systems and, ix, 4–5, 12, 28, 43, 53, 61, 78, 114, 186, 218; technology and, 3, 5, 6, 7, 9, 10, 11, 15, 16, 17, 20, 32, 35–37, 39, 44, 45, 47–53, 55, 57, 69, 76, 83, 88, 97, 102, 164, 186, 189, 199, 213–15, 244–46; traditional 18, 25, 47, 64, 65, 68, 71, 164, 179–80, 183, 197, 221, 222

theatron, 6, 8, 12

Thomas, LaRonika, 95

Tieck, Ludwig, 4

Toy Story, 29

transphobia, 150, 152, 232

trolls, 16, 82, 136–37, 141, 143, 150, 166, 174, 182, 186

Turner, Victor, 78

uncanny, the, 58, 64, 195, 196, 199, 202, 205, 207, 209, 213, 214, 215, 248

uncanny mountain, the, 195, 214

uncanny valley, the, 63, 199–200, 211–12, 214

Uncharted, 161, 219

van Kerkhoven, Marianne, 11, 12, 88

vast narratives, 29, 112–3, 240

Verdonck, Kris, 10, 41, 88, 93, 95

videogames, ix, x, 1, 3, 5, 15, 16, 19, 23, 25, 56, 57, 59, 67, 68, 77, 85, 87, 95, 102, 104–5, 112–13, 126, 132, 134, 141, 143, 157–78, 185–87, 190, 192, 196, 197, 199, 204, 205, 206, 210–11, 213, 218, 225, 236, 248

Index

violence, 14, 81, 86, 95, 126, 131, 137–38, 143–44, 146, 149–52, 166, 169, 171, 187, 191, 193–94, 196, 197, 199, 201–6, 209, 212, 215, 227, 233, 235, 236

virtual reality, 9, 24, 56, 76, 145, 159, 185, 188, 192, 243

Vitruvius, 8

Vogel, Paula, 185

Wagner, Richard, 8, 11, 44–45

walk-throughs, 195–96

Wardrip-Fruin, Noah, x, 21–33, 87, 169–70, 217–41, 245, 246

Weems, Marianne, ix-x, 10, 17, 18, 63–73, 217–41, 245, 246

Wolves, the, 93–94

Wooster Group, the, 41, 56, 63, 88

worldbuilding, 25

World of Warcraft, 25, 160, 185, 241

Wu, Brianna, 131, 132, 141, 146

Zeami, ix, 8, 11, 18, 36–37, 41- 44, 49–50, 52, 53, 54, 55, 58, 60, 77, 94, 118, 143, 156, 215, 233, 244–45

Zeydel, Edwin, 4, 119

Zimmerman, Eric, 14–15, 77, 84, 100, 102, 247

Zola, Émile, 9

zombies, 196–205, 209–11

Zylinska, Joanna, 243

MICHAEL MARK CHEMERS is a professor of dramatic literature at the University of California–Santa Cruz. His book *Ghost Light: An Introductory Handbook for Dramaturgy* has become a standard point of reference for dramaturgs all over the world. He was the founding director of the bachelor of fine arts in production dramaturgy at Carnegie Mellon University.

MIKE SELL is a professor of English at Indiana University of Pennsylvania. He has written extensively on the avant-garde, the Black Arts Movement, and the historical and performative dimensions of games. He is the founder and codirector of the Digital Storygame Project, which supports teachers in the incorporation of creative coding, design thinking, and ethically oriented decision-making in middle and high school curricula.

Theater in the Americas

The goal of this series is to publish a wide range of scholarship on theater and performance, defining theater in its broadest terms and including subjects that encompass all of the Americas.

The series is focused on the performance and production of theater and theater artists and practitioners. The series includes studies of traditional, experimental, and ethnic forms of theater; celebrations, festivals, and rituals that perform culture; and studies of dramatic literature; and acts of civil disobedience that are performative in nature. The series includes studies of theater and performance activities of all cultural groups within the Americas, including biographies of individuals, histories of theater companies, studies of cultural traditions, and collections of plays.

Scott Magelssen, Editor, 2014-2023

Founder and Editor, Robert A. Schanke, 2000–2014

Other Books in the Theater in the Americas Series

Shadowed Cocktails: The Plays of Philip Barry from "Paris Bound" to "The Philadelphia Story"
Donald R. Anderson

Adapturgy: The Dramaturg's Art and Theatrical Adaptation
Jane Barnette

A Gambler's Instinct: The Story of Broadway Producer Cheryl Crawford
Milly S. Barranger

Unfriendly Witnesses: Gender, Theater, and Film in the McCarthy Era
Milly S. Barranger

The Theatre of Sabina Berman: "The Agony of Ecstasy" and Other Plays
Translated by Adam Versényi
With an Essay by Jacqueline E. Bixler

Experiments in Democracy: Interracial and Cross-Cultural Exchange in American Theatre, 1912–1945
Edited by Cheryl Black and Jonathan Shandell

Staging Social Justice: Collaborating to Create Activist Theatre
Edited by Norma Bowles and Daniel-Raymond Nadon

*Messiah of the New Technique: John
Howard Lawson, Communism, and
American Theatre, 1923–1937*
Jonathan L. Chambers

*Composing Ourselves: The Little Theatre
Movement and the American Audience*
Dorothy Chansky

*Ghost Light: An Introductory
Handbook for Dramaturgy*
Michael Mark Chemers

*The Hanlon Brothers: From
Daredevil Acrobatics to Spectacle
Pantomime, 1833–1931*
Mark Cosdon

Richard Barr: The Playwright's Producer
David A. Crespy

*Stage for Action: U.S. Social
Activist Theatre in the 1940s*
Chrystyna Dail

*Women in Turmoil: Six Plays
by Mercedes de Acosta*
Edited and with an Introduction
by Robert A. Schanke

*Off Sites: Contemporary Performance
beyond Site-Specific*
Bertie Ferdman

*Rediscovering Mordecai Gorelik: Scene
Design and the American Theatre*
Anne Fletcher

*Californios, Anglos, and the Performance
of Oligarchy in the U.S. West*
Andrew Gibb

*A Spectacle of Suffering: Clara
Morris on the American Stage*
Barbara Wallace Grossman

American Political Plays after 9/11
Edited by Allan Havis

*Performing Loss: Rebuilding Community
through Theater and Writing*
Jodi Kanter

*Presidential Libraries as Performance:
Curating American Character from
Herbert Hoover to George W. Bush*
Jodi Kanter

*Unfinished Show Business: Broadway
Musicals as Works-in-Process*
Bruce Kirle

*Swim Pretty: Aquatic Spectacles and the
Performance of Race, Gender, and Nature*
Jennifer A. Kokai

*Staging America: Cornerstone and
Community-Based Theater*
Sonja Kuftinec

*Words at Play: Creative
Writing and Dramaturgy*
Felicia Hardison Londré

*Entertaining the Nation: American
Drama in the Eighteenth and
Nineteenth Centuries*
Tice L. Miller

*Memory, Transitional Justice, and
Theatre in Postdictatorship Argentina*
Noe Montez

*Theatre and Cartographies of Power:
Repositioning the Latina/o Americas*
Edited by Jimmy A. Noriega
and Analola Santana

*Documentary Trial Plays in
Contemporary American Theater*
Jacqueline O'Connor

*Working in the Wings: New Perspectives
on Theatre History and Labor*
Edited by Elizabeth A. Osborne
and Christine Woodworth

*Cuba Inside Out: Revolution
and Contemporary Theatre*
Yael Prizant

*Stage, Page, Scandals, and Vandals:
William E. Burton and Nineteenth-
Century American Theatre*
David L. Rinear

*Contemporary Latina/o Theater:
Wrighting Ethnicity*
Jon D. Rossini

*Angels in the American Theater:
Patrons, Patronage, and Philanthropy*
Edited and with an Introduction
by Robert A. Schanke

*"That Furious Lesbian": The
Story of Mercedes de Acosta*
Robert A. Schanke

*Caffe Cino: The Birthplace
of Off-Off-Broadway*
Wendell C. Stone

Teaching Performance Studies
Edited by Nathan Stucky
and Cynthia Wimmer

*Broadway's Bravest Woman: Selected
Writings of Sophie Treadwell*
Edited and with Introductions
by Jerry Dickey and
Miriam López-Rodríguez

*The Humana Festival: The History of
New Plays at Actors Theatre of Louisville*
Jeffrey Ullom

*Childhood and Nineteenth-Century
American Theatre: The Work of the
Marsh Troupe of Juvenile Actors*
Shauna Vey

*Our Land Is Made of Courage and
Glory: Nationalist Performance
of Nicaragua and Guatemala*
E. J. Westlake

*From Red-Baiting to Blacklisting:
The Labor Plays of Manny Fried*
Barry B. Witham